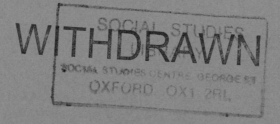

BRITAIN'S NAVAL FUTURE

BRITAIN'S NAVAL FUTURE

James Cable

In Old English there was no separate future; present and future were one.

Fowler

First published 1983 by
THE MACMILLAN PRESS LTD
London and Basingstoke
Companies and representatives
throughout the world

ISBN 0 333 34685 8

Printed in Great Britain by
Pitman Press, Bath

For Viveca as always

Contents

Preface and First Thoughts on the Falklands   ix

Introduction   1

1   The Trident and its Passing   10

2   The Causes of our Present Discontents   21

3   The Relevance of Sea-Power   36

4   Contingencies of Conflict   48

5   The Limited Deterrent   66

6   Alliance Naval War   I: the orthodox case   86

7   Alliance Naval War   II: choosing the threat   105

8   Alliance Naval War   III: tasks and resources   125

9   On the Fringes of Alliance   140

10   If Alliance Fails   150

11   Doing Without a Navy   165

12   Towards an Uncertain Horizon   174

Notes and References   189
Select Bibliography   205
Index   207

Preface and First Thoughts on the Falklands

'Admirals don't need advice'

Chatfield[1]

The author did, and is deeply grateful to all those admirals, British and foreign, who provided it so lavishly. Their juniors, officers of the other Services, academics, analysts, officials and politicians were equally helpful. The assistance, courtesy and encouragement of many busy people in demanding jobs made this book not only possible, but a pleasure to write.

So did the generous grant of a research fellowship by the Leverhulme Foundation, which alone enabled the author to travel to and fro about the country in search of enlightenment.

As most of those interviewed are still active in their professions, it seems more discreet not to identify them or to specify the extent to which their opinions may have contributed to the expression of controversial ideas. In three cases, however, gratitude must outweigh discretion. Vice-Admiral (retired) Sir Ian McGeoch, Professor Peter Nailor and Professor Bryan Ranft were all kind enough to read and comment on the typescript. None of the errors that remain, nor the inherent heresies, are attributable to them, but they prevented worse. Professor Ranft, however, must bear a heavier responsibility. He suggested the book, guided the author in his research and added to the weight of earlier debts. The contents are not his fault, but the book would never have existed without him.

An equal debt, of course, is owed to the many writers, living and dead, quoted in the pages that follow. One not actually cited offered an encouraging precedent for impudence. A Scot, a civilian, a landsman: his *Essay on Naval Tactics* was the first work of its kind to be written in

English. Whether or not John Clerk of Eldin influenced Rodney and Nelson, as some have claimed, his book is the first of many excuses for an amateur intervention in naval affairs.

In the quest for more recent books nobody, as usual, was more helpful than the Librarian of the International Institute for Strategic Studies.

NATO has been admitted to these pages as an exception to the principle that alphabet soup is a diet intolerable to the civilised reader. The acronyms lurking in quotations are risks inseparable from eating out.

A risk which the author has not avoided is the explosive impact of war in the South Atlantic. From the first page of the Introduction onwards it will be obvious to the reader that this book was completed before Argentina seized the Falkland Islands on 2 April 1982. Repeated references to naval conflict as a phenomenon without recent precedent now strike a jarring note. They could not, however, simply be removed without putting something in their place.

That would still be premature. The reports of the media make it clear enough that there are important lessons to be learned. Everything from the machinery of government to the characteristics of weapon systems has been exposed to the sudden flare of a new and harsher light. That does not mean that anyone can safely draw conclusions from reports that are inevitably incomplete, if not deliberately reticent, slanted or censored. The whole truth could not be told while fighting continued and will probably not emerge for some time after it is believed to have ceased. Even then it will be a slow and gradual process. The deficiencies in British gunnery revealed by the first battle of the Falklands in 1914 had not been corrected, or even fully appreciated, before the battle of Jutland in 1916.

The outstanding achievements of the Royal Navy in the recent conflict are more obvious and their celebration would be a more pleasing task. There again, praise, if it is to be discriminating, must await fuller information. It would be both foolish and presumptuous to offer a hasty encomium.

The most that the reader can expect, or that the author will attempt, is an answer to one inescapable question. Has even the inadequate information so far available of naval conflict in the South Atlantic made transparent nonsense of any of the arguments in this book?

With one exception the arguments specifically related to what was then a hypothetical contingency have stood the test of time and battle. It was a correct prediction that:

Such a war – for instance, one intended to recapture the Falkland Islands – would naturally be much more difficult, expensive, politically unpopular (both at home and abroad) and in every way damaging than prudent peace-time precautions. As these are, for a variety of reasons, unlikely to be attempted . . . the Chiefs of Staff might be asked for their proposals to deal with a situation which should never have been allowed to arise.

Unfortunately, if Chapter 4 correctly predicted the dilemma, Chapter 9 was unduly dismissive of a potential prophylactic. Much might have been avoided if the Ministry of Defence had actually sent 'a substantial naval task group on long detachment for visits and exercises in the South Atlantic'. The author was right in believing that cruises in balmier seas would be preferred. The 1982 Statement on the Defence Estimates admits, with courageous candour, the intention 'to deploy a naval task group of five warships and afloat support, headed by HMS INVINCIBLE, to the Indian Ocean and east Asia for six months'.[2] He was more correct than he knew in manifesting some scepticism of the utility of such tourism, but he would have demonstrated greater foresight by insisting that the South Atlantic was what was indicated by Nelson's dictum that 'the battle ground should be the drill ground'. The author shared the error of General Galtieri – and of many other foreigners – he did not believe that a British government would fight – or display advance readiness to fight – for distant islands they had declined to defend.

The Government's last minute change of attitude in no way deprives the Falklands' War of its naval interest, but the decision was one of several that gave the conflict an unusual political character. It was such an optional war. The cause of dispute could have been negotiated away long before. Alternatively, the precipitating attack might have been deterred by peacetime naval deployments. Even when the attack took place, a range of responses, whether political or military, was open to Britain. There were strong arguments in favour of the actual British reaction, but these might not have prevailed in different circumstances or under another Administration. What is significant is not that the war was unnecessary – most wars are – but that Britain had such freedom of choice. The very distance of the scene of conflict – otherwise so inconvenient – provided ample time for exploring alternatives and pondering decisions.

These are features unlikely to be repeated if the British Isles or vital British interests are threatened; if Britain's allies are involved, perhaps even more directly than herself; if the option of escalation is in other hands. As a dispute and even when it became a conflict, the Falklands offered a more controllable issue than most of those envisaged in this book as potential problems for Britain. When further evidence permits a more considered judgment on the quality of British decisions, before and after 2 April 1982, it will be worth remembering that future opportunities for the exercise of national control will probably be less extensive. This was an exceptional incident.

It would thus be doubly mistaken to rely on a hasty analysis of what is so far known of the Falklands conflict to support the wider arguments of this book. It is true that it enabled the Navy to demonstrate the value of flexibility and versatility; that the movement of warships gained time for the decisions of statesmen; that the fallacies of the single scenario were made manifest and islands shown to need navies. These are propositions that do not require the support of such a special case.

Naturally, once the facts are fully established, the Falklands operations will become an essential study for everyone concerned with defence and international relations in many countries beside Britain. For naval specialists, in particular, this conflict will be a precedent as important as the 1973 Arab–Israeli War has been for soldiers and airmen. In Britain it is, or it ought to be, inconceivable that this experience will not profoundly modify many aspects of defence policy. The very desirability of this process, the obvious need for fresh thinking, nevertheless makes it important not to waste such potent arguments by deploying them before their true nature has been properly established by fuller evidence.

This is not just pedantic caution. Opposition to learning from the Falklands experience is already entrenched and will exploit factual inaccuracies to demolish the arguments they were intended to support. It would also be easy, while still under the immediate influence of dramatic events, to get the proportions wrong and to press even a legitimate argument further than a special case would bear.

One such argument would be to maintain that the Falklands War has demonstrated the need not merely for a flexible and versatile ocean-going navy, but for a much larger and stronger navy. It certainly seems, from the information so far available, that the Royal Navy were only just able to meet the Argentine challenge and at crippling cost to the naval readiness of NATO. Even so they had to rely heavily on requisitioned auxiliaries, on warships due for disposal and on dockyard workers with redundancy notices in their pockets. It is an intriguing question. How long would General Galtieri have had to wait to be sure of success: until after the next British general election, until Mr Nott's economies had taken full effect, or only until HMS INVINCIBLE had reached East Asia?

This argument could naturally be reinforced by pointing to the losses and casualties which might have been avoided if specialised ships and aircraft or better weapons and equipment had been available. It could be sharpened by reference to those absurd weeks in which the Ministry of Defence were simultaneously organising the permanent reduction and the temporary expansion of the Navy. It is an attractive argument, but it is also vulnerable.

General Galtieri has shot holes in the conventional wisdom, but he has not broken the mould of British politics, nor eliminated the pressures on the defence budget, nor transformed Britain's international environment. The Falklands War was an aberration, even if General Galtieri ultimately made it a necessary aberration, from the primary task of defending the British Isles against the various threats which Soviet hostility could pose. There is a case – and it is argued in this book – for giving greater emphasis to the maritime component of Britain's defences. Experience in the South Atlantic should strengthen that case by providing fresh evidence of what the Navy can do. That experience should also be exploited to the full in seeking qualitative improvements. To go further – to demand a navy capable of combining a distant campaign with continued readiness in the Narrow Seas – would be unrealistic. It would also be politically counter-productive.

The objection has already been raised – and more will be heard of it once the smoke of battle has dispersed – that Britain would never have got herself into this unnecessary conflict if she had not still possessed an ocean-going navy. This is not the purely pacifist position it might appear, for it also enjoys some, temporarily tacit, support from those who regard the Soviet Union as the only enemy and the Central Front as the only theatre. They are mistaken, but they should not be fortified in their errors by any suggestion that the Navy exist for conflicts as distant as, to many, they seem anachronistic. The Navy can be proud of this renewed demonstration of their traditional ability to do more than they should ever have been asked, but they should not rest their future on the likelihood of a repetition. It will happen, one way or the other, but the argument will not persuade those who believe themselves capable of avoiding such errors and actually are able to control expenditure on defence.

The unassailable political lessons of the Falklands are that disregarding a threat does not make it disappear; that Britain can not exclude the contingency of limited war; that the constraints imposed by allies are at least as important as the assistance they provide; that a navy can offer an option not otherwise available; and that the single scenario is a certifiable delusion. It only remains, once the last death duties of our imperial past have been paid off and everyone has wriggled out of his previous errors, to apply these lessons to the problems, certainly more complex but hopefully more soluble than is often supposed, of our survival in the Narrow Seas. For what they are worth, the suggestions offered in this book require little modification in the light of recent events.

So much can not be said of that ill-fated document, *The Statement on the Defence Estimates 1982*. Published on 25 June and, so far as the naval programme is concerned, substantially modified by Mr Nott's speech of 1 July, it is a contribution to history rather than to debate, significant mainly for what it omits. The first volume (the second is statistical) contains 55 admirably informative pages about the matériel, the personnel and the logistics of defence. Legitimate curiosity concerning the design of submarines, the cost of weapon systems, the European balance, boarding schools in West Germany and the rescue of the Captain's wife from the Ecuadorean vessel BONITA is generously satisfied. One perfunctory paragraph out of 530 attempts some strategic justification for this immense expenditure and that paragraph, no. 102, is even less persuasive on the limited subject of the British nuclear deterrent than earlier official arguments. Anyone investing £ 8.50 in the hope of discovering what the Navy – or anyone else for that matter – could actually do will have wasted his money. The word 'strategy' does not even occur in an Index that finds room for 'Bessbrook police station' and 'cleaning'. After the real, if limited, improvements of 1980 and 1981 this is a sad relapse.

There is unfortunately every reason to regard the exclusion of strategic argument as deliberate. In his Introduction Mr Nott welcomed 'public interest in defence', but p. 17 makes it clear, as did Mr Nott in addressing the House of Commons on 1 July, that any such interest should be directed to the use of civil resources to strengthen the defence effort. The importance of this issue was emphasised by the utter dependence of the armed forces on civil resources during the Falklands conflict, which also demonstrated the need for 'adjustments or changes of emphasis . . . in the area of defence equipment'. Why, when, where and how Britain should fight are nevertheless questions in greater need of a public response than the inevitably technical problems of mobilising reservists, organising logistic support or modifying weapon systems.

These larger questions are also more likely to attract useful answers. In the Ministry of Defence, in Downing Street, in all the corridors of power, even throughout the armed forces, this is a heretical view. The Falklands War produced the usual crop of attacks on 'armchair strategists', but the complaint was doubly unfair. It did scant justice to the care devoted by the Property Services Administration to the comfort of the Chief of the Defence Staff or the Commander-in-Chief Fleet. It also revealed an inability, more regrettable than surprising nowadays, to discriminate between strategy and tactics. The latter was the subject of most of the suggestions offered by retired senior officers. Strategically there was one indecision – to neglect an obvious threat – and one decision: to counter-attack when it occurred. All the rest was tactics.

For twenty years the strategic component had been lacking in British discussion of the Falklands. Because strategy was not debated, within official circles or outside them, it did not exist. Options were neither pondered nor created. Argentina could thus confront Britain with a single choice: acquiescence or counter-attack. As earlier argued, it was an exceptionally voluntary choice and the slow passage of the Task Force kept it open unusually long. Even with these probably un-repeatable advantages, the narrow and unwelcome choice imposed by past neglect resisted every attempt at widening which sudden apprehension could suggest or belated ingenuity contrive. Those who refuse to consider alternative courses of action when they can – in time of peace – will be denied the chance when they want to. The next foreseeable contingency to expose options unexplored in public debate could be nearer home, faster-moving, more doom-laden in some of the choices it will open up. Breath then expended on opinions not put forward in advance – not formulated now, in 1983 – will be, even more than in the uniquely amenable Falklands crisis, the mere vapourings of the gaseous invertebrate.

It is not necessary to believe in democracy to deprecate such a state of affairs. If history teaches us anything, it is that governments, the establishment, the conventional wisdom are all prone to error. They need constant challenge and correction from equally fallible heretics. No normal ruler invites such an uncomfortable experience, least of all in those sensitive areas where the painfully revealing probe is most required. The initiative must come from outside.

That initiative is most needed in strategy and in the political purpose that should inform and direct strategy. The relative merits of missiles, radar, ships, aircraft and tanks may legitimately by regarded as matters for the experts, of whom only a minority are unofficial. No such excuse for confidence, acquiescence, indifference or apathy is available in approaching the larger issues. These are not the subject of systematic or professional investigation and resolution. It is uncertain, for instance, how far the latest Statement on the Defence Estimates commanded the approval, even the prior knowledge, of the Naval Staff. The strategic expertise – or motivation – of those who decided its shape is as much open to doubt as their ability to learn from experience. If there was a strategic rationale, it was unstated and it is never safe to assume that the calibre of thought can transcend the quality of its expression. On the evidence presented by the British Government – and the choice was theirs – a vacuum exists. No clearly stated and convincing purpose now animates the maintenance of the Royal Navy.

That purpose needs to be hammered out in a more open forum than the ledger-bound bureaucracy of Whitehall Gardens can provide. The Defence Debate of 1 and 6 July 1982 revealed a dawning political receptivity to new strategic thought, even if it confirmed ministerial reluctance to risk the chill of such unfamiliar waters.[3] This book does not even pretend to supply the answer. Its utmost claim is to offer that indispensable stimulus to intellectual activity, the intrusive scrap of grit that may, just conceivably, irritate the sluggish oyster of the conventional wisdom into the long-awaited gestation of one of its very occasional pearls.

Introduction

The rôle of naval forces in total war is somewhat uncertain.[1]

Threadbare by now from quarter of a century of quotation, these words still provide journalists with a theme, irritate admirals, perplex Ministers of Defence and await a comprehensive answer.

We should all be grateful that there has been no war to provide it. Not that naval forces have been idle in those twenty-five years. The Americans intervened in the Lebanon, protected Taiwan, employed blockade to prevent nuclear war over Cuba, changed the government of the Dominican Republic, preserved the existence of Israel – by the use of warships. The British defended Kuwait, intervened in East Africa, contested fishing rights off Iceland. The Soviet Union asserted their presence in the oceans of the world. Turkey had her way in Cyprus. Many political purposes were served – and others frustrated – by the use or threat of limited naval force.

But there was no naval battle, let alone a maritime war, to offer naval strategists the kind of object-lesson in modern combat that has been provided for the world's armies and air forces by the conflict in Vietnam or by the wars of 1967 and 1973 between Israel and her Arab neighbours. Navies have been designed, built, equipped, trained and deployed on a basis of speculation unsupported by any significant experience less than thirty-five years old. During that period they have also been transformed. In 1939 the Royal Navy was not very different from what it had been in 1918: most of the battle fleet had been at Jutland and more recent ships embodied little that would have puzzled Jellicoe. Today almost nothing is what it had been in the Second World War: not the ships, nor their classification, nor their armament, nor their propulsion and least of all the fantastic electronic equipment that accounts for so much of their cost. Admirals seldom go to sea; the Captain's action-station is no longer on his windswept bridge; uniforms have been altered and the rum ration

1

abolished. Bereft of applicable precedent a new navy must rely on conjecture to establish its rôle in an altered world.

To some extent this is a problem for all navies. The impetuous pace of technology has not merely left history far behind: it has out-distanced strategic thought. Such concepts of naval operations as emerge from the Soviet Union or the United States seldom carry entire conviction in their efforts to assign to war at sea its necessary and appropriate place in a wider conflict. Indeed, much of the limited attention that either Admiral of the Fleet Sergei Gorshkov or his American counterparts can spare from the increasing intricacies of their matériel has to be devoted to the rather different task of justifying the size and expense of their forces. Gorshkov's success in overcoming the opposition expressed in Khrushchev's celebrated complaint about 'metal eaters' has been manifested on the oceans, but even the anguish of American admirals at the decline of the United States Navy should not obscure its continued possession of ships that are more numerous, far more powerful and more widely deployed than in 1939. American naval strength may be inadequate to the present challenge, but it has more than maintained the traditional peacetime standard.

The British case is different. In 1939 the Royal Navy had four times as many major surface warships as it has today. This precipitous fall in British numbers has not been offset by the increased, but sometimes over-specialised, sophistication of those vessels that remain. By any test of power the Royal Navy is no longer in the first rank to which centuries had accustomed it. On the surface of the oceans the Soviet Union has four major warships for every one that flies the White Ensign. In their depths the ratios are even worse: almost ten to one in attack submarines; over twenty to one in strategic. Many of these Soviet ships are larger and armed with weapons of longer range. Some of them – the new nuclear battle-cruiser KIROV, for instance – are quite unmatched in the Royal Navy.

As for deployment, the oceans are misty with the ghosts of vanished British fleets: Grand, Home, Atlantic, Channel, Mediterranean, Pacific, Far Eastern; of the China Squadron, the South American Squadron, the West Indies Squadron. Rear-Admiral Yangtse has long ceased to fly his flag and the White Ensign is little more than a memory in Aden, Alexandria, Malta, Simonstown and Singapore. The ample houses, in so many scattered ports, with their flagstaffs, the piled cannon-balls, the neatly trimmed lawns, of commanders-in-chief, flag officers, senior naval officers, have other tenants. Now there is simply The Fleet and its Commander-in-Chief inhabits the London suburb of Northwood. In this staid environment of comfortable villas, far from the sound or scent of the sea, his headquarters is dignified by the name of HMS WARRIOR: an obsolete cruiser that perished after an encounter, of greater gallantry than utility, with the High Seas Fleet.

The retreat to Northwood is often depicted as no more than a logical consequence of the dissolution of the British Empire: the creation of the Royal Navy, for long its principal preoccupation and, in the eyes of some, its raison d'être. This last view is historically inadequate. An island-state needed a navy long before the Empire existed. Arguably that need still persists. Nevertheless the association between imperialism and naval power, canonised by Mahan and fortified by centuries of diplomatic and naval practice, nowadays operates to the disadvantage of the Royal Navy. Diminished requirements, it is often suggested, are necessarily reflected in reduced resources. Reduction, indeed, has not yet gone far enough. There are arguments requiring later scrutiny to support this view, but instinctive judgments are no less important. These long upheld the maintenance by Britain of a superior navy, but its relegation to the second division has not merely weakened popular sentiment, but threatens to change its direction. 'Only the best is good enough' can be a double-edged slogan in contemporary Britain. The sense of economic failure easily inclines the despondent to urge its extension, to make a virtue of what they suppose to be a necessity, to bleed the patient.

Metaphor is always suspect, but often revealing. It was significant that *The Times*, on 22 December 1980, gave pride of place to a letter arguing that the British people should cease struggling 'to go on living in the gradually decaying ancestral mansion' and opt for 'a drastic curtailing of the Royal Navy's high-seas rôle' in order 'to live comfortably within their means in a bungalow'.[2] The syllogism may be imperfect, but the sense was clear and the conclusion has doubtless been noted by house-agents in Northwood.

Such sentiments, metaphors, analogies are neither isolated nor irrelevant: they are sufficiently widespread to influence political attitudes and these may ultimately determine decisions. Little enquiry is needed to confirm the predominant rôle of instinctive preconceptions: not naval officers alone, but members of parliament who have served in the navy or represent naval constituencies; historians or journalists with maritime interests; critics of the European Economic Community; traditionalists or isolationists; these and many others may be no more objective in extolling the advantages of sea power than their opponents in denigrating it. There are also the larger categories of those who equate defence with motherhood or armaments with sin. A reasoned approach is a rarity.

Attainment of the rational ideal is naturally not facilitated by the orthodox arguments for the existence of the Royal Navy. For reasons which must be explored, these are no longer mainly concerned with preventing invasion or 'impeachment of our trades'. Instead they relate to the British contribution to NATO, whose naval strategy – maritime support for the armies in Europe – is as difficult to relate to a plausible scenario as is the successful execution by these armies of the tasks assigned to them by the doctrine of forward defence and flexible response. Both tend to be explained and justified on political rather than on military grounds and doubters are constantly reminded that NATO has kept the peace of Europe for more than thirty years. Whatever its historical merits, this is a disquieting argument: 'what is, is best' can be found engraved on every step of Britain's downward path for more than a century.

The difficulties inherent in NATO strategy will have to be examined, but the challenge to the British contribution springs from other sources. One of the most important is usually described as economic. For quarter of a century British defence expenditure has been confined to what the conventional wisdom regards as a tolerable level (not varying greatly in real terms) by offsetting reductions in the size of the armed forces against the ever-mounting cost of their equipment. This process was facilitated by progressive withdrawal from overseas commitments and, to a lesser extent, by the gratuitous renunciation or reduction of specific military capabilities: strike carriers, amphibious forces, airborne troops, reserves, strategic bombing. What remained was, with trifling exceptions, committed to the defence of the British Isles and the support of NATO.

Yet the pressure for defence cuts shows every sign of persisting. The cost of military equipment continues to escalate and the performance of the British economy to sharpen Socialist distrust of defence and Conservative opposition to government expenditure. In the Services, in government, in Whitehall, in Parliament and outside there is general scepticism about the chances of maintaining, for the rest of the eighties, let alone of the century, British forces with the range of capabilities, the strength, the efficiency – all of them already inadequate – they now possess. The validity of this scepticism – and the reasons for it – will also have to be examined, but it exists.

Two kinds of response may be distinguished. The minority view, but one which is held by people of great influence, calls for maintenance of the policy of 'equal misery', whereby the available resources are allotted on an equitable basis among the three Services. This doctrine is of ancient origin and found its most striking expression in 1933, when the Chief of the Imperial General Staff resisted an appeal from the Head of the Treasury to seek a *larger* army on the grounds that this 'would unbalance the report as between various items and as between three Services'.[3] In recent years the danger of 'unbalance' has been successfully avoided and cuts so distributed as to preserve the established share of each Service in the Defence Budget. If worse is to come then, so it is contended, 'we must go on slicing the salami ever thinner, to the consistency of rice-paper, till it can be seen through'. There is, in this view, no alternative to the present strategic concepts that require the maintenance by Britain of a range of military capabilities spreading across all three Services.

A different opinion – more widespread, but perhaps less influentially supported; more plausible, but with less appeal to traditional loyalties and less underpinning from institutional pressures – is that defence cuts across the board have reached, if they have not already transcended, the lower edge of military efficiency. If there must be more – even if cash limits merely constrain necessary increases in expenditure – then one of the present functions of British defence must be slashed in order to sustain the remainder. These functions are the nuclear deterrent; the continental commitment; the partly associated air defence of the British Isles; and naval defence in the Eastern Atlantic and Narrow Seas.

This opinion is intellectually attractive, but has two main weaknesses. The first is that its advocates do not agree among themselves about what should be cut and what conserved. Serving officers and civilians, politicians and officials, experts in one trade or analysts in another: they all have different priorities. He who listens may hear arguments, from foreigners as well as Britons, for the abandonment or curtailment of any one of what the Ministry of Defence are accustomed to call the four pillars of British defence policy. The second weakness is that nearly all these advocates have a sentimental axe to grind: they are loyal to the Navy, or the European ideal or NATO; they dislike Germans or nuclear weapons; they remember the Second World War; they believe in deterrence or exalt political factors. None, in the limited experience of this author, is prepared to complement his radical redistribution of British defence efforts with that necessary consequence: an alternative British strategy. One of the pillars is to be weakened without lightening the roof. 'The Germans can replace the troops we withdraw from the Rhine; the Americans can put more fighters into East Anglia; there is no conceivable contingency in which we could employ nuclear weapons; if there is ever a war in the Atlantic, the United States Navy can cope.'

A curious instance of this general myopia is offered by an otherwise rather respectable report commissioned by the Labour Party and entitled *Sense About Defence*.[4] This devoted considerable research to the economic implications of substantial defence cuts, mentioned political factors in passing, but remained silent on strategy. Enquiry revealed that this omission had been deliberate.

What the British armed forces might actually achieve in war seems to be the question least discussed even by those politicians most concerned to improve military efficiency or reduce defence spending. The characteristics of ships and their armament attract an interest that is keen and informed. So do the costs of defence, the problems of recruitment and training and all the comparisons to be drawn with other countries or different forms of expenditure. Painful choices are not excluded and the international as well as the domestic implications are realised. The nature of deterrence and of the Soviet threat are much debated. In these areas most points of view are represented and few interests lack their champion. But it is the instruments of power that excite controversy rather than their application. More scope for change is seen in the size and characteristics of the armed forces than in the nature of their tasks, nor is there much effort to define these in terms of expected achievements – that all-purpose panacea, deterrence, always excepted.

There are many reasons for this preoccupation with means rather than ends. Strategy, for instance, is officially proclaimed as a NATO rather than a national responsibility and everybody is familiar with the difficulty of reaching, let alone modifying, agreement in NATO. Politicians have some excuse for concerning themselves with the composition of Britain's armed forces, which they can hope to control, rather than with their employment. Moreover, they are offered little by way of alternative strategies or even of professional exposition of the existing strategy. Discussion within the armed services or in those official circles directly concerned with British defence policy exhibits much the same political, economic, technical, institutional bias. This is particularly true of the Navy. Naval officers are better educated, more expert, more widely sophisticated than they have ever been. The 'surly and ignorant sea-dog with a real and large hook instead of a hand' of whom Keynes wrote is an extinct species.[5] But there is no generally received doctrine of naval strategy. The subject is scarcely taught at Greenwich, where even naval history has been virtually abandoned. Heresy no longer abounds. Sixty articles in five consecutive issues of the *Naval Review* included precisely one devoted to naval strategy. The situation today is actually worse than it was before the First World War. In those days admirals may have claimed a monopoly of strategic thought, but some of them did at least exercise their privilege in vigorous and public debate. And Corbett lectured at Greenwich.

The explanation is both old and new. The intellectual demands of an escalating technology are exorbitant. Anxiety about survival – not against the enemy, but in the face of domestic political and economic pressure – is emotionally overriding. It is typical that students at Greenwich should be asked to write essays on 'The Navy of the Nineties'. Strategic speculation is no road to promotion and, in the thermonuclear age, presents formidable difficulties.

There has been no stampede of civilian analysts to fill this vacuum in strategic thought. Like guests at a cocktail party they have shunned the unfrequented corners and crowded together around the sticky dregs of debate on TRIDENT, on HMS INVINCIBLE, on the Soviet building programme, on submarine detection. Corbett's *Principles of Maritime Strategy* is out of date,[6] but so are the scanty works of his would-be successors. This is a pity. Without a contemporary concept of naval strategy the discussion of British defence policy lacks one of its dimensions. And that discussion is far-reaching. The pressure for change does not emanate only from economists. Proposals exist – and attract substantial support from the Labour Party, the trade unions and other sections of British public opinion – for the renunciation of British nuclear weapons and for the withdrawal from the British Isles of American nuclear weapons. The arguments for and against this idea may be reserved for later consideration, but one consequence of its application seems inescapable. The political impact on Britain's allies would be quite as significant as the alteration in the purely military balance between British vulnerabilities and defensive resources. A new international situation would have arisen and NATO strategy would be no more likely to survive unchanged than British. Before the last reverberations died away, different tasks might emerge for the Royal Navy.

To a lesser extent, similar consequences are conceivable for other radical proposals to alter the resources at present allocated to British defence. There is a point, however hard to define in advance, beyond which even the gradual whittling away of British forces must finally destroy the credibility of the strategy they are intended to support. The removal or serious weakening of one of the four pillars of British defence policy would, of course, precipitate the process. Even a Conservative Secretary of State for Defence could talk, in 1981, of a turning point in the history of NATO and of a transformation in the next ten years. His reasons were familiar:

> Technological change is accelerating and the public mood has become more questioning. Some of us are trying to spread our efforts too thinly over too many tasks and we are going to have to concentrate our efforts to achieve a more effective output.[7]

It is the function of strategic analysis, as long as the reduction of defence resources continues to be debated, to explore the alternatives. If major change does come, it will be helpful if a strategy to accommodate it has already been discussed. Even if such discussion reveals no alternative without grave disadvantages, this in itself will be material to the wider debate and may even influence its outcome. Defence policy does not make sense unless it produces a sensible strategy, but the merits and defects of any particular strategy can only be assessed by comparison with the possible alternatives.

This is not a popular notion among those responsible for British defence policy. They believe they already have the best strategy which allies, resources and circumstances will permit. Moreover, military opinion has always regarded the mere mention of alternative positions as damaging to the morale of those required to hold an exposed salient. Westminster and Whitehall are also agreed that naming the Devil is calculated to rouse him from slumber. The Ministry of Defence are less neurotic about NATO than the Treasury were about devaluation or the Foreign Office over the referendum on the European Economic Community. But taboo is potent and the cult of secrecy exaggerated; some contingencies are not for planning and certain speculations are in poor taste. Ideas exist and will emerge when the time is ripe, or rotten, but the discussion of radically different strategies needs to be initiated from outside. Without such discussion, of course, such strategies may not be accepted, if they are needed; or rejected, if they ought to be. The questioning mood of public opinion can be inconvenient, but its replacement by the spirit of disciplined acceptance is not a change which can be predicted with any great confidence.

Choices are a necessary feature of strategic argument, but the advocacy of alternatives is not the purpose of this book. It is concerned with general strategy as the setting for naval strategy and with naval strategy as one of the criteria for assessing the future utility to the British people of their navy. In practice, of course, the size and characteristics of the Royal Navy will continue to depend on the shifting cross-currents of

British politics; on perceptions of the international environment; on resource constraints, or what are seen as such, and on institutional pressures. It is rash to assign much influence to rational argument and presumptuous to attempt it. The concept of utility nevertheless has its attractions and, if applied to navies, is perhaps best measured on the basis of expected achievements. Such predictions are both difficult and uncertain. Without a strategic yardstick they are impossible.

Of course, strategy is the child of political purpose and the creature of circumstance and the tilth of strategy will need quite as much examination as its flowering. The rôle of the Navy can not be divorced from the character of the British people or the part they choose to play in the world. But one question is central to Britain's naval future. It would not be asked now if it had already been adequately answered. It would not have remained so long without a convincing reply if it was at all easy. It would have been better attempted by an admiral. It is posed here only because it imposes itself and sets the pattern for the book.

What could the Navy do?

1 The Trident and its Passing

> The kingdom of England is and must always remain strong at sea, since on this the safety of the realm depends.
>
> Philip II of Spain[1]

This book is about Britain's naval future. If it begins by glancing at the past, that is because the central question – what could the Navy do? – derives much of its peculiar resonance from the echoes of past years.

For centuries the sea has murmured in English ears unfamiliar with its harsher roaring. Not seamen or coastal dwellers only, but midland farmers, sedentary men of letters, scheming politicians have celebrated the importance of the sea and of the ships that sail it. In the earliest times it was from the sea that danger came and in a later era it was the sea that was the source of prosperity and power. The history, the literature, the political thought, even the folklore of England reverberate to the sound of the sea, to the sea as a moat and to the sea as the avenue of adventure.

In an island it seems an understandable preoccupation, but it was slow to assume the form of a special national characteristic. Mackinder has pointed out that 'the shipping of the Middle Ages belonged for the most part not to the English, despite their immigrant history, but to the inhabitants of the mainland'.[2] A mere eighty years have given his words a hollow ring.

When the mediaeval English began to turn more of their attention to the sea, these foreign mariners did not welcome imitators, still less interlopers in the commerce or the overseas ventures they had initiated. The sea soon became both the source and the theatre of conflict. Edward III had to gather ships to rid the Channel of pirates and the long wars with France early included a primitive naval battle (at Sluys in 1340). From small beginnings there developed a particular interest in the sea as something more than the road to France. As early as the beginning of the fifteenth century, for instance, *The Libel of English Policy* pro-

10

claimed that 'the true process of English policy is this . . . Cherish merchandise, keep the Admiralty, that we be Masters of the Narrow Sea'.[3]

This martial chord was somewhat prematurely sounded and would be slow to reach its final resolution, but the idea – it was then more of an aspiration – of mastery at sea was one that gradually began to take hold of the English imagination and intermittently to engage the attention of English governments. The encouragement of trade, the fostering, through Navigation Acts, of merchant shipping, the sponsoring of exploration and political action to ensure overseas markets were all early preoccupations. Presently these were joined by the notion that trade and shipping needed armed protection at sea. Henry VII built a royal dockyard at Portsmouth and Henry VIII a royal navy of fifty-three vessels.[4]

The achievements of Elizabeth I scarcely require enumeration, for the defeat of the Spanish Armada in 1588, together with the Battle of Hastings in 1066, is one of the few historical facts to have gained indisputable entry to the sparse dictionary of general knowledge. Nevertheless it is worth emphasising the connection between English prowess at sea and the country's growing prosperity, which now depended increasingly on seaborne trade, not only to foreign ports, but still more coastwise. The root of wealth was naturally immunity from invasion, but adventure further afield caught the popular imagination and also played its commercial part. Rowse, writing of the expansion of trade and of the minor industrial revolution that transformed the economy, has a striking, if unorthodox, example: 'A small portion of it [the booty from Drake's raid upon the treasure-route off the coast of Peru] was enough to float the Levant Company. Members of the Levant Company in turn fostered the East India Company, from which grew an Empire.'[5]

The connection between trade and the navy became even more explicit in the seventeenth century, when commercial rivalry provided the underlying motive for repeated naval wars. This was also the period when the search for profit and for commercial outlets began the establishment of actual colonies, not across the Narrow Seas, but beyond the oceans. But the purely naval record was patchier, the transitory triumphs of the Cromwellian era being preceded and followed by periods of neglect and consequent humiliation. It was often in vain that successive governments were urged to emulate the achievements of the Elizabethan era. But the idea of naval mastery persisted. Even in the lamentable reign of Charles II, a period of British history much resembling that which occurred three centuries later, the will was there, even if it often outran performance. In 1674 we find Mr Secretary Pepys 'insistent on the salutes due from foreign vessels to the King's flag as Sovereign of the Narrow Seas from Finisterre to Norway'.[6] The presumption of this claim, which had already provoked one war and which was now put forward – successfully – a bare seven years after de Ruyter had burned the English fleet at its moorings, is more of a tribute to the nation's survivability than to its sense. It was nevertheless a tradition that had been intermittently maintained since at least 1299 and was to continue until 1805.[7]

Although the seventeenth century, as Bryant has demonstrated, laid the administrative foundations of the navy, it cannot be said to have established English naval supremacy, even if it promoted English trade at the expense of the Dutch. The fortunes of battle, particularly against the Dutch, swayed this way and that, but it was the battle that was never fought that was decisive. In 1688 Dartmouth, dithering among the sands,[8] failed to intercept the Dutch invasion fleet and a foreign army was successfully landed to overthrow the established government. The significance of this loss of naval control has been somewhat obscured by the fact that many, but by no means all, English people wanted a change of government and that, in the event, this proved to have been advantageous, but the lesson deserves to be remembered in a time when potential usurpers lack even the relative benevolence of Dutch William.

The lesson was not forgotten in the eighteenth century, when the threat of a Jacobite landing was long a constant preoccupation. With a less vigilant navy, Prince Charles Edward might have brought more soldiers to Scotland and the Forty-Five have had a different issue. As it was, the naval victories of the War of the Spanish Succession (1702–13) had established a British naval supremacy which endured for most of the century. 'Before that war', Mahan wrote, 'England was one of the sea powers; after it she was *the* sea power, without any second.'[9] What is more, this power was no longer exerted in the Narrow Seas alone. The Navy was active, and often successful, in the Atlantic, in the Mediterranean, even in the Baltic. It was not unknown in the Indian Ocean. This extension of naval protection for an ever-expanding trade was soon reflected, not only in domestic peace and growing prosperity, but also in the popular imagination. In 1740 Thomas Augustine Arne transformed the indifferent verse of James Thomson into the song that was to fire his countrymen for two hundred years: 'Rule Britannia, rule the waves'.[10] In 1778 Dr Johnson, the arbiter of established English thought, pronounced the sentence that was to distinguish one British attitude from that of other nations. If he had merely said 'every man thinks meanly of himself for not having been a soldier', his sentiment would have found an echo in many languages. It took an Englishman to add the words: 'or not having been at sea'.[11]

This emphasis on popular sentiment, as opposed to what may seem the harder facts of swelling trade statistics, of an expanding Empire, of growing riches, is not unwarranted. If Britain – and after 1707 we must use that term – was usually willing to support a naval establishment superior to that of her presumptive enemies, popular sentiment must be given its due. The ruling classes might bear the main burden of taxation, but it was the mass of the people, in the coastal areas at least, who tolerated the operations of the press-gangs, without which the Navy would not have survived during the Napoleonic Wars. Without them Mahan would never have written his famous sentence: 'Those far distant, storm-beaten ships, upon which the Grand Army never looked, stood between it and the dominion of the world.'[12]

Without the sailors thus compelled – harshly described by a contemporary British admiral as 'miscreants of every description, and capable of every crime'[13] – Britain, inferior in 1789 alike in population, in national income and in the production of pig-iron to France, would never have emerged, even in the midst of war, as 'the manufactory and warehouse of Europe'.[14] Historians have rightly emphasised the extent to which British victory over Napoleon depended on British economic and financial strength. Since the days of Mahan they have not always sufficiently stressed how much that very strength, the product of fortunate centuries, was the legacy of immunity, thanks to sea-power, from foreign invasion. As Mahan himself put it: 'the strength of Great Britain could be said to lie in her commerce only as, and because, it was the external manifestation of the wisdom and strength of the British people . . . in their independence and untrammelled pursuit of wealth – they were secured by their powerful navy'.[15]

Nevertheless, it is from 1815, the year of the land battle of Waterloo, that a new era in British naval supremacy must be dated. Before then, in spite of all the glorious victories, there had always been a challenge to meet and overcome. The famous campaign of 1805 had been almost as much of a 'damned nice thing – the nearest run thing you ever saw in your life'[16] as Wellington's final victory. In the nineteenth century the Royal Navy saw much action, but never with anything approaching an equal fleet. British naval mastery might be resented, but it was not seriously disputed. The Navy might be liable to technological challenge – 'the French laid down the first sea-going iron-clad warship,

the GLOIRE in 1858';[17] the admirals might be unduly aged, as the
Crimean War demonstrated; British battleships might even be un-
seaworthy, as some have concluded from the collision of the VICTORIA
and the CAMPERDOWN in 1893.[18] There were also periodical invasion
scares and money was wasted on coastal fortifications, but the popular
instinct was correct: Britannia did rule the waves. What is more, she did
so at remarkably little expense until nearly the end of the century, when
alarm about the pace of foreign naval construction sharply increased the
estimates.

The waves that Britannia ruled also extended more widely than ever
before. The Royal Navy operated against slavers off West Africa and in
the Persian Gulf; it maintained squadrons on both sides of South
America; it intervened in Chinese rivers and it bombarded Japanese
forts. Every aspect of sea-power – trade, colonies, the merchant marine,
shipbuilding, the omnipresence of the Navy – attained a degree of
supremacy and a geographical extension unmatched in any other
century.

In retrospect it seems obvious that the nineteenth century was an
extraordinary era in the history of Britain. She had emerged from the
Napoleonic Wars with much the same economic preponderance as the
war of 1914–18 was later to confer on the United States. In industry, in
trade, in wealth Britain easily outshone countries with larger populations and greater natural resources. Her peaceful political evolution
contrasted with the domestic turmoil that preoccupied her rivals. At
home and abroad events seemed to conspire to create for Britain a
position of predominance as unique as, today, it seems inevitably
ephemeral.

It did not seem so then. On the contrary there was a tendency to
exaggerate the real strength of Britain, whether diplomatically, as in the
futile intervention in the Schleswig–Holstein dispute, or economically,
as in the neglect of industrial innovation in the closing decades of the
century. The music-hall song of 1878

> We don't want to fight, but, by Jingo, if we do
> We've got the ships, we've got the men, we've got the money too

became notorious, but it reflected a popular mood, not least in the
priority accorded to ships. At a more sophisticated level there was,
towards the end of the Victorian era, a general optimism about the
irreversibility of progress and a readiness to find in the history of the past
the inevitable causes, and thus the guarantees, of Britain's present
greatness.

By 1890, therefore, when Captain Mahan of the United States Navy published his book on *The Influence of Sea Power Upon History*, he found an appreciative audience for his twin propositions: that sea-power had made Britain what she was and that Britain was endowed by nature with special advantages in its exercise. His book was followed by others and his thesis was soon extended by British writers. They rationalised what, as we have seen, had long been a national instinct and they did so just as the concept of British mastery at sea was about to come under twofold attack: from the naval construction of rival powers and from such theorists as Mackinder, who delivered his celebrated lecture on 'The Geographical Pivot of History' in 1904.[19] He, too, was to found a school, but his theories had less immediate influence than those of Mahan or the long tradition of British thought or the obvious challenge of events.

Sea-power was still the ruling dogma when the end of the nineteenth century confronted the British government with the unwelcome fact that the Royal Navy was no longer equal to the combined navies of other powers. It was still received doctrine when it became obvious that Germany, where the Kaiser was an ardent reader of Mahan, was intending to pose a single-handed challenge to British naval supremacy.

This supremacy was already overstretched. The long preoccupation of Britain's rivals with their territorial affairs had allowed Britain, and the Royal Navy, to exert an almost universal influence that depended on the absence – periodical invasion scares notwithstanding – of any serious challenge at home. Once that bubble was pricked, sea-power had to be envisaged in different terms. In the metaphor so much favoured by writers of the early twentieth century, the legions had to be called home.

It would, of course, be exaggerated to maintain that the concept of preserving sea-power was the sole reason for the changes in British policy that followed: the abandonment of 'splendid isolation', the abortive efforts to reach agreement with Germany, the altered attitude towards the United States, the alliance with Japan, the entente first with France and then with Russia, Fisher's reorganisation of the Royal Navy. There was, for instance, the idea of the balance of power on the mainland of the continent of Europe. Nevertheless the maritime factor dominated. The fear that the British might no longer 'be masters of the Narrow Sea' shaped British policy from Venezuela to Japan. Everywhere could be discerned the desire to eliminate lesser causes of conflict, to concentrate all efforts on the North Sea, on that ominously nicknamed German Ocean.

The dogma of naval supremacy had become so instinctive to the British people that this vast reorientation of British naval policy, the withdrawal of so many ships from the oceans and the concentration in the Narrow Seas, could be said to be based more on an abstract principle than on a concrete plan. It was widely and automatically accepted that Britain had to be able to master German naval power, but British foreign policy was fundamentally altered and the constituents of the Grand Fleet created before any definite conception was evolved of the strategy to be pursued in a war against Germany: the contingency which the entire revolution in British attitudes was designed to meet. Fisher was an even more remarkable organiser of the British Navy than St. Vincent, but he was unable to put forward a convincing plan for the navy he had created to win a war against a continental power. Close blockade, diversionary raids and peninsular operations had offered a war-winning strategy in 1805: they did not a century later, nor was a satisfactory alternative identified to the argument of the General Staff that a British expeditionary force must join the main battle on the Western front.

Before war had even broken out, one interpretation of sea-power had been tacitly abandoned: its autonomy. It was no longer considered possible for Britain, as she had often but not always done, to sit behind her naval defences and subsidise others to do the fighting on land. Nor, as the war itself proved, could command of the seas be so absolutely secured in the absence of close blockade. Worst of all, as the Kaiser had earlier remarked of the French, the British Admiralty 'had not read their Mahan'.[20] At least they had ignored the verdict that two major wars were to confirm: 'the result of the convoy system, in this and other instances, warrants the inference that, when properly systematized and applied, it will have more success as a defensive measure than hunting for individual marauders . . . looking for a needle in a haystack'.[21]

The First World War thus delivered an ambiguous verdict on the concept of sea-power which, for Britain, had been its predominant cause. The Admiralty had been given almost all they wanted. The Fleet was ready, but for a dimly conceived pattern of events which failed to materialise in the expected form. True, Jellicoe did not lose the war in an afternoon, the German submarine offensive just failed to win it, the distant British blockade was eventually effective, but the decisive victory took place on land.

This is a verdict which should not be exaggerated. Britain would never have played her essential part in the land battles if the Navy had not controlled the Channel, a control that depended on the existence of the Grand Fleet, even if Jutland was no Trafalgar. Britain – and her allies – would not have survived if the Admiralty had not belatedly come to their senses and defeated the German submarines. In the First World War sea-power was ancillary, rather than positively decisive, but it was indispensably ancillary.

It was more than that between the wars. With army and air force neglected and the economy flagging, only an ageing navy and an empire that was as much of a liability as an asset maintained for Britain the status of a great power. In the Near East, in China, around Spain, in the Baltic, even in the Americas, British naval power was significant. It had again expanded from the Narrow Seas to the oceans. But from the early thirties there developed a problem. Britain's potential antagonists were becoming too strong. Even excluding the United States, even relying on alliance with France, there remained Germany, Italy and Japan. Chatfield, whether as First Sea Lord or as Minister for the Coordination of Defence, was always clear on one point: the Royal Navy was not fit to fight all three together. He did not even believe that his projected improvements – which, less fortunate than Fisher, he did not obtain in time – would eventually make this possible. In the crucial thirties he considered that Britain must reduce the number of her potential enemies. He was undoubtedly right, but the task was beyond the resources of diplomacy.

The Second World War, which confronted Britain with all three enemies, thus invited comparison with Mahan's earlier verdict on the Trafalgar campaign:

> the naval superiority of Great Britain lay not in the number of her ships, but in the wisdom, energy and tenacity of her seamen. At best her numbers were but equal to those arrayed against her.[22]

And this superiority, further impeded by defective armament and the crippling neglect of air defence, was not merely slow in attainment, but achieved against Germany and Italy alone. This time the government had not prepared the navy for anyone's war and the deterrence of invasion, the maintenance of supplies, the precarious ascendancy in the Mediterranean: all these were triumphs snatched from the edge of disaster. Once again the final victories were won on land but, if anything was needed to prove that islands need navies, it was Britain's survival during the prior conquest of Europe by the Germans, together with her eventual ability to return to that continent.

Blockade, however, was a failure and so were British naval efforts against Japan. The ships were simply not available and, when they could at last be spared, Britain had still to re-equip herself for the new kind of

naval warfare that had meanwhile developed in the Far East. The British
fleet despatched to the Pacific for the final months had to be provided
with a hastily improvised Fleet Train to ensure its logistic support at sea.
Neither in speed, nor in capacity, nor in training were these miscel-
laneous vessels the equals of the Americans they had come – at British
insistence and in the face of some initial reluctance from Admiral King
of the US Navy – to help. The part played by this fleet in the last
operations was not of major importance to their outcome.

Nevertheless the British Pacific Fleet deployed in 1945 deserves to be
remembered for its sheer size: 272 ships, including 4 battleships, 17
aircraft carriers of various types, 10 cruisers and 40 destroyers. Bearing
in mind the simultaneous existence of an East Indies Fleet of 168 ships,
which also included capital ships, and of substantial forces in home
waters and the Mediterranean, it could reasonably be assumed that
Britain was still a major naval power, even if a small proportion of these
vessels had been contributed by other members of the Commonwealth
and even by European allies. As a manifestation of political will, of the
traditional preoccupation with sea-power, the British Pacific Fleet was
truly imposing after five and a half years of the most devastating and
dangerous war Britain had ever experienced.

Unfortunately, when the United States Navy designated this mighty
British fleet Task Force 57, the title was flattering rather than otherwise.
The American Task Force 51 assembled for the attack on Okinawa in
April 1945 comprised 1205 vessels, including 10 battleships, 8 heavy
cruisers, 4 light cruisers, 18 escort carriers and 82 destroyers. And this
was merely an invasion force. The main American fighting strength was
in the separate Fast Carrier Task Force of 8 battleships, 16 Fleet
carriers, 19 cruisers and over 60 destroyers. When this was later
reinforced by the British Pacific Fleet, the latter could only contribute
1 battleship, 3 fleet carriers (only 6 were in commission in the entire
Royal Navy), 6 cruisers and 15 destroyers.

What was worse, British aircraft carriers were mainly equipped with
aircraft of American manufacture and the logistic support of the British
fleet depended heavily on American help. This was a curious reversal of
the situation in the First World War, when the US Army had depended
on Britain and France not merely for aircraft, but for artillery and
tanks.[23] In the final stages of the war against Japan the Royal Navy was
not merely a lesser ally: it was, to a considerable extent, a superfluous
ally.[24] This too was a curious reversal of the situation obtaining in 1917,
when Vice-Admiral Sims of the US Navy had been disconcerted to
discover that the Admiralty had no need of his new battleships.[25] The

trident had passed from Britain. The United States Navy, technologically and by an order of magnitude, was now supreme.

The persistence into the post-war era, indeed the exacerbation, of this supremacy could be excused by the vast economic advantage of the United States. By 1950 the American Gross National Product of 288 billion dollars was nearly eight times larger than Britain's. American naval supremacy could be made acceptable by belief in undying Anglo-American friendship – forgetting that, as late as September 1939, the US Naval War College was still studying the contingency of war with Britain.[26] But it was still a sea change, something that had never been admitted for one and a third centuries: that the Royal Navy was manifestly inferior, not to a combination of powers, but to a single rival. The mastery of the oceans, however narrowly this might recently have been interpreted, was something to which Britain could no longer aspire.

At this stage, after two exhausting wars and in the light of historical developments during the three previous decades, it seems a reasonable renunciation. The challenger, the aberrations of the twenties and thirties notwithstanding, was an ally as well as a Super-Power. To be second to a mighty friend was surely acceptable and, as disengagement from British imperial responsibilities began, progressively more in keeping with diminished needs. Even after 1815, in the era when Palmerston could grandly proclaim that neither Britain's friends nor her enemies were eternal, only her interests, it had been accepted doctrine that the navy should be no larger than was needed to meet the potential threat. Now that, for a variety of reasons, the United States had come to be regarded as a necessarily perpetual ally, there was surely no cause to attempt more.

Even if these arguments from political expediency and economic necessity are accepted, it is one thing to yield primacy to a powerful ally, quite another to surrender it to a formidable foe. The year 1953 marked an even more sinister stage in Britain's naval decline, when the Soviet Union became the possessor of the world's second largest navy,[27] a navy that had grown by 1960 to about twice the tonnage of the British.[28] For 1977/78 the statistics provided by the International Institute for Strategic Studies were brutally revealing: 82 strategic submarines against 4; 230 major surface combat ships against 75; 234 other submarines against 27; 450,000 men against 77,000.[29] Never since the days of the Vikings had Britain suffered such a crushing naval inferiority to the country generally regarded as her most likely potential enemy.

Sir Walter Raleigh concisely defined the essential problem centuries ago: 'There are two ways in which England may be afflicted. The one by invasion . . . the other by impeachment of our Trades.'[30] The second, as growing dependence on imported food, energy and raw materials suggested, and as the experience of two world wars had demonstrated, was now the more acute, but the danger of actual invasion had attained a degree that would have been acceptable to few British rulers since Ethelred the Unready. Even James II had good grounds for expecting naval victory over his Dutch brother-in-law. For hundreds of years of her history Britain had struggled, usually with success, to maintain supremacy at sea. In the early years of this century, when she reluctantly renounced the idea of superiority to the next two navies combined, she nevertheless maintained the standard of a sixty per cent advantage over her German rival. As late as 1919 she had indisputably the strongest navy in the world.

Quarter of a century afterwards she was outclassed by the United States. Another thirty years passed and Britain's naval strength was less by an order of magnitude than that of either the United States or the Soviet Union. Fifty-five years had effected a revolutionary departure from the traditional assumptions of four centuries. Nor was it only the number and strength of British warships that declined. They were progressively withdrawn from the oceans without thereby re-establishing supremacy in the Narrow Seas. They were supported by a diminishing merchant marine, an overseas trade of less relative import-ance and a shipbuilding industry almost in ruins. British sea-power seemed on the verge of eclipse.

History is largely a narration of the altered circumstances of peoples and the facts of change need not, in themselves, furnish cause for astonishment. But they do require an attempt at explanation. That will be the subject of the next chapter. They also provoke enquiry concerning the future. That will be the matter of this book. Is Britain's naval decline ephemeral or a continuing trend; must it simply be accepted or could some reversal be attempted; what, if any, future can be envisaged for the British navy and the concept of British sea-power?

2 The Causes of our Present Discontents

After the injuries of two of the severest wars that ever the Sea yet knew . . .

Samuel Pepys, 1675[1]

No student of history should expect the patterns of the past to be self-perpetuating, but the recorded insistence of the British on the maintenance of sea-power did correspond to certain obvious needs and opportunities. These were not diminished, but actually increased, by many of the trends that developed in the first three quarters of the twentieth century. A potential enemy had now emerged with much the same ideological incentive to the conquest of the British Isles as that once possessed by Philip II or the leaders of Revolutionary France. Growing British dependence on imports had sharpened the weapon, wielded in different forms by Napoleon, by Imperial Germany and by Hitler, of their denial. The identity and location of the enemy had reinforced the geographical advantage of the British Isles, that unsinkable aircraft carrier athwart the exits from the Baltic and the Norwegian Seas. On the face of it, there was more for the Navy to do than there had ever been. But there was also a very general acquiescence in its decline.

The explanations usually offered for this phenomenon fall into three categories, each of them overlapping and interrelated with the others, which it will nevertheless be convenient to consider separately, not for their historical interest alone, but as pointers to the future. They may be briefly described as political, economic and strategic.

The first, which tends to receive a sympathetic hearing among naval officers, attributes much of the decline to an unfortunate change in political priorities. The British people have become less interested in the security of their islands and of their essential imports than in their own immediate and personal welfare. This argument lends itself easily to statistical illustration. In 1905 £36.8 million was spent on the navy and only £28 million on all the civilian outlay of the state.[2] This, admittedly, was a ratio that could scarcely be expected to survive the progressive expansion during the twentieth century of governmental expenditure on social reform and welfare. Yet, as late as 1962, defence was still the largest single category of British public spending, only to be overtaken in the following year by social security benefits.[3] These have remained ahead ever since and so, from 1970, has education. Housing and Environmental Services joined the front runners in 1973 and by 1980 the National Health Service was a whisker ahead of defence, which then ranked fourth, receiving half as much money as social security benefits and one ninth of the total expenditure of central and local government. In 1967 the share of defence had been one seventh.[4]

In itself expenditure on the welfare of the nation can not be considered as inimical to defence. Correlli Barnett, in his brilliant and profoundly depressing book *The Collapse of British Power*, has demonstrated how often, and how seriously, British defence efforts in the first half of the twentieth century suffered from the deficiencies of British education. The inroads made upon the physical fitness of the British working class by poverty and inadequate medical care and unsanitary conditions at home or at work were reflected in the numbers of recruits rejected as unfit for service in the armed forces. Even before we come to consider the economic basis for military power, it is clear that only much increased civilian expenditure could have maintained the British people at an educational and physical level comparable to that of their potential rivals. The most fervent navalist must admit the necessity of civilian expenditure, but he may question the degree to which its priority is pushed.

In the third quarter of the twentieth century this priority was increasingly being exerted at the expense of the British armed forces. This was not unprecedented. Prolonged periods of peace – and this one is approaching the length of the interval between Waterloo and the Crimean War – have always been accompanied by reductions in defence expenditure and often by a dangerous neglect of naval strength. Moreover, as Mahan observed nearly a century ago, 'popular governments are not generally favourable to military expenditure, however necessary'[5] and British governments have become increasingly 'popular' in his sense of the word, meaning responsive to the immediate aspirations of a mass electorate. Under the influence of these two factors it is scarcely surprising that spending on the long-term security of the British people has been increasingly submerged by the mounting cost of their demands for medical care, housing and environmental services, education and social security. At 1975 prices civil expenditure increased between 1967 and 1977: defence expenditure declined during the same period, even allowing for an incomplete recovery from the nadir of 1974.[6] It is even remarkable that, as a proportion of the gross national product, it was still at the historically high peacetime level (compared with 3.7 per cent in 1913) – a higher level than that attained by richer countries such as France and Germany – of 4.7 per cent in 1979/80.[7]

Unfortunately it is not enough to compare defence expenditure with previous levels or with that of allies or even with the national income. The true comparison is between the strength of the armed forces thus produced and those of the obvious enemy. This is a subject to be explored in later chapters. Here it will be sufficient to assert what few British politicians would deny: neither singly nor in combination with allies are the British armed forces adequate for war against the Soviet Union. If this is true and insofar as it is the result of political trends in Britain, what prospect is there of reversing these trends? Could the British electorate be persuaded to accord a higher priority to defence, thereby allowing politicians to divert resources from other purposes to the strengthening of the navy?

At first sight the historical precedents are encouraging. When Mahan published his gloomy comment on popular governments in 1890, he added: 'there are signs that England tends to drop behind'.[8] He did not foresee that, under the spur of a foreign challenge, British naval expenditure would be more than tripled in the next two decades. He might even have been surprised that much of this increase was the work of the most 'popular' governments Britain had yet experienced: the Liberal administrations of Campbell-Bannerman and Asquith, with their extensive programmes of social reform. It was again a 'popular' government, Attlee's Labour administration, that raised British defence expenditure to the highest ratio of the gross national product ever attained in time of peace – 11 per cent in 1951.[9] That again was in response to the perceived threat of war. There is even the fact that, in 1979, the British Conservative party won an election on a manifesto that included the promise of an unspecified increase in defence expenditure, although public opinion polls reported few of their respondents as regarding defence as even among the important issues in the election.

Such arguments should not be ignored, but they are not enough to prove the case of those who believe that determined and enlightened leadership would suffice to awaken the British people to their danger and to win their consent to the measures required to avert it. The optimism engendered by historical instances must also be weighed against secular trends. The great naval rearmament at the beginning of the century had to be justified to a smaller, better informed, more patriotic and more deferential electorate. To the student of late twentieth-century politics it is astonishing to read Marder's account of the extent of popular agitation for more Dreadnoughts and of the massive support accorded to this campaign by the Press.[10] Moreover, the cost of this rearmament fell largely on those best able to bear it and, because of their proximity to the ruling class, most inclined to support it. Finally, because of the concentration of spending on the navy, the rise in total defence expenditure was modest: from 2.4 per cent of the gross national product in 1890 to 3.7 per cent in 1913.[11]

The corresponding efforts of 1950–3 were more easily accepted by voters who had recently experienced war and who were not yet accustomed to ever rising expectations of welfare. Today any British government must confront an electorate of whom the majority have known only peace and to whom the overwhelming threat is that of a reduction in the benefits they take as their due from the State. Nor does this government – any government – enjoy the authority and prestige of its predecessors in even the fifties of this century. There is no longer the same willingness to give the government of the day the benefit of the doubt: to assume that official pronouncements on foreign affairs, defence, the national interest deserve at least a degree of credence.

This scepticism, indeed cynicism, is not entirely unjustified, nor is it unprecedented. In the thirties, for instance, many of those anxious to resist Germany did not believe that the British government could be trusted to do it and many supporters of the government saw little need for resistance. Today, however, there is a possibly unique combination of widespread personal interest in priority for civil expenditure, of incredulity concerning the need for defence and of contempt for authority. In 1983 there must be added the peculiar paradox of a government ostensibly favourable to defence, yet hostile to those policies best calculated to sustain it: increased expenditure by the State and economic nationalism. This is a difficult atmosphere in which to seek popular support for a significant change in the allocation of scarce resources. Nor is it confined to Britain. Similar tendencies are discernible in all the nations to which Britain is at present allied. It is hard to resist the conclusion that there is a long-standing and persistent trend in the political evolution of the industrialised democracies which is adverse to the maintenance of an effective defence.

What is more, the factor which in the past served to reverse such trends, even belatedly, seems no longer to be fully effective. Fear prompted British rearmament, often needlessly, on many occasions during the nineteenth century. It did so again at the beginning of the twentieth century, during the late thirties and in the early fifties. It was potent in the United States in the early sixties. But the great accretion of Soviet strength in the seventies, together with their much increased activism throughout the world, has prompted little response from the Western powers. The more the Russians have become capable of victorious war, the more the conviction has grown among their potential victims that they would never attempt it. By comparison the complacency of the twenties seems justified and even the wishful thinking of the early thirties is understandable. One is bound to ask: is there anything the Soviet Union could do, short of war itself, that would convince the peoples of the West of the dangers that they face?

These are rhetorical questions and political developments are notoriously difficult to predict. The technological problems are more easily defined, but harder to surmount. When the British government were finally convinced, at the beginning of the century, of the German naval menace, it took less than two years, from March 1905 to December 1906, to design, build and commission a warship so revolutionary as to supersede all her rivals: HMS DREADNOUGHT.[12] Before a decade was out, this ship was only one of a British fleet of thirty vessels, nearly all of them more advanced than the prototype. Her namesake of half a century later, the nuclear submarine HMS DREADNOUGHT, drew heavily on American experience in design and manufacture, but still needed four years to complete and, twelve years after her commissioning, had only twelve sister ships.[13] Today it can take longer to introduce a new shipborne missile than it once took to build a fleet.

The political explanation of British naval weakness is thus more plausible than it is encouraging. On the one hand there are identifiable trends that have manifestly reduced the priority enjoyed by the navy: the enormous growth in the civil side of governmental expenditure; the dependence on this expenditure of a mass electorate; the diminished popular experience of war or belief in its likelihood; the scepticism accorded to the concept of the national interest and, above all, to calls for personal sacrifice in that cause. On the other hand there are the uncomfortable facts that public indifference to the necessity of defence has persisted during a period of unprecedented threat; that this threat has been more real, yet perceived as less immediate, in the seventies than it was in the fifties and sixties; and that the time required for any effective response to an increased perception of this threat would today be longer than it has ever been before.

Any purely political analysis, therefore, is likely to reach the conclusion that only an unexpected crisis would persuade the electorate to accept a significant strengthening of the navy and that, unless the Soviet Union is willing to sound a major alarm many years before a major strike, such a belated British conversion would have little practical effect. This could be too pessimistic. The government now in office might succeed in its declared intention of reducing public civil expenditure, of increasing spending on defence and even of restoring the economy: it might, therefore, reverse long-established trends and transform the political climate. Stranger things have occurred in earlier periods of British history. And the last three decades have been characterised by a remarkably slow and cautious exploitation of Soviet opportunities. At best, however, the question remains open: is there still time to re-create an effective British navy?

In part, the answer depends on two other questions. Is it economically possible and – political and economic constraints apart – is there still a useful rôle for the British navy?

Scepticism, even wilful incredulity, concerning the existence of a threat is nothing new. Even the younger Pitt produced a masterpiece of wishful thinking on 17 February 1792, when he told the House of Commons:

> Unquestionably there never was a time in the history of this country, when, from the situation of Europe, we might more reasonably expect fifteen years of peace than at the present moment.[14]

It was a remarkable prelude to almost two decades of war. By comparison the politicians and public opinion of the early twentieth century seem positively prescient. Yet, in the years before the First World War, even in the last days of peace, there were many influential Britons who refused to believe in the German menace. There were fewer who regarded it as beyond Britain's economic capacity to meet. The latter category had increased in number and influence by the thirties, but the majority, the consensus, still regarded the decisive question as being whether or not a threat existed. It was not widely supposed that efforts to meet the threat might be hopeless rather than needless.

Today the situation is different. It is not enough to convince the people that a threat exists. It is also necessary to demonstrate that an effective response is possible. The idea of making sacrifices in peace to ensure security and victory in war has always been unpopular. But, if no conceivable sacrifice will be enough for either security or victory, why make any? This is the question that has to be answered, particularly by the navy, before any final conclusion is reached about the political possibilities of reversing Britain's naval decline. It is a question that needs at least preliminary exploration in considering the next set of causes.

These were earlier given the cursory description of 'economic', but this all-embracing adjective covers two rather different sets of judgments. The first concerns the total capacity of the economy to equip and support armed forces; the second the extent to which this capacity can be so employed without side-effects liable to undermine the economy itself and thus its future ability to maintain the armed forces that have been created. It would be an over-simplification to say that the first is a criterion for use in wartime and that the second is more appropriate to a period of peace, but this is in practice often the case. Before the Second World War, for instance, the need to preserve British exports was recognised as a constraint on rearmament, but this consideration was largely abandoned during the war itself. Another way of looking at the distinction is to argue that the first kind of judgment indicates what is possible, the second what is desirable. The difference often depends on the time-factor or the urgency of the threat: in 1940 it was worth ordering military equipment without regard to the ability to pay for it; in 1938 it was not.

Unfortunately neither criterion can be determined with much pretence at objective accuracy. During the Revolutionary and Napoleonic Wars, for instance, and contrary to all expectations, British economic strength actually increased. Even foreign trade almost doubled between 1792 and 1802.[15] In the two world wars of the twentieth century Britain relied heavily on American logistic support, but her own productive capacity was nevertheless greatly expanded. Correlli Barnett, for instance, talks of the drift and decline of fifty years being reversed in three years of the First World War, of 218 new factories, of a doubling of electricity production, of the creation of a chemical industry.[16] Wartime experience undoubtedly fortifies the navalist view that where there is a will there is a way.

Even so, total capacity must impose some ceiling, however hard this may be to define with objective precision. Nobody would argue that the

British economy could support either the domestic production or the importation of ballistic nuclear missiles and their ancillary equipment on a scale comparable to the armouries of the United States or the Soviet Union. The most ardent of admirals would admit that, if the British gross national product is one eighth of the American and one third of the Russian,[17] the navies, to say nothing of the armed forces, of the three powers can scarcely be equally matched. This argument from capacity, relative as well as absolute, is well-established. Before the First World War the British government were satisfied that the economic capacity of the country enabled them to maintain a naval race with Germany (admittedly because the latter was also supporting a much larger army). After that war, when the American gross national product was probably about three times greater than the British, the government conceded that a similar race with the United States was impossible and thankfully settled for an agreed parity by the Washington Treaty of 1922. By 1950, when the American gross national product was eight times the British and the American alliance had been accepted as eternal, the question did not even arise. In 1976, however, the problem was slightly different. The Soviet Union was, according to the estimates of the International Institute for Strategic Studies, spending over eleven times as much on defence as Britain.[18] This represented a much larger share of a greater gross national product, but the efforts of various authorities to quantify either are conflicting. It may, however, reasonably be suggested that British defence spending could scarcely aspire to match the Soviet level. But the Soviet Union was subject to manifold handicaps: the need to rival the United States in preparations for nuclear war; the requirement for air and ground forces capable of conventional war on two fronts; the necessity of garrisoning and controlling the East European Empire; the desirability of an overseas intervention capability; the geographical inevitability of dividing her naval resources among four fleets with different tasks, widely separated bases and little possibility of unopposed cooperation.

In these circumstances, which meant that only a fraction of that part of Soviet efforts devoted to the navy could be directed against the British Isles, why should Britain be incapable of keeping the mastery of the Narrow Seas? She was not required, not least because of her allies, to match total Soviet strength. Only a fraction of a fraction was needed: to deny to the Soviet Union the possibilities of invasion or of 'impeachment of our Trades'.

It is here that the second category of economic arguments becomes important. The first criterion, that of total economic capacity, whether absolute or relative, is clearly flexible. It imposes some limitations, both quantitative and, as Correlli Barnett has demonstrated was true of armour-plate, guns and precision instruments in the late thirties, qualitative. Yet, as recently as 1981, Britain spent more on defence than West Germany, although the latter had double the gross national product.[19] In 1976 ratios of the gross national product spent on defence ranged from less than 1 per cent in Japan to over 35 per cent in Egypt and Israel and the two last-named countries maintained stronger forces than many larger and richer states.[20]

Unfortunately this very flexibility of choice becomes a weapon in the hands of those opposed to defence expenditure. The favourite argument of the British Treasury, particularly during defence reviews, is that economic performance is inversely related to defence expenditure. France, Germany and Japan, to say nothing of many lesser countries, so the Treasury maintained, have overtaken Britain economically precisely because they spent a smaller proportion of their gross national product on defence and could thus spend more on re-equipping their industry and promoting their exports.

It would take a separate book and the assistance of a team of economic historians effectively to expose the fallacies of this argument. Here a few brief comments must suffice.

In the first place, it is generally agreed that Britain's economic decline began over a century ago. To some extent this may have been inevitable. The British people had long been inferior in numbers, as in natural resources, to France and Germany, but in 1871 they were surpassed by the Americans as well. It was beyond all expectation that the British could long continue to produce, as they still did in that same year, more pig-iron than the rest of the world put together. Nor could they, even with their colonies, forever retain a foreign trade exceeding the combined totals of France, Germany, Italy and the United States. In the long run larger numbers were bound to prevail in the older, labour-intensive industries.

What is as surprising as it is deplorable, is that the British did not meet the challenge by diversification and innovation. Native genius was not lacking, but the aniline dyes (discovered in 1856 by an Englishman) were commercially developed in Germany; agricultural machinery (pioneered in Scotland) became increasingly American; the Scot who invented the telephone patented it in the United States in 1875; the manufacture of electrical apparatus, in the following decade, was dominated by Germany. Well before the end of the nineteenth century, in a period of historically low British defence expenditure, at a time when France and Germany maintained large armies, Britain had lost the commanding industrial lead she had established during the Revolutionary and Napoleonic Wars. In the production of steel, the dominant manufacture of the age, she had actually been overtaken by both Germany and the United States.

Neither the origins of this decline, nor its long continuation, had anything to do with British defence expenditure. Indeed, as Correlli Barnett has ably argued, the efforts demanded by the two world wars provided the main interruptions, if not reversals, to the downward trend. It is thus historically inadequate, when confronted by a phenomenon over a hundred years old, to explain it by comparisons drawn only from the third quarter of the twentieth century. And, even in this period, Germany's fastest growth coincided with her rearmament (her gross national product doubled between 1952 and 1962, but her defence expenditure trebled) and France's followed two wars – in Indo China and in Algeria – more debilitating than any suffered by Britain in this particular epoch.

Many causes can be suggested for Britain's economic decline – the educational system; the organisation of industry; the distorting effects of having, and the traumatic impact of losing, an Empire; the power of the trade unions; the conflict of classes; the lack of political leadership; the influence of the Treasury – but blaming it all on the maintenance, for a minority of the period, of a higher ratio of defence expenditure simply will not do.

This argument is nevertheless important, both because it exercises more influence than it should and because, in exceptional cases, defence expenditure can impose a genuine strain on the economy. In the late thirties, for instance, industry was so run-down that it could neither fulfil the rearmament programme from its own resources, nor provide a sufficient export surplus to cover the cost of purchases from abroad. Only the eventual grant of Lend-Lease then prevented the British economy from collapsing under the demands of defence. Admittedly the sorry state of British industry at that time was in part the result of the earlier neglect of British defence. A steady programme of re-equipment in the twenties would have retained the essential manufacturing potential developed during the First World War and prevented the crisis of the late thirties from assuming so acute a form. In a period of underused capacity and massive unemployment it would also have benefited the economy as a whole. Beatty who, as First Sea Lord, predicted in 1921–2 that failure to build warships would destroy the capacity to manufacture armour-plate was a better economic prophet than the Treasury mandarins.[21]

Nevertheless, the debating point of the politician who, when asked how he would escape the dilemma confronting his opponents, replies that he would never have got into it, is not available to the practical administrator, who must rearm as he can and not as he would. Today, as in the past, the legacy of neglect will afford the Treasury an easy opportunity to argue that increased defence expenditure will strain and distort an economy unprepared for this necessity.

The vulnerability of the British economy must be admitted, as must the superior wealth and growth achieved by other countries. Where the original argument fails is in its extension to the assumption that money saved on defence is automatically devoted to the kind of productive investment that stimulates economic growth. This scarcely emerges from the statistics. At 1975 prices, for instance, British defence expenditure was lower than it had been in 1967 in each of the following ten years. The decline in gross domestic fixed capital formation between 1967 and 1977 was even steeper.[22] It is at least plausible that the exact opposite may be true: increased defence expenditure demands new investment, particularly in high technology, which subsequently has a commercial spin-off. But for the demands of defence, would Britain today have a significant position in the petroleum industry, in chemicals, in aerospace, in electronics? And, whatever the political composition of the government that achieved major savings on defence, would there be more than two destinations for the money: transfer payments under Labour or increased imports of consumer goods under Conservatives?

Since 1919, therefore, two economic trends have powerfully influenced the decline in British naval strength. The first was the real regression of the British economy, relative to that of rival states. This was gradual before the Second World War, but has been precipitous in the last thirty years. In 1950 the British gross national product surpassed that of Germany and France alike; in 1965 it was inferior to Germany's and equal to France's; by 1973 it was half Germany's and much inferior to that of France. The second has been the bias, conspicuous in the Treasury but arguably reflecting a more widely shared view, against defence expenditure as such. This is of ancient origin, but it has been growing. In 1935, for instance, the then Head of the Treasury, Sir Warren Fisher, played an honourable part in urging the necessity of rearmament. He has had few successors. By the seventies a new challenge had been added to the familiar armoury of arguments concerning the inadequacy of resources, the existence of competing demands and the illusory nature of the threat. Did we, it was asked, actually need a navy? What could armed forces hope to achieve? What difference would it make if they did not exist?

In repetitive defence reviews the Treasury put the Ministry of Defence to the question: define the purpose of your expenditure and its expected results. This may be regarded as a legitimate interrogation, but it is inevitably a difficult one. Defence is a confusingly hypothetical problem for a country with no intention of taking the offensive. The intentions of the enemy can only be guessed. Moreover, if any defence depends on the cooperation of allies and if some forms of defence offer little hope of success, the question must arise: if you are not sure of victory, why try?

It is here that the economists join hands with the politicians in their criticism of defence expenditure. Each starts with different ideas about alternative uses of the money, but both are united in demanding that the utility of defence should be justified. This is scarcely surprising. Retention of an existing naval superiority – the issue before 1914 – had been a simple concept, enjoying wide popular appeal and only open to criticism on margins and methods: were four, six or eight new battleships necessary for salvation? Even in 1939 the idea of matching Germany and Italy, though difficult to attain, did not seem inconceivable.

More sophisticated arguments are needed today, when the British people have long been accustomed to two awkward ideas: that their navy is inferior in strength to its potential antagonist and that even a superior navy, if that were possible, would not suffice to prevent the destruction of the British Isles.

It is a painful dilemma for a staff officer. He realises the political futility of putting forward proposals to meet the full potential threat. But how is he to justify partial preparations for a lesser menace? What acceptable compromise is there between the assured superiority demanded before the First World War and the pacifist abnegation widely favoured since the Second?

In this dilemma the Treasury have undoubtedly secured a tactical advantage. They have arrogated to themselves the privilege of questioning the strategic judgments of the Ministry of Defence. I do not say they are wrong. The conventional wisdom should always be subjected to challenge. Unfortunately the process has not been reciprocal. The Treasury have successfully evaded any confrontation on the issue of economic judgments. This was partly a matter of those 'Treasury manners' about which Lloyd George complained,[23] but more the result of the absence of countervailing expertise. The Ministry of Defence have a Chief Scientific Adviser and any number of variously graded assisting scientists, but they do not have a Chief Economist, although in recent years and at a lower level in the hierarchy an Economic Adviser has appeared.

As a result the Ministry of Defence have fought the Treasury on unequal terms, unable effectively to present those alternative arguments which might suggest that, in conditions of depression, of unemployment, of under-utilised capacity, defence expenditure is a positive tonic to an ailing economy. This is a long-standing weakness. When one thinks of the follies of British economic policy between the wars and the devastating impact on the armed forces – even to the point of naval mutiny – of a misguided deflation, one cannot resist the idle query: suppose the Chiefs of Staff had then engaged Keynes as a consultant. Might not the combination of defence requirements and the 'pump-priming' theory of public works have been more effective together than was either in isolation?

This is fantasy, but the need is real. The effective Treasury monopoly of official economic argument has allowed them to reinforce the adverse political trends of the last fifty years. Ministers already convinced of the political unpopularity of defence expenditure have been fortified by the unchallenged advice of the Treasury that this would also be economically undesirable, if not impossible. Yet the historical record is clear: in the thirties Germany restored her economy through rearmament; Britain attempted neither objective until both were too late.

If the regeneration of the navy is to be possible, therefore, the political climate must be transformed by demonstrating the reality of the threat, by establishing the strategic possibility of meeting it and by overcoming the economic objections. The last could actually be the easiest.

On 24 June 1950, for instance, North Korean forces invaded South Korea. Today that episode is little remembered in Britain, but at the time it was acutely alarming, not least because it had been preceded by such indications of Soviet aggressiveness in Europe as the Communist coup d'état in Czechoslovakia and the blockade of Berlin. Even before the Chinese joined in the fighting and drove the forces of the United Nations into headlong retreat, there was real apprehension in Britain that the Korean incident might prove to be the start of a general war. It is scarcely surprising that, as early as 26 July 1950, the British Minister of Defence announced a programme of rearmament nor that, as one military setback in Korea followed another, this programme was progressively increased. The danger seemed evident and the needs of the British Armed Forces, which had been steadily reduced since the Second World War and had been living on their accumulated stocks, were obvious.

It was nevertheless an inconvenient moment for rearmament. The economy was just beginning to recover from the siege conditions of the Second World War. Both production and productivity had been steadily increasing, investments were being made, the social services developed. The standard of living was rising and wartime controls and restrictions were being cautiously relaxed. All this was fully occupying a still precarious economy. Unemployment was negligible and exceeded by unfilled vacancies. Demand was no problem, only supply and, as always, the balance of payments. The last thing anyone wanted – economists or politicians – was a return to those defence exigencies from which the country was escaping.

The record of achievement, in these particularly unfavourable circumstances, is thus impressive. In 1949/50, before the threat was apparent, defence expenditure had been reduced to £744 million or 7 per cent of the national income. In the following year this was increased to £830 million and the estimate for 1951/52 was £1300 million. Not all of this could actually be spent, the state of the economy imposing real constraints, but expenditure in 1952/53 rose to £1513 million. In three years, therefore, defence expenditure had been doubled and, on this occasion, without external aid.

Before taking this multiple – a doubling of defence expenditure in three years – as a yardstick of the economically possible, two further factors need to be considered. They are contradictory. The first is that this effort did damage the economy. The second is that this damage was inflicted on an economy already fully stretched rather than on one in which, for instance, shipyards were starved of orders, the automotive industry could not resist foreign competition, the steel industry was being forced into contraction and unemployment was reaching levels unknown since the thirties.

The first factor has, perhaps, since been given excessive weight, particularly by the Treasury. There was an economic crisis in 1951. Joan Mitchell,[24] in a very fair and balanced account, lays particular emphasis on the loss of $2 billion from the reserves, but she attributes much of this to factors extraneous to rearmament itself: the rise in raw material prices caused by the Korean War, for instance. The other penalties of rearmament she sees mainly as the sacrifice of rises in the standard of living that might otherwise have been attained. Moreover, so she argues, 'by the end of 1952, recovery from the crisis of 1951 can be said to have been completed'.[25] When one considers the extent and gravity of the other economic crises that have afflicted Britain since the Second World

War, usually in the absence of any special defence effort, one may perhaps conclude that this was a cheap price to pay.

The second factor – the difference between the impact of defence expenditure on a fully stretched economy and on one already in recession – is more difficult to analyse. The surplus capacity theoretically available in the latter often proves to be in the wrong kind of industry or in an insufficiently skilled pool of unemployed. This is a handicap even more likely to be encountered today, when the demands of defence would bear particularly hard on the highest technology.

It would thus be rash to argue that doubling defence expenditure would be more painless today than in 1951 simply because there is now more slack in the economy. Since 1951 we have lost control of our imports and of our currency. Even if these were regained and if the increased spending took place over a longer period, considerable strain would have to be expected. Nevertheless, if the example of 1950–2 is anything to go by, that strain need not be intolerable, not least because of the existence of a significant cushion in the form of arms exports and of the protection afforded by North Sea Oil to the balance of payments.

What is or is not tolerable depends, however, on political perceptions. Even if we assume that increased defence expenditure is, in the light of earlier precedents, economically possible, it still remains to be demonstrated that such expenditure is both necessary and useful: that politicians can reasonably be expected to tell the electorate that a stronger navy would actually achieve something of value to their country and themselves.

3 The Relevance of Sea-Power

What is the objective in naval warfare if command of the sea cannot be achieved?

Rosinski[1]

Before attempting to examine the prospective utility to Britain of the Royal Navy it seems desirable to consider briefly the general relevance of sea-power in a world that has undergone profound changes, political as well as technological, in the thirty-six years – the longest period in modern history – that have elapsed since two fleets last met in naval battle.

In doing so one temptation must regretfully be set aside. Space is lacking to discuss the argument, skilfully deployed in Chapter 7 of Paul Kennedy's admirable and often quoted *Rise and Fall of British Naval Mastery*, that a secular and adverse change has occurred in the relationship between sea power and land power. Two excuses may be advanced. First, Kennedy's argument is directed more to the British dilemma, which will be considered later, than to the general principle in question here. Secondly, as the legendary Chinese said of the French Revolution, it is perhaps too soon to judge. What is thirty-six years? As long as the two Super-Powers continue to spend more than ever before on their navies, the concept of sea-power must still deserve some thought on its maritime merits.

Sea-power has been very frequently and variously described, but Roskill's definition is concise:

The function of maritime power is to win and keep control of the sea for one's own use, and to deny such control to one's adversaries.[2]

36

Here 'control' is employed as the equivalent of the older 'command of the sea' which, so Corbett declared, 'means nothing but the control of maritime communications'.[3] In modern American usage, however, 'sea control' is often contrasted, as a separate naval mission, with the projection of naval power ashore. This is, if not a distinction without a difference, perhaps a juxtaposition of the whole with one of its parts. As Admiral Holloway pointed out, when Chief of Naval Operations in the United States, sea control is 'a prerequisite of all other naval tasks and most sustained operations by the general purpose forces of other services'.[4] It thus seems preferable, at least at the outset of the argument, to follow Roskill in treating control as a condition for using the sea.

This is a classical conception, primarily applicable to war and to nations aspiring to naval superiority, but capable of extension for other purposes. This process has to start with the reminder that, even in the light of historical experience and without considering the impact of recent developments, neither control nor its denial can reasonably be expected to prove complete, permanent or universal. It has often happened, whether in the seventeenth century or for much of the Second World War, that control has remained in dispute. Even when one fleet has established a clear ascendancy, this has often not been extended to all uses of the sea. In the Revolutionary and Napoleonic Wars, when British sea control reached its zenith, the depredations of enemy commerce-raiders were always substantial, even if convoy made them tolerable. In the First World War the U-boat campaign undermined British naval strategy and threatened actual defeat. The time taken by the US Navy to establish control of the Pacific during the Second World War was enough to permit the emergence of fundamental and lasting political changes in most of the limitrophe countries. The interruption of control, even for brief periods, has often been critical. In 1940 forty-eight hours of aberration by the Royal Navy sealed the fate of Norway. Finally, there are usually some seas – the Baltic in both world wars – in which the strongest navy does not even attempt to win control.

These inevitable imperfections of sea control are often aggravated by mere human error – Admiral Nagumo at Midway, for instance. Nevertheless they do not invalidate the concept: they illustrate the difficulty of its application. This has to depend on the resources available, the nature of the conflict and the priority attaching to the particular uses of the sea which it is intended either to protect or to deny. It is the first of these factors that has received most attention and traditional theory assumed that sea control and ultimate victory could be expected to reward the stronger navy. Even the experience of the two

world wars is often interpreted in terms of British failure to provide
matériel of the right kind and in sufficient quantity. Undoubtedly the
lack of secure bases (in both wars), the deficiencies of naval construction
and armament, the utterly inadequate provisions for defence against
mines (those pathetic sweepers in the Dardanelles), submarines or
aircraft can be attributed both to technical blunders and to resource
constraints. But the disappointing results of attempts at sea control or
denial, together with some of the deficiencies in matériel, had a more
fundamental cause in prior misconceptions of the nature of the coming
conflict and of the strategy required to meet it.

Before the First World War, for instance, neither the British nor the
German Navy could seriously complain that their demands had been
denied by their respective politicians. But the Germans had provoked
the British into war by building a battle-fleet for which they could, in the
event, devise no strategic rôle. Its deterrent function was not merely a
political failure, but a boomerang. When war came, the close blockade it
was intended to break, once attrition had reduced the superiority of the
British fleet, did not materialise. The distant blockade remained beyond
German reach and was ultimately effective. Yet the British neither
foresaw the German counter (which might have been much more
devastating without the wasted expenditure on the High Seas Fleet) of a
submarine war on trade nor, until the eleventh hour, reacted by
adopting the classical expedient of convoy and escort.

Two fortuitous events transformed, for Britain, the character of the
Second World War and obscured the extent to which strategic
misconceptions were responsible for British unreadiness for any kind of
conflict in 1939. The German invasion of the Soviet Union and the
Japanese attack on Pearl Harbor provided Britain with allies more
powerful than herself and created conditions in which the British army
and, more dubiously, Bomber Command could make an important
contribution to the defeat of Germany. The initial continental commitment and the bombing offensive seemed retrospectively – it was nearly
posthumously – justified. Yet neither the expeditionary force nor the
long-range bombers came near achieving the original objectives of
deterring Germany from war and preventing her conquest of Europe.
The continent was lost and with it substantial British forces. What is
more, the diversion, before and during the war, of resources to these two
unproductive tasks left too little to provide sufficient ships and aircraft
of the right kind to ensure the defence of the British Isles and their
seaborne communications. If Britain was neither invaded in 1940 nor
starved in subsequent years, it was in spite of British strategy, not
because of it.

It would be unconvincing to explore the hypothetical consequences of the adoption, in the early thirties, of a maritime strategy intended to ensure the defence of Britain, even to keep her in a state of peace, until such time as a change in the international situation offered a real prospect, which did not exist in 1939, of actually defeating Germany. This alternative strategy of insuring against a British defeat was rejected in favour of gambling on the chances of deterrence and ultimate victory. Fortune favoured the reckless decision and it can never be proved that the two options were mutually exclusive or that the first offered rather better prospects than the second. The possibility nevertheless deserves to be remembered, as does the subordinate rôle actually allotted to British sea-power, by anyone tempted to invoke past precedent as a guide to future choice. Naturally the governing factor will again be the political objective, which has to determine the general strategy, and the priority allotted within that strategy, to sea control or sea denial. There is nothing eternal or immutable about British strategic objectives and even for an island-state these two expedients do not have the same value in every conflict.

Nor are they necessarily exercised for the same purposes. It is the nature of the conflict which decides the relative importance of using the sea oneself or denying it to adversaries, of distant waters or the Narrow Seas, of the immediate outcome or an ultimate decision. In 1588, in 1688 and in 1940 what mattered was to deny the use of the Channel to an enemy invasion. Failure was irredeemable. On the other hand, German control of the Channel for the return of their warships from Brest in February 1942 merely humiliated the British without affecting the outcome of the war.

This discrimination between those uses of the sea, whether by oneself or the enemy, which can be decisive and those which are not, is inadequately reflected in traditional theory. This tended to follow Mahan in regarding command of the sea as in itself a sufficient objective and one to be attained by

the possession of that overbearing power on the sea which drives the enemy's flag from it, or allows it to appear only as a fugitive.[5]

Corbett, for instance, argued that:

A plan of war which has the destruction of trade for its primary object implies in the party using it an inferiority at sea. Had he superiority, his object would be to convert that superiority to a working command by battle or blockade.[6]

This is an interesting example of putting the cart before the horse, destruction of trade being rejected, not on its merits as a form of sea denial, but as an attribute of an 'inferior' (the word has moral overtones) navy. Admittedly, Corbett did not believe that war on trade would be effective: 'no Power will incur the odium of sinking a ship with all hands'[7] (again a moral judgment), but only Fisher dissented and British naval strategy in the First World War did aim at 'a working command by battle or blockade' without realising, until it was almost too late, that the imperfections of command could critically affect the outcome of the war.

The primacy for naval strategy of the priority attaching to particular uses of the sea emerges even more clearly from a comparison of the different campaigns of the Second World War. For Britain the mortal issue, apart from the threat of invasion during the summer of 1940, was the defence of her seaborne trade against submarines. In the Pacific the Americans and Japanese were almost exclusively concerned with the use of the sea for amphibious operations and aircraft carriers were the decisive factor. In the Mediterranean, which was essentially a side-show, the sea was primarily required for the logistic support of armies, whose ability to retain airfields for shore-based aircraft often did as much as navies to decide control of the sea.

The different ways in which these three campaigns were fought cannot be explained as reflections of the strategies natural to either a superior or an inferior fleet. The successful American submarine war on Japanese trade, for instance, followed rather than preceded the victories which established American naval superiority. These were different kinds of conflict in which discrepant objectives had to be pursued by methods appropriate to the specific use of the particular sea it was desired either to protect or to deny. Any more general command of the sea was the product of success rather than the prior condition of its attainment.

To some extent this need to specify functions has always existed, for no kind of power has any absolute value: it is merely the capacity to apply force about a given point and varies with the nature of that point. Trafalgar made the invasion of Britain impossible: it did not prevent Austerlitz. Nevertheless the need to specify functions has increased as the autonomy of sea power has declined. When based on the virtual invulnerability of a superior fleet, that autonomy meant, for an island-state, immunity at home and the ability to limit the extent of intervention abroad. In practice, of course, such intervention was not always limited and it was often unsuccessful, but the strategic choice was Britain's.

The first half of the twentieth century eroded that autonomy, as mines, torpedoes, submarines and aircraft challenged the invulnerability of the superior fleet. Whether the ideal fleet need have become quite as vulnerable as some actual fleets proved to be is debatable, but irrelevant, for the second half of the century introduced a qualitative change in the conditions of warfare that has so far proved irreversible. The advent of inter-continental missiles has destroyed the ability of the strongest navy, however skilled in anti-submarine operations and mine-hunting, whatever the extent of its support from seaborne or land-based aircraft, to guarantee the immunity of the homeland. It is no longer true that 'he that commands the sea is at great liberty, and may take as much and as little of the war as he will'.[8]

Naturally, even thermonuclear power is not an absolute and its relativities may conceivably continue to exclude its use. But its mere existence has profoundly modified the concepts of sea control or denial and could do so again if it ever became possible to locate and track submarines with sufficient accuracy to offer a reliable prospect of destroying them before they could launch their missiles. This might then emerge as the paramount use of the sea.

Even today, and at lesser levels of conflict, technological and political changes have greatly modified the conditions in which sea power can be exercised. More sophisticated forms of combat, for instance, have demanded greater specialisation in the functions of warships. As late as the Second World War destroyers could and did perform almost any task: hunt submarines or surface craft, escort convoys or capital ships, bombard the shore, land or evacuate troops, attack battleships. No single ship is equally versatile today.

The Americans prefer to employ a task force even for the low-level operations of violent peace and, in the view of some competent foreign observers, concentration on anti-submarine warfare has left the entire Royal Navy with a much reduced capacity for other kinds of combat. The difficulty and expense of combining the various weapons systems required to meet different forms of attack tend to favour sea denial at the expense of sea control. The commander who attempts denial can now add to the traditional advantages of selecting time, place and target that of the choice of weapons. Even the United States, who have contrived to retain a large, general purpose navy, can scarcely be expected to concentrate a balanced carrier task force – and nothing less could be expected to defeat all forms of attack – at every vulnerable point in a system of general sea control.[9] Nor is mere sophistication of equipment any guarantee of effectiveness, as the Royal Navy learned from the bumping contest between their modern frigates and the primitive Icelandic gunboats. Naval force has to be appropriate to the task in hand. Admirals have always had to worry that the only ship available might lack the armament or the speed or the protection or the endurance needed for the job: now they also have to wonder whether the ship is too valuable to be risked. Technical specialisation has only increased the need to predict the type of conflict and to specify those uses of the sea which most require either protection or denial.

It is easy to multiply illustrations of the incidence of change on the conditions of naval operations. This is a continuing, an accelerating and, worst of all, an ambiguous process, particularly ambiguous, because it is necessarily based on speculation in the absence of relevant combat experience. Satellite observation, for instance, has exposed the trackless wastes of the ocean to scrutiny. Surface warships can no longer expect their whereabouts to be veiled in uncertainty, nor count on surprise for their appearance. Yet nuclear power has enhanced these attributes in the true submarine. Endurance has been expensively increased in certain warships paradoxically armed only for 'the battle of the first salvo'. The KIROV is generally admired, but Western observers are puzzled to define her function. The hierarchy of warships – which can expect to sink which and in what circumstances – is more than obscure and nobody can produce a convincing scenario for a fleet action. Time, once the ally of sea-power in the exercise of its slow, cumulative, autonomous pressure, now seems captive to the foreseeable exigencies of land warfare and of escalation to nuclear conflict. Unprecedented resources for the projection of naval power against the shore are now liable to encounter cheaper means of resistance and, in time of nominal peace, new political obstacles.

The pace and extent of change have focussed the attention of analysts and naval officers alike on the significance of technical innovation; on the trends in naval construction; on the mounting cost of both; on the study of deployments and manoeuvres; on the analysis of political constraints. If so much research seems to have led to few positive conclusions, the cause may lie in the inadequate response of the strategists. The onset of naval change – iron for wood, steam for sail, breech-loading for muzzle-loading – was the prelude to a seminal era of strategic thought concerning the nature of sea-power, the purpose of naval warfare and the proper objectives of particular navies. Not all this thinking was fruitful – least of all in its impact on naval officers – and the ingenious ideas of Grand Admiral Tirpitz proved an international disaster, but the intellectual foundations laid in the decades before the

First World War have since received insufficient addition, let alone challenge. Between the wars the new doctrines of air-power and the armoured Blitzkrieg found their only naval parallel in Japan and, since the turn of the century, strategists have been so preoccupied by nuclear weapons that the very word 'strategic' has lost its sense.

As a result both of the forces of change and of relative neglect of what were once termed the more 'sublime' aspects of naval thought, contemporary notions of naval strategy lack the clarity and the sense of purpose which Mahan and Corbett sought to impart. Earlier concepts have gradually become distorted without necessarily being discarded or replaced. A case in point is control or command of the sea. Admiral Holloway seemed to give it no less primacy than the classical writers, even if he added that sea denial was cheaper. Yet Admiral Turner, one of the most thoughtful senior American naval officers, argued in 1974 that the objective should be 'realistic control in limited areas and for limited periods of time'. He contended – and nothing in the unfolding balance of naval strength has since appeared to refute his view – that 'it is no longer conceivable, except in the most limited sense, to totally control the seas for one's own use or to totally deny them to an enemy'.[10]

His words found a Norwegian echo at the following year's conference of the International Institute for Strategic Studies: 'The term "sea control" today connotes control in limited areas for limited periods of time . . .'.[11] As Soviet doctrine has long rejected the idea of command of the sea, Admiral of the Fleet Sergei Gorshkov is unlikely to disagree. Indeed, MccGwire quotes him as defining a rather similar objective: 'to create a situation whereby the enemy is either paralysed or constrained in his actions, or weakened, and thereby hampered from interfering with our execution of a given operation, or the discharge of our operational tasks'.[12] Admiral Eberle of the Royal Navy made no significant departure from this consensus, when he declared, also in 1975:

> I am quite clear that naval force is to establish control over certain sea areas. The first sea area that it is necessary in the national interest to establish control over is one's own backyard.[13]

There is thus contemporary authority, quite apart from the experience of two world wars and the indications of the present naval balance, for the proposition that sea control is an objective limited in both time and space. But is this any more the concept advanced by Mahan and Corbett, the achievement of the Revolutionary and Napoleonic Wars, the conceivable purpose of the Royal Navy in the First World War? The command of the sea, with trifling exceptions, is one thing as a prize from which all else flows. It is quite another as a transitory and local triumph. The difference emerges between an intrinsic good and the means to a particular end, the general goal of naval strategy and a tactical expedient.

This is more than a philosophical distinction. The old doctrine, as this was actually understood, not always as it was preached, often assumed practical importance, not only in determining the naval share in the general strategy, but also in influencing tactical decisions. If command of the sea is attainable and the supreme objective, admirals may give priority over other tasks to the destruction of the enemy fleet or to the conservation of their own. Such considerations have sometimes led, even if they were not the only factors, to the abandonment of convoys or allowed transports to reach their destination. If a dominant strategic principle exists, it must be expected to influence difficult choices made in haste. If the demotion of sea control is once thoroughly assimilated into the working doctrine of naval officers, this must produce a major change in one of the preconceptions with which they approach the increasingly rapid decisions likely to be required in future conflicts.

This change depends on more than the naval balance. Naturally it is significant that the United States Navy, after some heart-searching among their principal commanders, no longer claim an assured margin of superiority over their Soviet rivals, but that could doubtless be remedied. What is past praying for is the order of magnitude ascendancy needed to offset the inherent advantages, which have been growing all this century, of sea denial over sea control. At sea it is the defence that needs the massive superiority once demanded of an offensive on land. The United States Secretary of Defense may have declared, as recently as 1978, that

in the event of a major emergency, we would want to be able to provide sea control forces sufficient to maintain our lines of communication in the Mediterranean, the Atlantic and the Pacific'[14]

but this is not an immediately attainable objective in war. The United States Navy are thinking in terms of sequential operations, in which naval forces 'surge' into one sea area, fight a campaign for control and, so it is hoped, move on to the next. Even assuming the utmost success – and the enemy may have his own views about where and when to accept battle – this could be a long process. Will it be concluded, will general sea control be established, before the advance of armies, to say nothing of nuclear escalation, has entirely transformed the international situation? A whole chain of rather improbable assumptions is required to support the proposition that sea control, in the sense this has always been understood, could be both feasible and, in the likely time-scale of general war, relevant.

The ideal of sea control is not dead and still has its Western devotees, but the rational arguments are against it. Even for the world's strongest navy – just – the command of the sea is a dubious objective. For lesser navies it is fantasy alone and improbable even in combination. No strategy has yet been advanced, let alone agreed, which offers the NATO navies – the only naval alliance that adds anything of importance to the strength of its principal member – the assurance of virtual control, whether generally or in a defined sea area, in time to determine every course of events. The feasibility and the value of sea control depend, as at this stage of the twentieth century they must, on the nature of the conflict and on the significance of the particular uses of the sea which it is desired either to control or to deny.

This is not an entirely new situation. In the past many navies have accepted that command of the sea, individually or in foreseeable combination, was not a feasible objective. They adopted alternative strategies: the war on trade or coastal defence or the over-sophisticated, as it ultimately turned out, risk-policy of Tirpitz. The new factor today is that command of the sea is no longer the automatic and attainable solution to anyone's problems.

Nor has any alternative principle emerged to offer a simple and obvious answer to the question: what are navies for? Gorshkov, admittedly, has certain suggestions to offer:

At present, a fleet with its strikes from the sea is capable of changing the course and outcome of an armed struggle even in continental theatres of military operations.

Today, a fleet operating against the shore is able not only to solve the tasks connected with territorial changes but to directly influence the course and even outcome of a war.

The chief goal of a fleet is becoming . . . action against enemy ground objectives and the protection of one's territory from the strikes of his fleet.[15]

These are not isolated opinions. The projection of power ashore has already been noted as a major task for the United States Navy. NATO hope to have a Strike Fleet in the Atlantic. Gorshkov's propositions can nevertheless not even be debated without specifying the fleet in question, the identity of the adversary, the nature of the conflict and the theatre of operations. In some circumstances Gorshkov might be proved correct, but his assertions cannot be regarded as a basis for the kind of general rule which Mahan, Corbett and Roskill thought they had found in the concept of command of the sea. Executing or preventing strikes from the sea against the land, amphibious operations, controlling or denying a particular area of the sea, convoy and escort, blockade, the political application of limited naval force: these and others are types of naval operation which may or may not prove both feasible and useful. None of them is the sure, sovereign and universally applicable remedy that command of the sea was once claimed to be for the superior fleet. The relevance of sea-power and the answer to Rosinski's question at the start of this chapter depend on the nature of the conflict.

If, therefore, the simple clarity of Roskill's classical formulation is to be adapted to modern conditions, there are two courses. One is to relapse into a prudent vagueness:

The function of maritime power is to secure for oneself, and to deny to the adversary, those uses of the sea which are important to the outcome of the conflict.

The other, which will be attempted in the rest of the book, is to abandon the search for general principles in favour of a more detailed examination of the different types of conflict in which Britain might be involved, of the importance which various uses of the sea might assume in each case and of the possible approaches to securing or denying them. If any view emerges of the function, in the last decades of the twentieth century, of maritime power, it will be one specifically geared to British requirements and British resources. As such, it will have to take account of many factors besides those listed by Mahan among the elements of sea-power. To the geographical position and configuration of the British Isles, for instance, must be added the extent to which these have been or may be exploited, not only by the British, for more than naval purposes. The national institutions are more variously influential than those known to Mahan. The character of the people is more complex and less easily defined. The character of the government fluctuates considerably and is more susceptible to outside influence than for centuries past. What constitutes sea-power is a question quite as difficult, and even more wide-ranging than what can sea-power do?

For the moment two assertions will suffice. The function of sea-power is to influence conflict concerning the use of the sea. Its existence depends on a national judgment that the influence is important and a national will to create the resources for its exercise. Neither condition is self-evident.

4 Contingencies of Conflict

> The want of omnipotence is no reason for abstaining from such choices as are available.
>
> Grant Hugo[1]

If the importance of sea-power depends on the nature of the conflict, it goes without saying that the identity of the participants is also significant. An import-dependent island-state is more likely to be involved in the kind of conflict in which sea-power matters than is a land-locked country enjoying a high degree of self-sufficiency. But this book is about Britain and this chapter is uniquely concerned with the kind of conflict in which Britain might be involved. When these contingencies are later examined in more detail, there will be opportunity enough to emphasise the specifically maritime aspects of British national interests. For the moment these can be taken for granted: they are familiar. Nor will this chapter scrutinise the oceans for future sources of conflict. There is already enough trouble to be getting on with. Instead, a series of predicaments will be briefly examined. In each case the purpose will be to identify, for later analysis, any significant contribution which might be expected from British sea-power. Where none can be found, then the hypothetical situation in question, however important, lies outside the scope of this book.

The first of these contingencies, quite obviously, is total nuclear war. This is an option which Britain would have no power to reject and which she could only doubtfully, and in rather unlikely circumstances, be said to have the ability to choose. By total nuclear war is meant a war in which there is no agreement, tacit or overt, between the Super-Powers to restrict their use of nuclear weapons, whether territorially, or by the nature of the targets, or quantitatively or otherwise. This does not mean – and it would be very unlikely to mean – that both Super-Powers would immediately discharge all the nuclear weapons they possessed,

48

but that no obvious limits would exist to the escalation of their initial nuclear exchange.

In these circumstances it is easy to argue that the nuclear capability of the Royal Navy would be irrelevant. A small, crowded island cannot hope to win a nuclear war against a continental state and the loss of Moscow would not prevent the Soviet Union from destroying the British Isles. Nor would a threat to Moscow constitute a deterrent if the Soviet Union was ready to accept the much greater risks of a nuclear exchange with the United States. Whether one considers the minimum threat from Britain – 16 missiles each carrying three 200 kiloton warheads from one submarine[2] – or a possible maximum three times greater, the deterrent effect must be reckoned as insignificant by comparison with the 2142 delivery systems and the 11,000 warheads at the disposal of the United States.[3] Nor will any likely improvement or expansion of British nuclear forces significantly alter the stark contrast of the relative figures. In any situation in which the Soviet Union is prepared to accept the risk of American nuclear bombardment, prospective British efforts cannot be expected to count, either for warfighting or for deterrence.

This is nevertheless a proposition which rests upon an improbability: Soviet readiness to fight a nuclear war with the United States. It is conceivable that such a state of mind might possess the Politburo and one popular scenario will be mentioned at a later stage of the argument. But it seems unlikely, bearing in mind the popularity of Clausewitz in the Soviet Union, that total nuclear war will ever be deliberately chosen as a true political instrument, a continuation of political intercourse carried out by other means.[4] This catastrophe may be threatened, or risked, for political ends, but it will scarcely be deliberately selected, as happened with earlier wars. The cost of even victory, however this might be defined, in nuclear war is simply too great. Both Super-Powers might go a long way towards the brink, but, before deciding whether to pass it, they would surely first exhaust every process of delay, menace and pressure, particularly if the burden of such processes could be made to fall on their allies rather than on themselves. It is in this kind of crisis, with both Super-Powers reluctant to pass the brink yet escalating towards it, that an ally with nuclear weapons might have larger, albeit rather desperate options, than one without. What is more, a submarine-launched deterrent is not merely survivable: it is hard to identify. Both Super-Powers might have cause to reflect that, if the pressures of escalation were too grievous for Britain to bear, the Royal Navy had a potential trigger as well as an actual weapon.

This strained and rather artificial scenario, this last and desperate resort, would not apply to a direct confrontation between the Super-Powers of such intensity that one of them seriously contemplates attacking the other, even expects to derive advantage from making the first assault. The most dramatic contingency of this kind at present envisaged is that, in the early eighties, the Soviet Union might be tempted by their numerical superiority in accurately deliverable war-heads into contemplating a disarming strike against the vulnerable land-based missiles of the United States.[5] The objective would be to deprive the United States of their counter-force capability and to present the President with an appalling alternative: either to strike back with the balance of his nuclear forces against Soviet civilian targets, thereby exposing his own people to a similar second strike from the Soviet Union, or else to surrender to whatever political demands might be made on him.[6] Improbable but conceivable.

In such a contingency, it might be argued, the Soviet leaders would expect compliance from the United States and would wish to avoid any extraneous risk of major casualties to their own population. They would not, therefore, make a nuclear attack on Britain or France for fear of retaliation from the submarine-launched ballistic missiles possessed by these two countries.

This may seem a dubious argument, depending on the assumption that the Soviet leaders would perceive the governments of Britain and France as readier than that of the United States to resort to the desperate use of force. Such a perception is not impossible, because a nuclear attack that eliminated attainable military targets would leave Britain with little to lose, much less than the United States. It can unfortunately also be argued that the Soviet Union would prefer the extra insurance of using those missiles that could not, in any case, reach the United States to reduce not only British retaliatory capacities, but also American facilities in Britain. This would be a hazardous move, for a disarming strike against Britain and France could only reduce and not destroy their ability to riposte. Nevertheless, the analogy of the German attack through Belgium in 1914 suggests that, once a decision for war has been taken, great risks may be run in order to maximise the immediate military advantage. Moreover, if the Soviet leaders see some risk that their pre-emptive strike against American land-based missiles might, contrary to their expectations, lead to a full nuclear exchange, they would have to reckon that any nuclear forces left intact in Britain and France might be more significant at the end than at the beginning of such a total nuclear war. It is difficult, therefore, in this particular scenario, to predict whether lesser nuclear forces would be perceived by the Soviet Union as a deterrent to simultaneous strikes or as a positive incentive.

Similar difficulties apply to all scenarios which assume the readiness of the Soviet Union to risk total nuclear war. In spite of all the sophistication which has been brought to the analysis of such contingencies, there is an inherent irrationality about the entire concept which makes it difficult to believe that leaders capable of such appalling decisions would be guided by the nicely reasoned calculations that occur to professors in the tranquillity of their studies. Nor is this scepticism merely speculative. Decades of analysis of the decisions that led to the two world wars – decisions taken under less pressure of time and even emotion than would be likely on the next occasion – have caused reputable historians to question whether they can be satisfactorily explained in terms of rationally expected advantage. If the choice of warlike acts defies, as it often does, retrospective analysis, it is necessarily even harder to predict in the hypothetical future.

It is unfortunately conceivable, however unlikely, that the Soviet leaders might decide on a disarming strike against the United States: it is not credible that such minor details as whether or not to accompany this by action against Britain, France and China are rationally more predictable than the reaction of the United States. The assumption that American ability to devastate the Soviet Union might fail to deter a Soviet nuclear attack on the American mainland necessarily implies a degree of scepticism concerning the efficacy of lesser deterrents. On this hypothesis, therefore, the only assured rôle for the Royal Navy's submarine-launched ballistic missiles is the ability to deliver the last sting of a dying bee. This is a difficult argument to present either to the Treasury or to the British electorate.

If the Super-Powers find themselves, perhaps inadvertently, in an escalating confrontation, yet shrink from a direct nuclear exchange, Britain might conceivably encounter such mortal danger that a desperate threat became credible and gave the Royal Navy a deterrent rôle. If either Super-Power is ready to risk total nuclear war, the Royal Navy is likely to be irrelevant to the survival of Britain. Its nuclear capability could as easily provoke the Soviet Union as deter it.

The aftermath of an actual nuclear bombardment of the British Isles would be scarcely worth considering, if it were not for the notion, once fashionable, of conducting 'broken-backed' naval warfare in such circumstances. Human beings do linger with worse than broken backs, but they are seldom willing, or able, to take out insurance against such contingencies. The idea of providing a navy that might feebly maintain an uncertain struggle after most of the British people had been destroyed will always exert even less popular appeal. Nor is it a useful argument to suggest that, in such circumstances, skilled and disciplined naval personnel might mitigate the sufferings of the survivors by supervising the landing of supplies across the beaches. Fighting services can and do administer first-aid in catastrophes, but this is not the purpose for which they are maintained and, if it were, these services would have a very different character. For Britain total nuclear war is a disaster which the navy can do little to avert and nothing of significance to repair.

Limited nuclear war might be another matter. Admittedly the entire concept of limited war attracts greater theoretical acceptance in the West than in the Soviet Union. Nevertheless limited conventional wars have happened – in Vietnam and in the Middle East. They would not have been limited without the tacit acquiescence, whatever the reasons, of the Soviet Union. It is not certain that the use of nuclear weapons – by crossing the 'fire-break' established since 1945 – would necessarily and automatically lead to total nuclear war. Professor Erickson has argued, for instance, that Soviet doctrine admits the possibility of a 'politically' limited war and that this might even extend to a 'high-speed theatre campaign in Europe' which the Soviet Union might envisage as being conducted without entailing a nuclear exchange with the United States.[7]

Some scenarios, admittedly, are less plausible than others. A purely quantitative limitation, in which the Super-Powers exchanged individual missiles as bargaining counters, can scarcely be regarded as durable. Theoretically it might lead to the early capitulation of one side or to the overthrowing of bellicose leaders lacking a secure power-base. In practice the casualties – and the emotion – generated by even a single missile could equally well lead to rapid escalation towards total nuclear war. An enemy nuclear missile exploding on the metropolitan territory of a Super-Power confronts decision-makers with the choice between double or quit. Double is a simple executive decision: quit can probably only be chosen under the slow-acting and often ambiguous pressures of popular revulsion.

A slightly different objection applies to an attack ostensibly limited to nuclear strike capabilities. For the Super-Powers, particularly the United States, the lower density of population in the vicinity of missile bases confers on this so-called 'counter-force' strategy a degree of significance largely absent in the case of the United Kingdom. Nevertheless, however careful the targeting, the side-effects on the civilian population would probably be too devastating for a rationally controlled response to be reliably predictable.[8] Impulsive reaction would be not merely possible, but likely. It is also doubtful whether a counter-force strategy, even if this were to be deliberately adopted by both sides, would be perceived by both as reliably confined to the means of delivery alone. If either side feared that its capacity for surveillance, communication and control was threatened, there would be a strong incentive to escalate before the power to do so was lost.[9] Most theories of limited nuclear war between the Super-Powers depend on the assumption of a degree of mutual understanding which, if it existed at all, would surely prevent the occasion arising.

There is nevertheless one form of limited nuclear war which does seem quite plausible, because the limitation would have a simple and unambiguous character eminently suitable for brief communication on the 'hot-line', offering some advantage to both Super-Powers, yet preserving their escalatory options in the event of any transgression, which would be instantly identifiable, of the accepted limits. This special case is a war in which, tacitly or by more or less express agreement, the territory of the two Super-Powers is exempted from nuclear bombardment. A Soviet offensive in Central Europe, for instance, might be accompanied by the use of nuclear weapons in the theatre of operations only. The Western response might also be confined to theatre nuclear weapons aimed at targets outside Soviet territory. Such a limited exchange may seem inconsistent with Soviet military doctrine and with American obligations, but both governments will presumably be anxious not to put their own populations at risk and will have strong incentives to proceed step by step. And, to political leaders, steps which kill only their own soldiers and foreign civilians are likely to seem less irrevocable than steps which inflict destruction on the homeland. As long as the metropolitan territories of the two Super-Powers remain immune, it is not inconceivable that conversations on the hot-line might cause stalemate to be conceded in Europe, or a local defeat to be accepted, as an alternative preferable to total nuclear war.

This is not a new idea. A similar situation was envisaged by Dr Kissinger long before the Soviet strategic threat to the United States reached anything approaching the present level.

What if the Red Army attacks in Europe explicitly to disarm West Germany and offers to the United States and the United Kingdom immunity from strategic bombing and a withdrawal to the Oder after achieving its limited objective? Is it clear . . . that an American President would trade fifty American cities for Western Europe?[10]

Twenty-two years later, after an unrivalled experience of these matters, he gave an answer that was not confined to the special case of his original question:

> the European allies should not keep asking us to multiply strategic assurances that we cannot possibly mean, or if we do mean, we should not want to execute because if we execute, we risk the destruction of civilisation.[11]

In the same speech he said that:

> the secret dream of every European was . . . if there had to be a nuclear war, to have it conducted over their heads by the strategic forces of the United States and the Soviet Union.

He was careful not to describe the secret dream of every American, but some of his countrymen have been less discreet.

The possibility of a territorially limited nuclear war will not be excluded by the installation in Western Europe of theatre nuclear weapons capable of reaching the Soviet Union, as long as the targeting of these weapons and the decision to fire them depend on the United States. No American decision-maker can safely expect the Soviet leadership to take a different view of a nuclear explosion on Soviet territory merely because the missile responsible was launched by Americans outside the continental United States. Impact provides an immediate and obvious argument: the origin, nature and motive of the launching may remain debatable too long to influence the response.

A Soviet decision, which might well be expressly announced, to attempt a territorially limited nuclear war, would not alter the underlying strategic balance, but it would imply a major shift in the political priorities governing Soviet strategy. At an earlier stage in the argument it was assumed that the Soviet Union might accept the risk of American nuclear retaliation against Soviet territory, might even court this risk by a pre-emptive attack against American land-based missiles. In these circumstances, it was argued, lesser nuclear forces could as easily constitute a provocation as a deterrent. That was because the added risks represented by these forces would be less significant, militarily speaking, in the initial than in the closing stages of a total nuclear war. If, however, it becomes a major objective to preserve the invulnerability of Soviet territory and if the military advantages of pre-emptive attack against American land-based missiles must be sacrificed as a necessary condition, then it becomes doubtful whether the minor gains to be expected from attacking Britain and France are worth the price of putting Soviet territory at otherwise avoidable risk. If a historical analogy may be permitted, there was a case in 1914 for disregarding the 'contemptible' British Army because an invasion through Belgium would facilitate the destruction of France. But, if the Germans had decided not to attack France, the General Staff would surely not have invited British hostility. An altered Soviet attitude towards the United States is thus likely to entail a different evaluation of the significance of lesser nuclear forces.

The difference would be political as well as military. Having once taken the decision that hostilities should be confined to a foreign battlefield, it would be logical to deprive not only the United States, but also lesser nuclear powers of their strongest incentive to extend that battlefield into the Soviet Union. If the United States could be persuaded that the immunity of the homeland should be reciprocal, the Soviet Union would have little reason to expect a different attitude from Britain or France. French doctrine has been sufficiently explicit; British official ambiguities and hypocrisies concerning NATO scarcely veil the obvious truth: a suicidal British threat to launch a nuclear attack against Moscow is credible only if the alternative is the destruction of Britain herself. On the other hand, any military planner would have to regard it as highly probable that the descent of nuclear missiles on either Britain or France would elicit an automatic response, perhaps even without political direction.

In these circumstances, the possession of a survivable force, however small, of submarine-launched ballistic missiles could preserve both British and French territory from nuclear attack.

This would not protect the troops of either country in the operational area. Nor would it necessarily offer any immunity against conventional attack on British and French targets, still less against the consequences of the main battle. The British position, for instance, would scarcely be enviable once the central front had been overrun in Europe. Nevertheless, initial immunity from nuclear bombardment might mean the difference between immediate life and death and would at least offer some hope of ultimate survival for the nation. The possibility of limited nuclear war in Europe thus represents one plausible contingency in which sea-power could be important to Britain. No other means of nuclear delivery offers the same assurance to a small, crowded island of posing a survivable deterrent to the most dangerous form of attack.

If the Royal Navy succeeded in this first task, there would naturally be others. The nuclear deterrent would have to be preserved, for its importance would actually increase as the Soviet Union expended its non-strategic nuclear capacity against the mainland, and the British Isles would have to be defended against conventional attack. This could be expected to begin at the same time as an assault on the central front and would not necessarily be suspended even if that front quickly collapsed.

Before we descend to conventional war – and it must be emphasised that none of these hypothetical situations is watertight: one could develop into another in days rather than weeks – a further contingency of limited nuclear war deserves a word. It is sometimes suggested that this might be confined to the oceans: that nuclear weapons might be targeted exclusively against ships, thereby creating less risk of retaliation against civilian populations and inflicting less collateral damage, whether immediate or from fall-out.

This seems improbable. It is not supported by the observable strategic doctrine of either Super-Power, nor does it correspond to their apparent interests. The Soviet Union can scarcely be expected to choose or accept a purely maritime war in which the balance of forces would be less favourable to them than in a general engagement. The United States might hope for naval victory, but would have to realise that this would not greatly impair Soviet ability to strike at the United States or American allies. Naval war is thus most likely as a complement to operations on land, whether in contesting reinforcement and supply or as a direct contribution to intervention. It is admittedly likely (political constraints apart) that, in a major naval war, tactical nuclear weapons would be employed from the outset. What is hard to imagine is how either the war or the weapons could be confined to the sea. The Soviet Union would have an obvious incentive to accompany maritime operations by an offensive on land, while the crossing of the nuclear firebreak at sea would reduce political objections to an American response involving the use of tactical nuclear weapons on the ground. A more plausible hypothesis than a purely maritime war is the extension of the concept of a territorially limited nuclear war to the sea. The governing principle of such a war is in its being exclusive rather than inclusive: no nuclear attacks against the homeland of nuclear weapon states.

Descending, therefore, from the contingency of a nuclear war, limited, for political reasons, to a particular theatre of operations (which could include sea as well as land areas), we arrive at the concept of a conventional war – of a war, that is to say, which remains conventional as long as the losing side does not resort to nuclear weapons.

This is a notion which seems to be exercising a growing appeal for the Soviet Union, as their long-standing quantitative superiority in conventional forces (at least on land and in the air) has come to be matched by a quality that, in many respects, is at least equal to anything possessed by their opponents. In the European theatre, in particular, it has long been assumed that the United States would have a more obvious incentive to make the first use of nuclear weapons – to redress a conventional defeat – than the Soviet Union. Indeed, the insistence of Soviet doctrine that all arms should be employed from the outset has often seemed to stem from the assumption that such an American reaction was inevitable and ought, accordingly, to be anticipated. Whether this assumption still holds good is uncertain.

Western experts on Soviet military doctrine differ. Some contend that the Soviet leaders believe they could fight and win a nuclear war. Others argue that the concept of deterrence as constituting the raison d'être of nuclear forces is making headway. Where the experts differ, the non-expert, as Bertrand Russell plausibly maintained, will conclude that no opinion is certain. The changing balance of nuclear forces has made American resort to their use less likely: the developing Soviet advantage in conventional forces has made their use of nuclear weapons less necessary. Either Super-Power might prefer a limited nuclear war in Europe to total nuclear war, but the choice between limited nuclear war and conventional war seems to present unequal opportunities. It could be argued, for instance, that war in Europe offers the Soviet Union the chance of acquiring new assets, which should not, therefore, be needlessly destroyed, whereas the United States, already enjoying all the advantage and influence they require in Western Europe, would be primarily concerned to deny these assets to the adversary. This argument naturally has two weaknesses. The first is that the continuing Soviet deployment of heavy missiles capable of reaching European targets but not those on the mainland of the other Super-Power suggests a different purpose. Secondly, the leaders of states engaging in war are always exposed to strong temptation to make the fullest possible use of the military means at their disposal regardless of the political consequences. The possibility that either Super-Power, let alone both of them, might be ready to refrain from the first use of nuclear weapons during a war in Europe, or elsewhere, can not, therefore, be regarded as more than a possibility. As such it nevertheless deserves consideration. It happened in Korea and again in Vietnam.

Before considering this possible conventional war it may be useful finally to dispose of the red herring of tactical nuclear weapons as a mere adjunct to the conventional battle, whether by land or sea. These weapons cover a wide spectrum of range and destructive power, but they have two essential characteristics: they are readily distinguishable from conventional weapons and, if they explode within the metropolitan territory of either Super-Power, they cease to be tactical. They may be employed to threaten escalation to a strategic exchange or to initiate a limited nuclear war, but their use effectively deprives war of its conventional character. Any resort to nuclear weapons entails the crossing of one obvious fire-break and the next may not come until there is a nuclear explosion on the territory of a Super-Power. In between those two boundaries there are no obvious limits to escalation except a credible threat to pass the second.

A conventional war, therefore, is one in which no nuclear weapons are employed. It also exhibits other significant differences. In the present state of the world – and in the foreseeable future – only a Super-Power can win a nuclear war (leaving aside the rather unlikely case of one minor power exercising the undisturbed use of nuclear weapons against another) and the victory of even a Super-Power might not be very meaningful. Conventional wars, on the other hand, still permit clear-cut results. The United States were decisively defeated in Vietnam. Israel undoubtedly won the wars of 1967 and 1973. If Britain were involved in conventional war, the differing consequences of victory or of defeat could be significant to the British people. What is more, the outcome of such a war could be significantly influenced by British efforts, even if Britain fought as part of an alliance.

It scarcely needs repeating that Britain can neither win nor significantly affect the outcome of a total nuclear war, but rather strained and improbable assumptions must be made to predict any British influence even in limited nuclear war beyond the single vital function of deterring its extension to the British Isles. And even that would not necessarily affect the outcome of the war for the alliance or the ultimate consequences of that outcome for the British people. Conventional war could be a different matter, particularly for the Royal Navy. Britain may be greatly inferior in total naval strength to both the United States and the Soviet Union, but neither Super-Power is likely to deploy more than a fraction of its navy in a single theatre. The Royal Navy, on the other hand, would presumably concentrate its efforts on the approaches to the British Isles, where its total strength would be more significant when compared with the partial deployments of the American and Soviet navies.

This is admittedly a complex and controversial issue. Some American naval thinking assumes that the US Navy could fight an Atlantic war single-handed – and might have to. But the combination of circumstances which would produce war in the Atlantic, yet deprive the United States of European support while allowing the US Atlantic Fleet to deploy anything approaching its full strength is a little hard to envisage. A more likely contingency is a dispute originating outside Europe, which would already have diverted to distant seas a substantial proportion of American naval forces, followed by a direct Soviet threat to Europe. In such a situation American carriers, already rather thinly stretched in the peacetime conditions of 1980, might not be readily available as the essential core of the Atlantic Strike Fleet.

A common assumption, to be further considered at a later stage, is that the Soviet Northern Fleet (which might itself have had to provide reinforcements for some more distant confrontation) would have two objectives in an Atlantic war: to deny access to the Norwegian Sea and to prevent American seaborne reinforcement and resupply of the land front in Europe. Whether or not Western offensive operations are feasible at all, it seems most unlikely that the US Navy could, unaided, combine these with a successful defence of seaborne communications to Western Europe. Indeed, even if the latter were the only task, it could be argued that the US Navy would have to denude the Mediterranean, the Pacific and Indian Oceans, perhaps even the Arabian Sea, for this purpose. Without British ships and – equally important – the intelligence, technical and logistic facilities provided by the British Isles – the prospect is scarcely encouraging. Without anticipating later discussion of the adequacy of the British contribution to allied naval efforts in the Eastern Atlantic, it may reasonably be argued that, even if British participation might not ensure victory, British abstention would nevertheless invite defeat. There is a case, even if it requires further examination, for the proposition that the Royal Navy could make a real difference to the outcome of a naval war between the Soviet Union and the North Atlantic Alliance.

And even this argument, whatever its naval merits, neglects the political factor. If there is no substantial Royal Navy to offer significant assistance in the maintenance of seaborne communications between the United States and the United Kingdom, why should the US Navy attempt the task?

Naturally, naval efforts would not be enough in themselves. It would not be enough to counter mining, bombing, submarine attacks in the Western Approaches. If ports in Britain, in France or in the Low Countries could be destroyed from the air or if Western Europe could be quickly overrun by Soviet armies, then naval success in the Eastern Atlantic might be as irrelevant as the safe transit of American re-inforcements. A continental attack cannot be countered by a purely maritime response. Nevertheless, in so far as there is a chance of the air and ground forces of the North Atlantic Alliance withstanding Soviet assault in conventional war, this depends on the arrival of seaborne reinforcements from the United States and, to a lesser extent, from the United Kingdom.

This discussion of seaborne reinforcement, indeed the whole of the preceding analysis of the contingencies for either nuclear or conven-tional conflict, has so far rested on the unstated assumption of general war, whether initiated by a direct attack on the United States or by an offensive against the Central Front in Europe. There are nevertheless other possibilities of conflict between the two alliances. Norway, Turkey and Greece are relatively isolated members of NATO, who might be picked on and whose territory might even become the focus of a limited war, if this did not spread. All would need seaborne reinforcement. So would Yugoslavia, if Soviet intervention ever drove her to seek Western assistance – a problem that NATO has been notoriously reluctant to consider. Some of these contingencies would involve the Royal Navy more directly than others, but all would affect it, if only through the diversion of American warships.

The demands of NATO, to which 'most of our surface vessels and all our submarines would be committed',[12] thus confront the Royal Navy with heavy and variegated tasks. Formally, at least, these are restricted to 'the territory of any of the Parties in Europe or North America' and to 'the North Atlantic area north of the Tropic of Cancer'.[13] This last restriction has attracted some surprising criticism from British admirals lacking sufficient forces to ensure the defence of even the Narrow Seas, but it will unfortunately not inhibit more extensive demands on the Royal Navy. In the autumn of 1980, for instance, the British destroyer COVENTRY and the frigate ALACRITY were diverted from a Far Eastern cruise to the Gulf of Oman in a gesture of support for the more substantial American naval forces deployed to deter any attempt by the belligerents in the Iran–Iraq war to interfere with transit through the Straits of Hormuz.[14] Although intended as a response to the exigencies of violent peace, a set of contingencies requiring separate and later consideration, the arrival of COVENTRY and ALACRITY brought them into contact with more than American warships: the Soviet Navy were also present in force. This kind of deployment thus suggests the possibility that British warships might become involved in hostilities outside the North Atlantic area. This is certainly not excluded by the official statement that 'our defence policy should also be designed to help protect, wherever possible, our own and more general Western interests over a wider area, including those outside the NATO area'.[15] Some of the implications, which could extend to limited war overseas, will be considered in Chapter 9, 'On The Fringes of Alliance'.

Alliance war, nuclear or conventional, general or limited, is nevertheless not the only contingency to be considered in connection with the Royal Navy. It would be preferable if it were, for neither the state of the navy nor that of the nation permit the prospect of an isolated struggle to be viewed with anything approaching encouragement. Nevertheless, there do exist residual British commitments overseas – to Gibraltar, for instance, or the Falkland Islands, to Belize or even to Hong Kong – which, if they were ever to encounter an armed challenge, would have to be defended, if at all, without much expectation of assistance from allies. It is to be hoped that limited naval force would suffice and that the bounds of violent peace would not be transcended, but such situations always carry a finite risk of escalation. Nor are these the only possibilities: a major worsening of the situation in Northern Ireland might attract foreign meddling while leaving Britain as bereft of assistance from her allies as France during her Algerian troubles.

These, it may be argued, are contingencies which common prudence should never allow to reach the level of war and against which only limited naval insurance would be appropriate. This is true up to a point, but the point is an awkward one. If some disputed overseas asset is obviously defensible by limited and preferably local force, then no attempt will be made on it unless the adversary is prepared for war. But, if the objective can be seized without significant resistance, there could be a strong temptation to create a fait accompli and confront Britain with the unwelcome choice between acquiescence and escalation. Therefore, the lower the capacities of the Royal Navy for the exercise of limited force in conditions of nominal peace, the greater will be the risk that these capacities may be required in actual war. Such a war – for instance, one intended to recapture the Falkland Islands – would naturally be much more difficult, expensive, politically unpopular (both at home and abroad) and in every way damaging than prudent peacetime precautions. As these are, for a variety of reasons, unlikely to be attempted, it is reasonable to bear in mind that a number of awkward contingencies could develop in which the Chiefs of Staff, not least the First Sea Lord, might be asked for their proposals to deal with a situation which should never have been allowed to arise.

The inconvenient legacies of a vanished empire and, of course, the unforeseen are not the only challenges to isolated combat of which the Royal Navy must take account. No alliance is eternal or entirely reliable and the third quarter of the twentieth century has produced a high incidence both of mortality and of fallibility. Britain's oldest ally, Portugal, received little help over Goa or in Africa or in Timor. CENTO and SEATO were, at most, surprisingly long in reaching the disintegration predicted from their birth. The mutual loyalty that bound the members of NATO was, from the very outset, strained by the usually unsuccessful attempts of different governments to extend to more distant continents the obligations which the North Atlantic Treaty had restricted, at least in its more usual interpretation, to Europe and North America. The Netherlands, Britain, Portugal, France, Belgium and the United States all had cause for disappointment (still felt by the last-named) on this score, though perhaps only Greece and Turkey (over Cyprus), Britain and Iceland (over fishing rights) and France (over Algeria) could complain of clear-cut breaches of the Treaty.[16] If Canada, Denmark, Luxembourg and Norway have so far had few grievances, they have also manifested a cautious approach to their obligations. Germany is a special case.

Legalities, however, are not the essential issue. There will always be an international lawyer to support any argument. What counts is that on a succession of international issues of great importance to individual members of the Alliance, NATO has been divided. The rights and wrongs do not matter: the United States may have acted prudently in opposing Britain and France over Suez in 1956; certain European members in refusing facilities for American assistance to Israel in 1973. Over the years the signatories of the North Atlantic Treaty have become less 'resolved to unite their efforts for collective defence and for the preservation of peace and security',[17] more preoccupied with a single contingency nowhere mentioned in the Treaty: a direct Soviet attack against themselves. Even in peacetime preparations to meet this specific threat, there have been such differences of attitude and so many reservations, express or tacit, as to leave room for doubt concerning the reactions of the various governments to any *casus foederis* that was at all ambiguous. It cannot, after all, be assumed that the Soviet Union would be so obliging as to launch a massive assault against all the members of the Alliance simultaneously. If only one or two members are threatened, and that indirectly, if the trouble starts outside the Treaty area or over some dispute attracting little general sympathy, there could again be a divided response. Even without such a crisis, it would not take much to persuade some members of NATO to withdraw from the Alliance or to make damaging reductions in their commitments: a change of government; another allied failure to support a particular national interest; the sudden fear of involuntary involvement in an avoidable war. The unravelling of NATO may be a nightmare, but it would be unrealistic to regard it as an impossibility or to exclude from our analysis of sea-power its possible utility if alliance fails.

The spectrum of possible conflicts thus briefly sketched is a wide one. It may strike some readers as exaggerated, others as extending speculation far beyond the bounds of practical utility. Navies, it may be argued, are built and their strategies shaped for simpler and more specific purposes. Ships designed for one kind of war may, admittedly, have to fight in quite another, but the initial choice is inescapable and any attempt to meet all possible needs risks ending in failure to cope with any.

There is much force in that argument, but the record of the past suggests that choosing the threat to meet is a process subject to error, both political and naval. The submarine threat to maritime trade was neglected before the First World War, the menace of the air to surface ships before the Second. Thereafter, the political conception of the navy's rôle tended to focus on a kaleidoscope of vanishing bases: Haifa, the Canal Zone, East Africa, Cyprus, Malta, Simonstown, Aden, Singapore. Not the Navy alone, but all of Britain's armed services, suffered from the lack of a clear-cut rôle commensurate with their resources. Even when tasks were defined, their requirements were not met. The Statement on Defence of February 1956 declared that 'the forces required to support our present strategy . . . must be capable of dealing with outbreaks of limited war, should they occur'. Admittedly, it was only the Army that was specifically expected to 'bring force to bear quickly in cold or limited war',[18] but it might have occurred to somebody that rapid intervention would need more than the two landing ships (tank) which the Navy maintained in commission.[19]

The ineptitude of Britain's political leaders has rightly attracted so much of the blame for the débâcle of Suez that it is sometimes forgotten that they were never offered the only option that stood any chance of working: immediate military intervention. That the British armed forces were not prepared for this was also, but only partly, the fault of the politicians. The responsibility must be shared by the military hierarchy of the fifties, just as their successors cannot escape some of the blame for British impotence, this time perhaps too readily conceded by the politicians, in the Cyprus crisis of 1974. In each case prior Service attention had been concentrated on the gravest threat rather than on those contingencies which were both likely to arise (and, in the case of Cyprus, the subject of a specific obligation) and susceptible to a British military solution.

Defence, particularly for a country with Britain's limited resources, is a question of priorities. These are confusing. Does one prepare for the worst that could happen, realising that only in exceptional circumstances would useful action be possible, or should attention be focussed on lesser challenges that are nevertheless probable and to which responses appear to exist?

The choice has many ramifications: between balanced defence forces of all arms and concentration on particular tasks; between a few highly sophisticated and specialised ships and a larger number of simpler vessels; between the optimum contribution to alliance strategy and a policy of national insurance. It is complicated by more than strategic considerations. If these favoured greater specialisation or the renunciation of certain capabilities, for instance, the effect on morale or domestic political attitudes might be adverse. Naval officers naturally want ships capable of the highest levels of combat; politicians or public opinion may prefer ready availability for the lesser contingencies of peacetime. Various kinds of navy can be envisaged for Britain: one tailored to the specific requirements in general war of the Supreme Allied Commander Atlantic; one designed to police Britain's Exclusive Economic Zone; an ocean-going navy intended to meet every low-level threat to British interests; a navy exclusively concerned with the maintenance of the nuclear deterrent. Economic constraints will make it difficult to have a navy equally capable of all these tasks and of others that the unpredictable future may pose. Whatever the strategic decision, moreover, the level of combat capability will always have to be flexible: the frigate designed for the utmost sophistication of anti-submarine warfare may have to tackle seaborne terrorists; the coastguard hydrofoil could need support against the challenge of a superior warship.

These considerations will receive later analysis, but one point needs to be made at once. In the second half of the twentieth century navies continue to be designed for hypothetical wars, but are actually used to meet the exigencies of violent peace in the political application of limited naval force. Whether as victim or assailant Britain is likely again to face this challenge in the years to come. It is one of the contingencies for which the Royal Navy must be prepared.

That these should range from deterring the nuclear annihilation of the British Isles to the mundane task of securing diplomatic advantage, or averting loss, without provoking war, is inconvenient but probably inescapable. The navy has many potential duties. Their probability, their feasibility, the economic and technological demands they will pose, the extent to which either their execution or their preparation will attract political support: all these are questions which require examination. And not these alone. It cannot be repeated too often that the case for having a navy does not depend merely on the existence of a potential threat. The possibility of an effective response must also be clearly established. It will not be easy to suggest convincing answers, but the effort is a necessary condition of any attempt to project Britain's naval future.

5 The Limited Deterrent

Whatever happens, we have got
The Maxim gun, and they have not

Hilaire Belloc[1]

If the Super-Powers decide not to use nuclear weapons against each other's metropolitan territory, then, so it was suggested in the previous chapter, the possession of an independent and survivable force of submarine launched ballistic missiles could preserve the British Isles from nuclear attack in limited war. In these circumstances deterrence would be a useful task for the Royal Navy.

This is a view which encounters widespread opposition for many different reasons. To some extent this is an understandable reaction to the confusion created by a succession of official apologists. The latter, admittedly, had a difficult task. British nuclear weapons were produced, in great secrecy, before any clear strategic conception of their employment had been articulated; indeed, before the aircraft intended to deliver them were ready.[2] They were produced because those responsible took it for granted that Britain should have what was latest and best in weaponry. The rationalisations came afterwards. Deterrence was mentioned as early as October 1945.[3] Independence was always implicit. In 1947 came the idea 'of offsetting the enormous Russian preponderance in conventional armaments'.[4] The notion that nuclear weapons might provide Britain with an 'equaliser' was far-fetched rather than far-sighted, but it continued to exert a subliminal influence long after it had become apparent that both Super-Powers had entered a nuclear dimension that transcended Britain's by more than an order of magnitude. The number of weapons, the means of delivery, the sophisticated techniques, the vast industrial investment, the intelligence resources: these had soared beyond Britain's reach. As a nuclear weapons state she seemed to be imitating the example, in the years before 1914, of those South American countries who had purchased a dreadnought each.

'She seemed', because successive governments preferred not to offer a rational explanation of their conduct. The contrast between the wide-ranging, well-informed, uninhibited debate in the United States and the needless secrecy, the obfuscation, the timidity in this country reflects no credit on British politicians, their military or civilian advisers or, with a few illustrious exceptions, the academic community. After 'a far-reaching examination of the nation's defence needs in the next decade', the 1966 *Statement on the Defence Estimates* included one singularly uninformative sentence on the subject: 'the Royal Navy will take over from the Royal Air Force full responsibility for the British contribution to the nuclear forces of the NATO alliance'.[5] In 1970 the Statement extended to 109 pages, but provided no additional information.[6]

Later that year a new government claimed to have 'reviewed defence objectives and priorities', but again found one sentence sufficient: 'the contribution of the British Polaris force to the Western strategic deterrent will be maintained'.[7] When they had found their feet in 1971, the story was the same.[8] Another new government and another defence review expanded the 1975 Statement to 125 pages and four sentences, each as void of strategic rationale as the one they had replaced.[9] 1979 produced a reversion to the single sentence: 'the Polaris submarines . . . provide a continuous patrol as the United Kingdom's contribution to NATO's strategic deterrent'.[10] In those thirteen years the student of nuclear strategy would have found more to read in Moscow.

Secretiveness was not the only cause. The subject was as unwelcome to Labour ministers, conscious of the hostility of many of their followers, as talk of sex to the traditional Victorian wife: they submitted themselves in silence to nuclear weapons for the sake of NATO. Conservatives, temperamentally more inclined to robust speech, were constantly restrained by an apprehensive Ministry of Defence: on no account must American susceptibilities be ruffled. Such debate as took place (there was none in the House of Commons) often focussed on side-issues: the possession of nuclear weapons was said to give Britain 'a seat at the top table'; their renunciation would send a British foreign secretary 'naked into the conference chamber'. These were perhaps not very appealing arguments for a weapons system that could kill millions and, in its latest projected form, cost billions. The ministers, officials and serving officers of that era lack any right to complain of the irrelevance, the emotional-ism and the superficiality of much British opposition to the maintenance of a nuclear capability: they did not offer public opinion a reasoned case to consider.

Nor should their successors believe that they have made sufficient amends in the Statements of 1980 and 1981.[11] Admittedly these represented an immense advance on anything available under those previous prime ministers, of both parties, who professed their belief in 'open government'. Although concentrating, in a manner now familiar, on the economic and technical aspects, there is one explicit strategic statement – [British nuclear forces] 'can be used only on the express authority of the British Government'[12] – and several reasonably clear hints – 'The Government has great confidence in the depth of resolve underlying the United States commitment . . . But . . . ';[13] 'Even if in some future situation Soviet leaders imagined that the United States might not be prepared to use nuclear weapons . . . ';[14] 'to be a credible deterrent our strategic nuclear force . . . must clearly be under ultimate United Kingdom control'.[15] There is also a miniature essay on 'Nuclear Weapons and Preventing War'.[16] There is no truth in the story that this was written by a bishop.

Unfortunately these laudable efforts are vitiated by a continuing ambiguity, a needless reticence and an underlying hypocrisy. The susceptibilities of Britain's allies still receive more consideration than the anxieties of the British public. The worst feature is the implication – it is never directly stated – that Britain might launch her nuclear missiles, even if the United States refrained, on a suicidal attack against Moscow in response to Soviet aggression against Britain's allies on the mainland of Europe. This, if anything, is what the argument about 'the second centre of decision'[17] means. If any sanity remains in the British Isles, it is not true. What is more important, it is unlikely to be perceived in Moscow as plausible. Mr McNamara, no mean expert in these matters, once remarked: 'one cannot fashion a credible deterrent out of an incredible action'.[18] Nevertheless, the mere suggestion that Britain might go it alone, in circumstances that caused the United States to prefer a prudent inaction, is enough to justify the doubts, not merely of British pacifists, but of British patriots. The Ministry of Defence would do better to come clean. France did and emerged with increased credibility and prestige. Admittedly she had both General de Gaulle and weapons of her own.

As it is, thirty-six years of official British obscurantism have not merely encouraged such extreme statements as 'deterrence might itself be defined as the biggest and most expensive Lie in history':[19] they have also left many serious objections without a convincing response.

These objections, if the purely ethical arguments may be left to those better qualified to address them, are of two kinds: to the concept of an independent nuclear deterrent and to the particular weapon systems now employed or envisaged. This book being more concerned with strategy than with matériel, the emphasis will be on the first. The basic assumption is – and the reader should be aware that this is not undisputed – that only submarine-launched ballistic missiles offer a second-class power in a small island even the possibility of exercising nuclear deterrence. The arguments against other forms of delivery system are convincingly deployed in 'The Future United Kingdom Strategic Nuclear Deterrent', a little known monograph by the Ministry of Defence which is most informative on the matériel aspect.[20] If a small deterrent is worth having at all, which is debatable, it must be as survivable and as reliable as the state of the art permits. Quantity being impossible, quality is indispensable.

The first objections to be addressed, therefore, will be those to the principle of the nuclear deterrent. These fall into five main categories:

The contingency that would lend credibility to a British threat to employ nuclear weapons could never arise.

Britain's nuclear force is so small as to be vulnerable to pre-emptive attack.

The added incentive to enemy attack provided by the possession of nuclear weapons outweighs their potential deterrent value.

Not being truly independent, Britain's nuclear capability would not be reliably available for national purposes.

The retention by Britain of nuclear weapons will encourage their proliferation to other countries, whereas their renunciation would be a stimulus to wider disarmament.

The first and last of these arguments may be briefly dismissed. The remainder deserve serious consideration.

The previous chapter outlined a plausible scenario in which British submarine launched ballistic missiles could provide a credible and effective deterrent. Naturally this contingency *may* never arise and certain constraints will be examined later in this chapter. To say that it *will* never happen demands either the gift of prophecy or a degree of faith in the good intentions of the Soviet Union or the sacrificial loyalty of the United States that strains ordinary credulity. There is a risk and it is probably insurable. What has to be determined is the balance between probability and the cost of the premium (which is not only financial). This can more easily be attempted after consideration of the other arguments, which may also reveal further opportunities for, or obstacles to, the exercise of deterrence by Britain.

As for proliferation and disarmament, this is an argument which rests on an inflated idea of British international influence and a deficient sense of political realities. The other nations with nuclear weapons are the United States, the Soviet Union, China and France. None of these would follow a British example. Nor would this influence such potential nuclear weapons states as Argentina, Brazil, Chile, Egypt, India, Indonesia, Iran, Iraq, Israel, Japan, Pakistan, South Africa, South Korea, Spain and Taiwan, all of whom have more on their minds than the attitudes of those islanders in the North Sea. British policy should be decided in the light of British needs and not in the vain hope that it will change the world as Britain desires.

The balance between nuclear weapons as an incentive and as a deterrent to attack presents more serious problems. Some of these can not be discussed to much effect without access to particularly secret information. Could an enemy, for instance, hope to destroy all four British submarines before these were able to launch their missiles? The available evidence makes this seem most unlikely – geography, for one thing, favours the British – but naturally nobody would admit the possibility even if it did ever arise. All that can be done is to accept official assurances that at least one submarine is always at sea and that, while at sea, none has ever been trailed. The possession of more submarines would naturally increase survivability, but so far this does seem just sufficient to deter a prudent enemy in the circumstances envisaged. Indeed, the most serious threat yet established to the British deterrent has come from disaffected British civil servants and that ought to be remediable.

Of course, if total nuclear war ever becomes a serious option then, as already explained, at least those British submarines in port would be obvious targets and the deterrent value of the remainder would no longer be significant. Scrapping the British missile-firing submarines, however, would not be enough to remove the British Isles from the target maps of the Soviet Strategic Rocket Forces. Even the Labour Party proposals for the elimination of all American nuclear weapons based in British territory might not suffice. There are other installations in the British Isles of sufficient military value to the United States to make worth while targets for those Soviet missiles that could not, in any case, cross the Atlantic. No government proceeding to the terrible extremity of total nuclear war can be expected to observe any kind of self-denying ordinance precluding nuclear attacks on states without nuclear weapons.[21] Military advantage would be the only criterion.

To obtain immunity from Soviet nuclear attack in the event of total nuclear war, it would accordingly be necessary to ensure that there was nothing in the British Isles that the Soviet Union considered worth destroying. This would take Britain rather far down the path of disarmament and neutralisation, certainly far enough to forfeit the prospect of assistance from her allies in resisting other forms of Soviet aggression and pressure. The extent of such pressure would accordingly be at the discretion of the Soviet Union. Speculation about its possible results is scarcely profitable: so much would depend on the repercussions elsewhere in Europe of Britain's altered attitude and on the reactions of the United States. It would, for instance, be foolish to predict that Britain would necessarily end up as a Soviet satellite and thereby become as much exposed, in the event of total nuclear war, to the danger of American bombardment as she is now to Soviet attack. That is a fantastic hypothesis, but it is one of many possible results of the radical change of course we have been considering.

If one postulates as the supreme object of British policy the avoidance of Soviet bombardment in the course of total nuclear war, then it is true that the removal from the British Isles of all military targets of any significance offers better prospects than anything the Royal Navy, or anyone else in Britain, could do. Once embarked on that path, however, great changes would be inevitable in Britain and in Britain's international position. The nature and extent of those changes would largely depend on factors beyond British control. The price to be paid for immunity from Soviet nuclear attack could be very high and might ultimately include exposure to American. Even the most extreme courses, therefore, offer no certain or painless way of avoiding the catastrophe of total nuclear war. Some compromise policies do, however, carry higher risks than others.

One such policy would be to permit an American monopoly of nuclear weapons in British territory. It has already been argued that such weapons cannot be launched at the Soviet Union without risking a Soviet riposte against the United States as well as the British Isles, but it is uncertain how thoroughly this argument is accepted in Washington. Indeed, American, to say nothing of British, motives for wanting missiles in East Anglia that could reach the Soviet Union are obscure[22] and have not been illuminated by paragraphs 215–20 of the 1981 *Statement on the Defence Estimates*. The explanations offered by officials tend to be metaphorical rather than precise: 'a useful extra rung on the escalatory ladder'; 'to the Russians they will be a visible link between tactical nuclear weapons and American strategic forces'. One is driven back to the masochism of the 1980 Statement: 'it is politically important that all allies should share the risks and burdens of providing for deterrence and defence'.[23]

This sentence would be slightly less alarming if, either in 1980 or in 1981, there had been a clear description of any measures which may have been adopted to ensure that these weapons can not be fired without the express approval of the British Government. Not that it is obvious how such measures could be fully effective. It is no discredit to American soldiers that they can be expected to obey the orders of their own government, nor could that government be blamed, if faced with the supreme emergency of nuclear war, for regarding the national interest as transcending all consideration of agreements or undertakings. British governments have so conducted themselves under less provocation and will doubtless do so again. If technical devices can be overridden, as one suspects a competent electrician could, there would probably not be time, between an order from Washington and its disapproval in London, to surround every missile (160 are projected) with British troops.

This is a worst case, an improbable contingency. It is more likely that the British and American governments will be in agreement and act, or refrain from action, in concert. But we are talking of the supreme test of national independence: the ability of the British government to decide whether or not to risk the existence of the British people. If there is any possibility, however remote, of a government of the United States regarding the discharge of weapons from East Anglia, perhaps only against targets west of the Soviet border, as an intermediate measure of escalation that would confine the Soviet response to the British Isles, then the British government need an effective power of veto. There should be – perhaps there even are – other ways of exercising it. But, if all else fails, the knowledge that Soviet retaliation against Britain could elicit a response from submarine-launched ballistic missiles not readily distinguishable from those of the United States, and thus capable of triggering total nuclear war, should constitute a deterrent as effective in Washington as in Moscow. Without POLARIS or TRIDENT the fate of the British people would be too exclusively at the mercy of every American missile on British soil.

Of course, it would be better not to have these missiles at all. The argument in the 1981 Statement about deterring 'the Soviet Union from thinking that it could fight and win a nuclear war confined to Europe'[24] has only to be spelt out step by step to reveal its flaws. These missiles would constitute a more credible deterrent to such a war than the much more powerful Strategic Forces of the United States. Why? Because they would be more readily fired. Why? Because the Americans would not expect the discharge of these missiles to invite retaliation against the continental United States. Why? Because these missiles would not be directed against the metropolitan territory of the Soviet Union.

If this chain of reasoning is accepted in Moscow, then the Soviet Union will presumably regard the presence of these missiles in East Anglia (and of others in West Germany, perhaps elsewhere) as confirmation of American willingness to fight a territorially limited nuclear war. Is this a deterrent or an incentive? The first view is possible, if the Russians think the adverse effect of these missiles on the outcome of a territorially limited exchange would outweigh the increased chance of avoiding total war. From everyone's point of view the interlocking assumptions required add up to a gamble but the odds are clearly more favourable to the Super-Powers, who could at least hope that their territory would remain immune even if deterrence failed, than to the Europeans, for whom hope would be minimal and its disappointment terminal.

These odds are particularly adverse to Britain whose submarine-launched ballistic missiles would otherwise offer the chance of opting out of a territorially limited nuclear war. This chance, as earlier argued, is not destroyed by the presence of American missiles in East Anglia, but it is certainly impaired. What might have been seen in Moscow as a simple proposition – British POLARIS missiles can more effectively be neutralised by threatening a nuclear attack on the British Isles than by making one – becomes a complex equation capable of suggesting that it might be easier to degrade the American missiles by a first strike than to deter the United States (whose own territory would have been promised conditional immunity) from using them. Cold calculation, admittedly, might still convince the Soviet Union that it was better to accept the risk to Soviet troops and to the territory of Soviet allies represented by these missiles rather than expose Moscow to British retaliation, but the case for excluding Britain from the nuclear battlefield would have been weakened. This weakening might be decisive if American missiles were fired before Britain had been attacked. Emotion might then reinforce the argument that a limited response, coupled with the reminder that much worse was available, might be a better deterrent to the British than mere threats – as long as Britain was left with something still to lose.

A determined British government might, as earlier suggested, succeed in convincing both Super-Powers that American missiles in East Anglia could not be attacked (or, by logical extension, launched) without serious risk of escalation to a strategic exchange, but it is scarcely desirable for Britain to be placed in the position of having to rely on so desperate an expedient. Even assuming the utmost Anglo-American identity of purpose and harmony in decision-making – and it is only fair to say that Americans are probably much less inclined to use any kind of nuclear weapon than is often supposed – the mere presence of these missiles must increase the risks to Britain and limit her freedom of manoeuvre. It is all very well for the Ministry of Defence to argue that 'in time of tension they would be quickly and widely dispersed',[25] but are we expected to consider the Russians capable of everything but surprise attack? Mobile missiles that have to be deployed in time of tension are less secure, yet more provocative, than a POLARIS submarine on constant patrol. Indeed, no state of tension is more readily predictable than that between the politicians, who would want to defer deployment for fear of exacerbating the crisis, and the military, who would want to hasten it for fear of inviting a first strike. And both might well be right.

On a purely strategic calculation of British interests the optimum solution for Britain would be a British monopoly of nuclear weapons in British territory. A small, survivable force controlled by a single government is a more credible deterrent (if total nuclear war is excluded from the argument) than a larger force with a mixed allegiance. It is a fallacy to suppose that uncertainty increases deterrence. If there is any truth in the idea at all – and the precedent of 1914 is not encouraging – it applies only to the penalties of aggression, not to the rewards of abstinence. Both are more readily predictable – and nuclear war does seem more likely to result from miscalculation than from deliberate choice – in the case of a single government than an alliance. A British monopoly of nuclear weapons in British territory would considerably reduce the scope for misunderstanding in Moscow about the most advantageous policy to pursue towards Britain. If political and economic factors had allowed Britain to follow the same line in previous years as France, this happy result – misunderstanding is usually more of a menace than guile – might well have been achieved without incurring any significant penalty in other respects. Now it may be too late.

What makes the projected installation of American missiles in Britain – not in itself an unprecedented step – particularly significant is that it will take place, if it does, at a time when the international environment has been modified by increased perception of the possibility of limited nuclear war. This is the risk the British Government have elected to share with their European allies, the risk they even hope these missiles will somehow help to avert. This is not, however, the most compelling reason for British consent. Accepting these missiles is the latest payment due on the long bill for the Anglo-American special relationship, in which American relief of Britain's necessities is balanced by British deference to American wishes.[26] After forty years this is so engrained in British policy, so integral a component of the mental processes of successive British ministers, officials and serving officers that few could now hazard a guess whether the practical or the psychological impediments to change are more potent. Both are conspicuous in everything relating to Britain's nuclear capability.

Britain's past debt to the United States for the economical acquisition and maintenance of the POLARIS system and her prospective debt for its replacement by TRIDENT are sufficiently familiar to require neither exposition nor emphasis. The medium term prospect for Britain has been, and will continue to be, one of dependence on the United States for the British nuclear weapons capability. Naturally the purely strategic significance of this dependence should not be exaggerated. In a sudden and desperate emergency the British Government could launch their missiles against Moscow or, for that matter, New York in defiance of American wishes. At any given moment Britain has nuclear independence. In the long term, by great efforts and at vast cost, she could theoretically recover it, as she did in the forties and fifties after the Americans had disregarded their wartime undertakings. It is in the medium term that the United States could degrade the British deterrent by cutting off intelligence, targeting information, spare parts, know-how, testing facilities and the concealed financial subsidy.

How long it would take before a British nuclear threat lost its credibility is a subject on which secrecy is justified and speculation would be otiose, but the prospect is naturally a formidable deterrent to British policies which the United States might consider unfriendly. Its psychological impact is enhanced by British memories of having to placate Admiral Rickover and the Joint Congressional Committee. There is thus a strong predisposition among the orthodox to regard the acceptance of American nuclear weapons in the British Isles as a necessary condition for the continuing effectiveness of the British nuclear deterrent. This linkage is not necessarily imperative and might be broken by, for instance, a German revolt against similar American missiles, but, in purely British political terms, those most inclined to risk American displeasure are also those least attached to the concept of an independent nuclear deterrent.

It is thus probable, not certain, that optimum solutions will be irrelevant and that, in the medium term, the practical choice will lie between having both an American nuclear presence in the British Isles and a British nuclear capability or else neither. The probability is perhaps increased by the prevalence of corresponding attitudes in the two main political parties in Britain. In terms of national survival the best option is not obvious, so there is something to be said for deferring a decision as long as the new American missiles are prospective rather than actual. Neither American submarines nor their aircraft pose so acute a danger. They are part of an established pattern, not the instruments of the new concept of territorially limited nuclear war.

This examination of the problems that might be created by American missiles in East Anglia has been more than a necessary digression. It has helped to answer the earlier question about the probability of a situation arising in which American strategic forces were not available to deter a nuclear attack on the British Isles. Clearly the United States would not be willing to incur the substantial financial costs, nor the British Government the political, of installing 160 missiles, unless both considered a territorially limited nuclear war to be a serious possibility. The risk exists and, until these missiles are actually in place – which may never happen – it will arguably be insurable. The risk that even a limited strike against Britain might provoke British retaliation is likely to loom larger in Moscow than the relatively slender advantages of inflicting mass destruction. It is far from certain that the Soviet leaders would reason in this way, but the chance of their doing so depends on British ability to punish an attack or reciprocate an abstention. The arrival of American missiles would complicate the Soviet choice, reduce British freedom of manoeuvre and thus impair the effectiveness of the British deterrent. Even then, Britain would still retain the rather desperate expedient of threatening a trigger-effect. In strategic terms, therefore, a risk exists which is now insurable and which might just so continue.

There is a further consideration. The international environment is not immutable. Its character could alter or its balance tilt or Britain's ability to rely on her allies be called in question in less time than would be needed to refashion a nuclear capability that had once been renounced. The existence of this time-lag between perceiving a new military need and completing preparations to meet it is an established and familiar argument. It has been applied to all kinds of naval strength and deployed, often in vain, by every writer on naval affairs in this century. It has not lost its validity merely by becoming hackneyed. If British nuclear weapons offer Britain a measure of insurance against risks now apparent, these are unlikely to be the only dangers in the womb of time. Cover against the unforeseen is also worth considering.

The question which remains is whether that insurance, which must always be both fallible and confined to a narrow range of mortal contingencies, is worth the premium.

Statistically, the cost of the POLARIS system has not been high. Of course, the figures that appear in annual statements by the Ministry of Defence (in 1981 these were: 2.2 per cent of the defence budget, 0.7 per cent of Service manpower and 1.8 per cent of civilian manpower)[27] need to be taken with a pinch of salt. That Ministry's cosmeticians may enjoy less scope than their Soviet counterparts, but they are equally skilled, particularly in their emphasis on the costs of upkeep rather than on those of acquisition. The original development of Britain's nuclear weapons and the £1 billion spent on the recent CHEVALINE improvement programme are only two examples of important expenditure on nuclear weapons that never appeared in the defence budget when it was undertaken. With research and development costing six times as much as the POLARIS force and the same amount as the rest of the navy,[28] it is not too easy to be sure of the true financial cost of Britain's deterrent. Nevertheless, even taking account of such useful estimates as those in Ian Smart's seminal paper of 1971,[29] the historical cost of POLARIS has been low, whether this is compared to the British gross national product, to the defence budget or to French expenditure on a comparable system.

Nor, in spite of an initial – and in some quarters persisting – absence of enthusiasm in the Navy, is there conclusive evidence that the maintenance of POLARIS has been seriously detrimental to British conventional forces. Ian Smart's estimate, for instance, shows that the cost of POLARIS (£994 million for seven years)[30] was roughly comparable in the late sixties to that predicted by the Ministry of Defence for the maintenance of a carrier force (£1400 million over ten years),[31] but it has not been proved that carriers were sacrificed in order to keep the deterrent, though the cost of the latter doubtless contributed to the total budgetary argument. Today the admitted expenditure of £269 million on the upkeep of the nuclear strategic force can be contrasted with £594 million on destroyers and frigates or £603 million on service pensions.[32] Even the CHEVALINE programme seems slightly less exorbitant, at £1 billion, when one remembers that the initial order for the Challenger Main Battle Tank, only one item in a range of equipment for the army, came to £350 million[33] or that estimates for the total cost of the RAF Tornado programme have soared over £10 billion. If money alone had to be offset against the chance of national survival, POLARIS

might be judged a better investment than British forces in Europe, which
cost £821 million in local expenditure alone,[34] perhaps £4525 million in
all, compared to David Greenwood's unofficial, but probably realistic,
estimate of £540 million for POLARIS.[35]

The political costs have nevertheless been substantial and not only
because emotional opposition to nuclear weapons has extended itself to
defence in general. The acquisition and maintenance of a relatively
cheap nuclear deterrent has compromised British independence. Some
readers may regard this argument as having already been accorded
undue weight. Orthodox opinion attaches more importance to
interdependence – it used to be called 'collective security' – than to an
independence which technological developments, no less than economic
decline and the altered political and strategic environment, have
rendered illusory. There is much force in the view that Britain must
stand or fall with NATO. It is nevertheless a view which has little
relevance to the case for a British nuclear capability. This would not be
needed in total nuclear war and, if plans for the installation of new
American missiles in Europe are implemented, would be superfluous –
to the Alliance – even in territorially limited nuclear war. Europeans
cannot win such a war and, if it must be fought, there would be enough
American warheads to orchestrate the last act of Götterdämmerung.

As for deterring it, the notion that Britain could, if the Americans
withheld their nuclear hand, prevent or arrest an attack on her allies by a
credible threat is simply preposterous. Either POLARIS is a weapon of
last resort for Britain herself or it is not worth the money it costs and the
debate it causes. That is why the preceding arguments have had so
nationalist, even Gaullist, a flavour. That is why one of the side-effects of
the POLARIS programme – its tendency to lock Britain into NATO
strategy and American policy – must be reckoned as a political debit. It
may or may not – the point will later be examined – be an advantage for
Britain to be thus committed, but it is inconsistent with the essential
purpose of an independent nuclear deterrent.

The future cost of this deterrent, now that the British Government
have decided on TRIDENT, has been much debated. The official view is
intended to be reassuring. In 1981, when the TRIDENT I C4 was the
chosen system, the figures given were £5 billion over fifteen years, not
more than 3 per cent of the defence budget on average and about 5 per
cent in peak years. The TRIDENT programme 'involves no dramatic
change in the allocation of our defence resources' and 'will not prevent
continued improvement in other areas of the United Kingdom's
contribution to NATO'.[36] In 1982, when the choice had been switched,

following the American lead, to the TRIDENT II D5, the estimate was £7.5 billion or just over 3 per cent of the expected defence spending during fifteen years.

The reader may well regard all these figures (and the different comparisons that can be drawn from them) as more than a trifle unreal, depending as they do on assumptions about future costs, inflation and defence spending that experience has shown to be unreliable. 'At September 1980 prices, therefore, we will spend on TRIDENT about £6000 million. Updating the price basis to September 1981 prices . . . adds a total of about £1500 million.'[37] If twelve months can increase the bill by 25 per cent, albeit in a depreciating currency, it is a little difficult to attribute more than symbolic importance to conflicting estimates of the budgetary cost of a fifteen year programme exposed to incalculable vicissitudes: political, economic and technological.

Much ingenuity has nevertheless been devoted to analysis of the official view that TRIDENT, in either version, would be financially compatible with the maintenance of unreduced conventional forces. The sceptics, who include serving officers and officials as well as politicians and analysts, challenge these predictions. The main thrust of their argument, expounded in careful detail by David Greenwood,[38] is that there is no prospect of a sufficient increase in British defence expenditure to accommodate the cost of even the original TRIDENT programme, which will accordingly have to be financed by savings elsewhere in future defence budgets. Indeed, Greenwood goes further. He argues that the NATO target, endorsed in the 1980 Statement,[39] of a 3 per cent annual increase in real terms represents the maximum to be expected in future years. He also contends – and, as earlier noted, many informed observers agree – that 'salami-slicing' has reached its limit as a source of significant savings. Therefore, if the TRIDENT programme is carried through, it can only be at the expense of the other three pillars of British defence policy and he illustrates his argument with specific figures for hypothetical cuts in either the naval rôle in the Eastern Atlantic or the continental commitment. These predictions received at least partial confirmation in *The Way Forward*, which is discussed in Chapter 8.

Greenwood's basic assumption of a ceiling for future defence expenditure was essentially political. As such, it was plausible: defence expenditure at constant prices varied very little from 1970 to 1977 in spite of the change from Labour to Conservative and back again to Labour during those years.[40] It was nevertheless conceivable that a new Conservative government, having forsaken consensus on so many other aspects of policy, would also make a major increase in the accepted level of defence spending, as Mr Nott claimed, on 23 February 1982, to have done.[41] The more optimistic advocates of this course often argued that increased perception of the threat would transform political priorities; that a dramatic rise in oil revenue would permit higher expenditure without adding to inflation or the tax burden; even that government policy would regenerate the economy. As late as April 1981 it was possible to believe that ministers realised the implications of their statement that TRIDENT would involve 'no dramatic change in the allocation of our defence resources', meant what they said and hoped that, when the time came, they would be able to find the extra money. Such a sanguine approach, indeed the strategy of Mr Micawber, has many precedents in British defence policy and the TRIDENT programme is intended to take fifteen years. As this period will necessarily include at least three general elections, a degree of optimism at the outset would not merely have been permissible but mandatory.

Such optimism has become difficult to sustain since the events of May 1981. A sudden flurry of press stories, some rather selective ministerial denials, the dismissal of a Parliamentary Under Secretary for voicing his apprehensions and an inconclusive debate in the House of Commons made it obvious that the future structure of British defence was again undergoing a 'far-reaching examination'. The Secretary of State for Defence did not admit that the purpose was to save enough money to pay for TRIDENT, but he did say: 'Of course, money spent on TRIDENT is money that is not spent on something else.'[42] In the charged atmosphere of the defence debate this was rather more than a statement of the obvious.

It will accordingly be necessary to analyse further the likely cost of TRIDENT in terms of conventional defence and, more particularly, of its impact on the navy. The time to do that will be when we come to consider the remaining contingencies, other than the deterrence of nuclear attack, for which naval forces might be required. The strategic advantages to be expected from maintenance of a nuclear deterrent must be weighed against any equivalent benefits which might have to be foregone. This, rather than the loss of ships or men or even capabilities, is the true defence cost. In doing so, account will also have to be taken of possible changes in strategy, whether as a result of political developments at home or abroad or as a necessary response to major alterations in the structure of British defence forces. Even if analysis were to suggest that British strategy would have to be transformed to accommodate TRIDENT, this would not constitute a net cost unless the change was likely to be for the worse.

Meanwhile a note of caution is needed. Given the plausible concept of a political ceiling for defence expenditure, persistence with TRIDENT is likely to reduce the money available for the rest of the armed forces. The growing preference, confirmed in the defence debate of 19 and 20 May 1981 in the House of Commons, for reconsidering priorities rather than maintaining equal misery may even translate financial shortage into structural change. It would nevertheless be foolish to suppose that change would not occur, or that the penalties of TRIDENT could be avoided, if the project were cancelled. A ceiling to defence expenditure is plausible: that this is also the floor is not.

The Secretary of State for Defence declared on 20 May 1981: 'I am looking at all the options. Nothing, including TRIDENT, has been sacred.'[43] No doubt all the options have been, and will be, examined, but some options are more equal than others. Little enquiry is needed to confirm the existence of a profound political disparity between two contesting ideas: reducing certain aspects of conventional defence in order to find money for TRIDENT; and cancelling TRIDENT to ensure the continued maintenance of effectively balanced conventional forces. For a Conservative government TRIDENT has acquired a political, indeed a symbolic, importance which could not readily be redistributed among more humdrum tasks. Experienced men, steeped in caution by years of disillusionment, foresee a risk that a Conservative government, if once reluctantly persuaded to abandon the concept of a British nuclear deterrent, might find other uses than conventional defence for the money saved. This is not an uncontested view, but the repercussions of so traumatic a sacrifice are not readily predictable.

Moreover, Conservative partiality for defence has usually been balanced by hostility to government expenditure and has often needed the glamour of dreadnoughts or bombers or nuclear weapons or whatever was latest and strongest to tip the scales. As early as 1934, for instance, Chamberlain was eager to cut expenditure on the army and navy in order to create a deterrent force of bombers larger than even the Royal Air Force wanted.[44] Today, so it is argued, the sacrifice of TRIDENT could be such a wound as not merely to preclude the increased spending on balanced conventional forces that rising costs of equipment will anyway require, but actually to provide a fresh incentive for the kind of major restructuring that might produce appreciable savings.

The Labour Party, of course, have more than financial reservations about TRIDENT and few members would feel the same bereavement at its loss. But, if they were in power, the sacrifice of TRIDENT would be even less likely to ensure the future maintenance of effectively balanced conventional forces. David Greenwood, who argued that the TRIDENT programme constituted a threat to conventional strength, had earlier been a major contributor to *Sense About Defence*, which reflected an emergent strain of party views when it set out various options for a 20 per cent cut in defence spending *in addition* to the withdrawal from service of the POLARIS submarines.[45] This would bite deeper than the consequences he predicted for completing the TRIDENT programme at substantially unchanged levels of defence spending. Many different political combinations could, of course, emerge from the three general elections that are the minimum to be expected before TRIDENT is finished, but the 'official' Labour Party, if there is such a thing, seem to be committed to a reduction in defence expenditure; Mr Benn's 'new non-nuclear defence strategy'[46] has yet to be spelt out and the intentions of Liberals and Social Democrats are uncertain. Political perceptions would have to change substantially before the loss of TRIDENT became a reliable source of equivalent funds for defence.

TRIDENT is obviously not cost-free, even in the narrow terms of its impact on general British defence capabilities. This will later be examined on the only basis – however improbable – that permits any useful analysis: that the present government mean what they say and that their successors will be of the same minds. But the fundamental paradox must be remembered. Just as renunciation of the British nuclear deterrent would not, of itself, remove the danger to which, indirectly, it has exposed the British people; so the same sacrifice would be inadequate to guarantee the maintenance of effectively balanced conventional forces. Salvation, if it is attainable at all, is to be sought in policy and strategy rather than in the choice of matériel. It thus seems sensible to give more weight to the admittedly conflicting political and strategic arguments than to economic predictions that depend on a wide spectrum of political assumptions. Defence is about survival and, before costing the options, there is something to be said for ascertaining which, if any, offers some prospect of achieving it.

Given the general preoccupation with hardware, it is scarcely surprising that the objection most carefully analysed is to TRIDENT as the wrong choice of nuclear weapons system for Britain. Alford and Nailor, Freedman, Greenwood and, of course, Ian Smart are all worth reading on the subject, while Rodgers provides a political view.[47] Except to note that some of the theoretical alternatives to TRIDENT – continuing POLARIS or installing cruise missiles in launch platforms of various kinds – have their partisans among serving officers, officials and politicians as well as analysts, these complex arguments need not be recapitulated here. Now that the British government have signed an agreement for the acquisition of TRIDENT,[48] they are probably irrelevant. If the TRIDENT programme is cancelled, which might be the result of a change of government, of mounting financial pressure or even of unforeseen technological change (failure of the American weapon system or a breakthrough in submarine detection), it is politically unlikely that any British government would start again from scratch on a new system. POLARIS might be continued or nuclear capability renounced, but it is hard to envisage a repetition of the switch, twenty years ago, from SKYBOLT to POLARIS.[49] Moreover, whatever the cause for this hypothetical abandonment of TRIDENT, the repercussions would be enough to create a new situation in which factors not readily predictable could swamp existing arguments.

For our purposes these arguments can be simplified to a single assertion: TRIDENT is a needlessly sophisticated and expensive method of providing Britain with a minimum deterrent. Disagreement is sufficiently widespread for the layman to withhold judgment, but the merits of the debate are relevant only to the choice of weapons system, which has already been made, not to the strategic utility of nuclear deterrence. Insofar as this exists at all, nobody has yet convincingly argued that it will be diminished by TRIDENT.[50] Most commentators admit that it is even likely to be increased. The objection is to its cost, not only financial but in terms of side-effects. It may thus be better to accept that cost as a fact, without considering whether or not it should have been incurred, and to treat it as the premium against which the future value of nuclear insurance must be weighed.

It is unfortunate that there should be so many imponderables on each side of the equation, but this is inherent in the political process. The idea of a fixed economic cost is as much a fantasy as the notion of a reliable strategic benefit. Uncertain fears have to be balanced against doubtful hopes.

Perhaps it would be best to begin groping for a conclusion by tackling the latter. Ruling out total nuclear war as a catastrophe beyond the reach of British influence, limited nuclear war is the contingency in which a British nuclear capability has most chance of proving useful. If war in Europe is conceivable, then a territorially limited war is at least as likely as any other variety: it would exempt both Super-Powers – the ultimate arbiters – from nuclear bombardment and would offer one of them a less one-sided prospect than conventional war. Both sides possess, or are developing, the weapons such a war would need and both envisage, beneath the customary smoke-screen of 'deterrence' and 'defence' and 'arms control', the possibility of being forced to fight it. Some indications of American and, for what these are worth, British attitudes have already been mentioned. Those of the Soviet Union may be discerned, with all the caution inseparable from this kind of speculation, in McConnell's interesting analysis of Soviet thinking on 'Eurostrategic war'.[51]

The official NATO response is to deter it by matching Soviet ability to fight it. The historical precedents are not encouraging, but the expedient now contemplated has an added weakness. The deterrence exercised by theatre nuclear weapons will not be inescapably directed against the Super-Powers: it will be applied, in the first instance, to their allies and only inferentially, by creating the risk of escalation, to themselves. For the Super-Powers, therefore, these weapons offer a *limited* deterrent to any kind of war in Europe, but also a degree of encouragement for the hope that such a war, if it could not be avoided, would at least remain *limited*. For Europeans, East or West, the concept of *limited* nuclear war can have no significance and a *limited* deterrent not under their own control little value. Either they must rely on their protecting Super-Power for an *unlimited* deterrent or else they must provide a *limited* deterrent of their own. The concept of the 'Eurobomb' bristles with alarming difficulties and objections and, East or West, is politically inconceivable in the likely currency of this book. But both Britain and France now possess a *limited* deterrent.

The obstacles (greater for Britain than for France) to the exercise of limited deterrence have already been sufficiently discussed. This will not work in total war or in the face of less than mortal danger. The target is the enemy capable of conquest or destruction but unwilling to attempt either at the cost of his capital. The most plausible contingency is a territorially limited nuclear war. Neither Britain nor France could prevent this, but they might be able to exclude their own countries from the nuclear battlefield. Exclusion would offer the best hope of national survival and it is hard to think of a better expedient for securing it than a national deterrent. It may be limited, but it may also be better than nothing.

The prime cost for Britain is political. This was predicted from the outset.

Late in 1947, when it was suggested that Britain might rely on the United States for the maintenance of her nuclear striking force, Lord Tedder, Chief of the Air Staff, voiced a general feeling when he replied that this would involve a close military alliance with the United States in which Britain would be merely a temporary advance base, would involve complete subservience to United States policy and would render Britain completely impotent in negotiations with Russia or any other nation.[52]

The full price envisaged by Lord Tedder has not been paid, because a substantial British investment has preserved, at any given moment of emergency, a minimal British independence and has thus avoided complete impotence in negotiations. Broadly speaking, however, he was right: Britain has paid a price which France found excessive.

The economic costs are more hypothetical. In 1979, for instance, the Treasury regarded 2 per cent as the average margin of error in predictions of the British gross national product.[53] In any one year, therefore, this might vary, other factors apart, by about half the cost of the fifteen year TRIDENT programme. Whether or not this bill is tolerable is economically unpredictable: it will depend on political perceptions at the time it is incurred. Three general elections offer no less scope for volatility in that respect. What does seem likely is that future decisions – to maintain TRIDENT or to cancel it, to fall back on POLARIS or to renounce nuclear deterrence – will be determined by political factors. These factors will also dictate the choice of economic arguments advanced in support of whichever decision is taken. Much the same, of course, could be said of the strategic arguments. Both kinds of reasoning are ancillary to the political process and both are fallible.

Indeed, at this moment of time and at the present stage of the argument, it would be hard to resist the proposition that political considerations not only will be decisive, but perhaps ought to be so. The economic case depends on political perceptions and the strategic case will be inconclusive as long as policy remains ambiguous. The political attractions of British nuclear forces, their credibility and their effectiveness are all functions of British political independence, with which they must rise or fall. So, unfortunately, must their price. This is a dilemma which strategic and economic arguments can sharpen, but which only political decisions, perhaps even political developments not now predictable, can resolve. Meanwhile British submarine launched ballistic missiles offer a degree of advantage in certain contingencies which seems rather more reliable than the equally hypothetical benefits to be expected from their renunciation. So far – remembering that some of the potential defence costs have yet to be analysed – the insurance seems worth the premium. It is a limited deterrent, but probably better than none.

6 Alliance Naval War I: the orthodox case

> It is not in the continental struggle that the final decision for this country – if there is to be war – will be taken . . . The crux . . . is our ability . . . to command the air and sea above and surrounding these islands.
>
> Enoch Powell[1]

The ifs and buts of deterring strategic nuclear attack seem almost simple by comparison with the complex uncertainties of war at sea. Nuclear forces are permanently in presence and their relative strength, which is known in considerable detail, does not significantly depend on mobilisation, deployment or reinforcement. Defence is unimportant and, for Britain, non-existent. Only attack, counter-attack and escalation count in nuclear war and these are the acts which, when credibly threatened, constitute deterrence. There are not many scenarios and very few of them offer Britain any choice at all.

War at sea, on the other hand, even alliance war, presents planners with a kaleidoscope of contingencies and choices. As already argued, such a war is unlikely to be fought for command of the sea. That is no longer a self-sufficient or readily attainable goal. Instead the objective will be to secure or deny some particular use of the sea. What that use will be is by no means self-evident. Even the identity of the sea is not. The Mediterranean, after all, is in the Treaty Area[2] and so is the Norwegian Sea. A conflict beyond the Tropic of Cancer would impose no obligations on the Alliance and might not involve many of its navies, but it could simultaneously heighten tension in Europe and alter the naval balance in the Atlantic. Even in that ocean, often regarded as the obvious theatre of naval war, different kinds of conflict are not merely conceivable, but likely.

Two variables are particularly productive of uncertainty at sea. One is the theatre naval balance. This can fluctuate more considerably, more easily and more rapidly than on land. Admiral Hays, for instance, pointed out that the carrier battle-group reassigned from the Mediterranean to the Arabian Sea in January 1980 'represented a 50 per cent reduction in our commitment of naval forces to NATO'.[3] Even this was an understatement, for much NATO planning assumes that four carrier battle-groups will be available in the Treaty Area and that all four, operating together, might be needed either in the North or in the South. The flexibility and mobility of naval forces is one of their advantages, but the whereabouts of those carriers could profoundly affect the nature of Alliance naval war. On land, in Europe at least, the strength of NATO forces only determines the duration of their necessarily defensive operations. At sea the range of options is wider, but the balance less predictable.

Critics of the Navy often complain that neither nationally nor on an alliance basis is there the same clear-cut strategy that exists for the army and air force. To some extent there cannot be, because the admirals do not know what ships they will have. The American carriers may be available for offensive operations or they may be fighting off the Gulf or needed in the Pacific or off the coast of South Africa when hostilities unexpectedly spread to the Atlantic or the Mediterranean or to Norway. And those carriers are the intended core of the naval strength of NATO. They are also among the principal assets of a navy which is primarily, as all navies are, the instrument of a national policy.

The second variable is the objective: the use of the sea which the nature of the conflict demands should be secured or denied. The orthodox view, particularly in Britain, has been that the main naval task will be to protect the seaborne reinforcement and resupply of the Central Front against Soviet submarine attack. This is a possible scenario, but its near monopoly of official attention is uncomfortably reminiscent of the confident expectation that 1914 would bring a fleet action in the North Sea. Seizure of the Danish Straits, of the Norwegian airfields, of Iceland, the Faeroes, even of the Shetlands are also contingencies to be considered. Some naval officers have coined the phrase 'Central Front myopia' to describe the general assumption that alliance war can only come in response to an avalanche of Soviet armour across the North German plain. It is at least conceivable that conflict will arise, and be mainly prosecuted, outside Europe, which will itself be subjected to pressure, threats, even localised interventions, rather than massive invasion. Visible naval concentrations might be needed in the North

Sea, lest the oil platforms should appear defenceless hostages, or across the Greenland–Iceland–United Kingdom gap: not to fight – NATO, as such, might not initially be at war – but to display resolution. There are many contingencies in which the neutralisation of Europe could seem more attractive to the Soviet Union than its conquest and the ambivalent deployment of the Northern Fleet a better method than manoeuvring the Group of Soviet Armies in Germany. Alliance navies may have to attempt the support of the Central Front, but there are other potential tasks.

The orthodox view nevertheless deserves examination, for it has hitherto dominated strategic thought and provided most of the official justification for the size, structure and building programmes of the Royal Navy. The argument starts from the premise that:

> the transatlantic reinforcement of Europe would be crucial to Alliance strategy. A major allied naval and air effort would be needed to protect this operation and the continued shipment of essential supplies. Unless NATO can show itself capable of mounting and protecting this reinforcement, the military credibility and deterrent effect of allied forces stationed outside continental Europe would be compromised.[4]

The Statements on the Defence Estimates for 1980 and 1981 mention other naval tasks as well, but both give priority to the protection of reinforcement and both explain that

> Our maritime forces are primarily designed for anti-submarine warfare, as the most dangerous threat is from Soviet submarines.[5]

The necessarily brief official exposition rests on a number of assumptions, which deserve careful exploration. Some are political and fundamental: that only the fear of nuclear conflict with the United States deters the Soviet Union from using military force against Western Europe; that nuclear deterrence can only be made credible by the maintenance of a high threshold of conventional defence; that this defence must include American troops on the ground; and that these troops will not be kept in Europe unless the collective efforts of the Alliance are sufficient both to satisfy the American conception of burden-sharing and to offer a reasonable prospect that conventional defence will be sufficiently protracted to obviate the need for a snap decision on total nuclear war. It is the final assumption that is invoked to justify naval efforts: without the prospect of reinforcement and resupply the prognosis for defence of the Central Front would be so dismal that it would not even be attempted and deterrence would fail.

Although political developments inside Britain or internationally could cast doubt on some of these assumptions, there is no point in querying them at present. They are not all particularly reasonable, but neither are human beings or their governments. Imperial Germany had more to gain from peace than war in 1914. Hitler's invasion of Poland in 1939 was as unnecessary as Chamberlain's prior decision to make it a *casus belli*. Both proved unprofitable. As long as governments maintain an offensive capability, it must be assumed that the prospect of immediate advantage will tempt them to employ it and the examples of Belgium, Denmark, Finland, Luxembourg, the Netherlands and Norway suggest that neutrality is an insufficient safeguard. It would be foolish of the Soviet Union to invade even a defenceless Western Europe: the Eastern half is enough of a headache. But the Politburo are no more immune from folly than Her Majesty's Government, who can not be wholly blamed for trying to protect the British people against what the Russians could, rather than against what they rationally should, do.

The strategic assumptions are another matter. Suppose the Soviet Union does decide to attack the Central Front. It is unlikely, because any such operation would increase the risks run by the Soviet Union to a greater extent than any advantages now foreseeable. But, people being what they are, it is conceivable. The Soviet Union would then have a range of options. They could choose invasion combined with total nuclear war, in which case all bets would be off for Britain. They could attempt a territorially limited nuclear war, which would allow Britain the chance to try limited deterrence. They could go for a full conventional invasion, with or without chemical and biological weapons. Or they could restrict themselves to securing defined objectives with a view to exploiting deliberately limited military success as a means of extracting political concessions.

Only the last two contingencies have much naval significance – except for the POLARIS/TRIDENT force. To the orthodox that significance depends on a controversial question: will there be time to reinforce the Central Front before military victory or defeat has been decided on the ground?

There is naturally no official pronouncement worth considering on this question. The 1981 Statement on the Defence Estimates analyses in some detail the advantage enjoyed by the Warsaw Pact in ground and air forces before predicting an offensive

> led by a large concentration of tanks supported by mechanised infantry, artillery, assault helicopters, helicopter gunships and close support aircraft, all concentrated on a narrow front. It would be the task of 1 (BR) Corps to break up the momentum of such an advance and then to defeat it.[6]

Clearly this is easier said than done. Indeed, it is widely believed that NATO forces on the Central Front, being both numerically inferior and, for political reasons, condemned to the militarily unsound strategy of forward defence, would be pierced by a Soviet Blitzkrieg in a matter of days. In less than two weeks the situation on the ground could be so desperate as to leave NATO with no options but negotiation or escalation to a strategic exchange. Resort to tactical or theatre nuclear weapons would not improve matters, for these are available to both sides and might well be employed from the outset by the Soviet Union.

Nothing, of course, is certain in war and predictions of rapid success have proved more fallible than most. These, however, now have the distinction of being made by the side that expects defeat. Naturally there are caveats. Some of the pessimism is the inevitable ground-bass of strident demands for larger forces and better equipment. There are even optimists who argue that the Central Front could survive if political warning time – and political resolution – allowed mobilisation and reinforcement to begin well before hostilities, although there is much dispute about the relative impact on the military balance of mobilisation by both sides. Depending on the assumptions made, there could be moments on the unpredictable time-scale between mobilisation and hostilities when the prospects of an offensive would be less favourable, but the calculations so far published seem highly speculative.[7] There are also the imponderable implications of new conventional weapons: will these be deployed in time; do they favour attack or defence and what were the true lessons of the 1973 war? Finally, and perhaps most important of all, we can not be sure which armies will actually fight with any enthusiasm. Poland and Czechoslovakia are reckoned as contributing nearly two fifths of Warsaw Pact manpower before mobilisation; Belgium, Canada, Denmark, France and the Netherlands – all of whom have reservations of one kind or another – account for more than a quarter of the Alliance forces expected on the Central Front. The fighting qualities of British soldiers and airmen may be depended on, but the attitude of a future British government is more susceptible to political developments.

The only safe conclusion is that the survival of the Central Front against Soviet attack is unpredictable, but unlikely to be protracted. Without reinforcement and resupply, however, its speedy collapse would be probable. This is not only because most Alliance ground and air forces, particularly One British Corps, need reinforcement to operate at full efficiency. It is also a matter of supplies. In theory stocks are held for thirty days. In practice everybody skimps and cheats. Ammunition – and the 1973 War did at least establish that unprecedented rates of consumption must be expected – would run out long before that – 'in a matter of days rather than weeks', a Congressional Committee concluded in 1979.[8] The chance of maintaining a conventional defence – and it is a fairly slender chance – depends on replenishment.

Now there are soldiers who argue that the cumulative effect of all these chances is too much: the Central Front is a deterrent and, if deterrence fails, it can not be defended – reinforcement or no reinforcement. The next move must be the threat of total nuclear war. The idea of ships crossing the Atlantic is fantasy: at best a political device to persuade the United States Congress to keep American troops in Europe; at worst a chimera that diverts scarce resources from the army and air force in Germany to the wholly imaginary concept of a seaborne reinforcement that could never arrive in time or survive for long. There is a strong school of thought that maintains that war in Europe must be either over or total in two weeks. Doubtless it was this kind of thinking that prompted the Secretary of State for Defence to contradict the earlier opinions of his own government by the rather off-hand remark that 'if we lose on the other fronts reinforcement is irrelevant – it will be too late'.[9]

This prognosis is predominantly European. Americans tend to argue, understandably, both that they expect Europeans to hold out longer and that any President of the United States would be slow to take irrevocable decisions. There is the military possibility that the impetus of the Soviet offensive would exhaust itself and the political option of a Soviet decision to consolidate limited gains and negotiate from strength. After a week or two weeks or even three, the allied armies might have been driven back a considerable distance, yet still be holding certain positions and capable of continued resistance. Threats of escalation would doubtless have been freely exchanged and nuclear weapons might even have been employed on the battlefield, but it would be apparent that the Super-Powers wished to avoid total nuclear war. In such circumstances – and considerable variations are more than conceivable in this scenario – there could be a need, even a continuing need, for the seaborne reinforcement and resupply of the allied ground and air forces, a process which the Soviet Union would wish, at least until negotiations were seriously engaged, to prevent. It is not, perhaps, the most likely contingency, but it can scarcely be altogether excluded from consideration.

Various expedients suggest themselves for the Soviet Union, if compelled to envisage the development of such a situation: launching their initial offensive as a surprise attack from a standing start, in the hope of decisive victory before reinforcement could be organised;[10] destruction of European ports by nuclear bombardment or, if the air battle had gone well enough, even by conventional means; the threat or use of nuclear weapons to terrify European governments into surrender. Any of these would be faster-acting, surer and less likely to encounter effective defence than attacking ships at sea. Moreover, the interdiction of maritime communications, though less neglected now than it used to be, is seldom mentioned in Soviet strategic writing or practised in Soviet naval manoeuvres.[11]

There are two respectable reasons for considering that the Soviet Union might nevertheless be tempted to imitate the examples of Imperial and Nazi Germany. The first is that, unless and until Genghis Khan enters the Politburo, the Soviet Union must be assumed to have some rational motives for initiating war in Europe. These ought to include the wish to exploit the resources of Western Europe for Soviet advantage and thus provide an incentive to minimise the kind of avoidable destruction that might deprive the Soviet Union of economic assets – including skilled manpower. It is arguable that the remaining, though diminishing, emphasis of Soviet strategic doctrine on maximising the intensity of war derives from an earlier era of defensive reaction to perceived vulnerability and is no longer fully applicable to a situation that offers the Soviet Union the prospect of meaningful victory in limited war. It could be, therefore, that the Soviet Union would attempt a carefully prepared conventional campaign with the object of establishing political dominance over a Western Europe of substantially undiminished economic utility. In that event the political attractions of maritime interdiction might outweigh its military disadvantages. It would be the natural complement of limited war on land.

The objections to a surprise attack, perhaps the best military means of securing Soviet objectives in limited war and eliminating any reinforcement complications, are of a different order. Rare though the successful instances are, the Soviet Armed Forces could probably do it. But could the political leadership? The Soviet régime is not as monolithic, as consistent in the pursuit of defined objectives, as swift and as resolute as frustrated Western staff officers often suppose. Soviet dithering over Czechoslovakia in 1968 and Poland in 1980–1 was well up to British standards. Stalin's vacillation and wishful thinking during the first half of 1941 were enough to justify a portrayal of Neville Chamberlain as a leader of iron will and instant decision. There will have to be considerable changes in the Politburo before the idea of that body ordering a bolt from the blue becomes fully credible. Of course it is possible and precautions ought to be taken against it, particularly during weekends and public holidays. After all, war did come to Britain in 1914, just as Fisher had predicted, on a weekend crowned by a Bank Holiday.[12] But a surprise attack is not so probable, nor its success so certain, as to justify the exclusion of seaborne reinforcement and its protection from the list of contingencies deserving consideration and preparation.

The second reason is simply that the Russians could attempt the interdiction of maritime communications. They have a lot of submarines, and Western naval officers sometimes find it difficult to imagine what else all these submarines could be meant to do. This is not an entirely convincing argument. The Russians also have numerous surface ships, whose wartime rôle is even more puzzling. No Western naval officer, for instance, could offer the author anything but a peacetime scenario for the employment of the KIROV: an expensive ship to build only for gunboat diplomacy and also one that might be rather difficult to sink in conventional war. There are other tasks for the Red Navy than sinking merchant shipping. Nevertheless, the argument from capability and historical precedent cannot be neglected. It is conceivable, particularly if it is not restricted to the single scenario of an offensive against the Central Front.

Moreover, it leads on to a third consideration. The principal objection, from the Soviet point of view, to attempting the interdiction of maritime communications is that this is the strategy which NATO is best organised to meet. If war comes, this objection may or may not prevail. But, if the objection did not exist, if submarine war on trade was the Achilles heel of NATO, then the political attractions of this expedient might tempt the Soviet Union to employ it not merely to complement operations on land, but even instead of them. Britain, as past experience has amply demonstrated, is particularly vulnerable to this form of attack and would have great difficulty in deterring it by a

credible threat – which would also be a suicidal threat – of nuclear
retaliation. Nor is it likely that Britain's allies would be able and willing
to assume the burden of anti-submarine defence in the Eastern Atlantic,
now so largely borne by British forces, even in general war. Their
reluctance would be still greater if a Britain that had divested herself of
this form of defence were then to be singled out as the victim of more
limited forms of maritime pressure: blockade, say, or selective sinkings.

To Britain, indeed, reinforcement of the Central Front is only a
secondary reason for attempting the defence of maritime communications. For Britain 'the problem of sea shipments is a question of
survival' – the words are Gorshkov's[13] – in any circumstances short of
nuclear attack. The Central Front is an outpost – an important
outpost – guarding the vulnerable flank of those communications in the
Narrow Seas. The collapse of that front would have disagreeable and
dangerous consequences, so much so that it is worth Britain's while to
make great efforts and run considerable risks to deter any major attack
on that front. But, if the worst happens, if both deterrence and defence
fail, if the Soviet armies flood through Germany into the Low Countries,
the consequences to Britain, however unpleasant, would not necessarily
be fatal – as long as her sea communications survived and she escaped
nuclear attack. The forward deployment of Soviet air power would be a
necessary prelude either to invasion or to massive conventional
bombing. This would take time, particularly in the light of the probable
damage to continental airfields, long enough in all probability, to permit
the arrival of reinforcements from the United States. If conventional
war persists after the collapse of the Central Front, a 1940 situation
would be conceivable, but one much improved by the availability of
American troops and aircraft – if their heavy equipment can get to the
British Isles without running prohibitive risks on the way and if they can
be supplied after their arrival. That is the use of the sea which could be
crucial for Britain. The relative security of transatlantic communications will determine whether Britain is an advanced base worth
reinforcing or a Dien Bien Phu swallowing troops that are useless
because they cannot be supplied.

This is admittedly a contingency which Mr Nott, who seems a
thoroughgoing convert to the doctrine of a short war and a nuclear
cataclysm, appears to reject:

the Channel would not protect the United Kingdom base from, for
instance, the highly trained Soviet special forces in the same way as it
protected us in 1940.[14]

This is an odd remark. The Channel did not protect us in 1940 or at any later stage of the Second World War: it was the ability of the Royal Air Force and the Royal Navy to defeat either airborne or seaborne invasion that was responsible. Nor is there any obvious reason for regarding 'Soviet special forces' (which presumably means air portable forces) as more 'highly trained' than the German forces which, in 1940, had already demonstrated their skills in the Low Countries. In 1940 the issue was determined by three factors: the priority belatedly accorded to the air defence of Great Britain before the war; Dowding's insistence on witholding enough fighter squadrons from the continental battle and the availability of superior British naval forces. Mr Nott, his predecessors and his advisers do not seem fully conscious of these lessons, but they are still applicable today. So is the importance of that other condition of survival in 1940: the transatlantic lifeline.

Of course, in the interests of alliance solidarity and allied morale, public emphasis has to be placed on sea-power – and its associated air-power – as something that supports the Central Front and thereby preserves the integrity of continental Europe, but it would be regrettable if anyone in Britain ever forgot that the opposite is actually the strategic truth.

For Britain this ought to be obvious, but even for the Alliance the primacy of the Central Front is less absolute than is sometimes supposed. The rational Soviet objective – and the one most easily deducible from Soviet policy during the last thirty years is not to destroy Western Europe, nor to conquer it, but to divide it from the United States and thereby to subject it to Soviet influence. So far the military contribution to this end has been the threat, generally only the implied and latent threat, of direct attack, whether nuclear or by invasion. This has been neither immediately relevant to the presumed Soviet purpose, nor productive. It has driven Europe and the United States closer together. To divide them, in peace or war, the Northern Fleet could be a better military expedient. All that has prevented its use or threat has been the fact that the defensive capacity of NATO has hitherto been more convincing at sea than on land. 'Untune that string. And, hark! what discord follows.'

Fortunately the two lines of argument – for anyone unwilling to attempt the impossible task of sacrificing everything else to make the unreinforced Central Front impregnable – tend towards the same conclusion. The defence of maritime communications has to be attempted for its own sake; because it helps to keep American troops in Europe; because it might conceivably assist the survival of the Central

Front; because it will become even more important – to Britain – if that front collapses; because it is a form of defence which can only be considered redundant if, and as long as, it is effective. The real question concerns its effectiveness.

The answer bristles with enough imponderables to baffle a computer and most of them are not even naval. Time and circumstance predominate. Will reinforcements and supplies be readily available in the United States when they are wanted or will they already have been diverted to another theatre of operations? Will there be time (allowing for the inevitable delays in deciding on mobilisation) to assemble and load – two months is the period often suggested – the vast quantity of merchant shipping required? The much simpler problems of One British Corps prompted the Expenditure Committee to the remark that:

> A cardinal assumption, on which this [NATO] strategy rests, is that any act of aggression would be preceded by a period of rising political tension of sufficient duration to enable reinforcement to be carried out and to allow front line forces to be brought up to battle establishment.[15]

Would the Soviet Union be so obliging? And, if they were, would all those NATO governments directly concerned take sufficient heed of the Committee's further comment: 'the main constraint on the speed of reinforcement was a political one, namely the need for a timely Ministerial decision'?[16]

Many major assumptions are thus required to support the proposition that seaborne reinforcements and supplies could even be sailed in time to affect the survival of the Central Front. Some assumptions are needed if their departure is still to be timely enough for Britain.

Let us make them. Suppose that hostilities do not actually begin before the first ships set out. What then happens at sea?

The best published estimate is probably to be found in a recent American book: *Securing the Seas: The Soviet Naval Challenge and Western Alliance Options*.[17] This makes the obvious point that the immediate reinforcement of the Central Front is best attempted by flying in men to use pre-positioned equipment.

> More Americans fly to Europe each summer as tourists than we would send as soldiers to fight the next war.[18]

This air-lift would be difficult to attack except at the receiving airfields and, on moderately optimistic assumptions about the availability of political warning-time and the willingness of allied governments to act on it, might even be completed before hostilities began. There are, however, political, economic and even military limitations on the extent of pre-positioning in Europe. Some heavy equipment, to say nothing of fuel, food and ammunition, will have to come by sea after the crisis is manifest. American plans envisage the movement of ten million tons of war supplies and fifteen million tons of oil in ninety days – for the use of United States forces alone. This would require a thousand merchant vessels.

This formidable undertaking, so it is suggested, could be protected by the United States Navy. Indeed, it is possible to meet American naval officers who would cheerfully assume the responsibility unaided. Others, including the authors quoted, have certain caveats. Thirty to forty-five days would be needed for the redeployment from the Pacific to the Atlantic of US naval forces, for the Second Fleet in the Atlantic is usually at the lowest strength and state of readiness of any of the four active American fleets (the opposite being true of the Soviet Northern Fleet). Not that this move can be regarded as assured. Quite apart from the possibility of conflicting operational exigencies, the idea of priority for the Atlantic over the Pacific is popular neither in the United States Navy nor in American political circles. It is scarcely surprising to read that:

> without NATO (or at the very least British) assistance, we might be hard-pressed to provide escorts for any sizeable number of noncombatant ships[19]

even before allowance is made for the possible needs of other recipients than the American armed forces.

The short answer, even on optimistic assumptions about the availability of the United States Navy, is that the Americans will at most look after the provisioning of their own forces in Europe. If the inhabitants of that continent require any transatlantic imports – and the British can hardly do without them – the naval protection needed will be their own responsibility. That is why the great majority of the naval forces likely to be available to NATO in the Eastern Atlantic at the outset of war are provided by Britain and her European allies. Clausewitz was not cynical, merely realistic, when he remarked:

> We never find that a State joining in the cause of another State takes it up with the same earnestness as its own.[20]

The task of allied forces would be to attack Soviet submarines leaving their bases in Northern Russia (a job for nuclear-powered attack submarines); to locate and destroy them as they penetrate the Greenland–Iceland–United Kingdom Gap (sensors, submarines, mines, surface ships, aircraft and helicopters); and to hunt down and destroy those that get through to the Atlantic or were deployed there before the outbreak of hostilities (surface ships, towed arrays for detection, dunking sonars, helicopters, aircraft and perhaps also submarines). Opinions are divided about the best tactics in the Atlantic itself: convoy and escort or protected sea lanes or hunting for individual submarines. Every historical precedent favours the first and casts doubt on the last, but computerised analysis is said to demonstrate that the established advantage of convoy – compelling the submarine to en- counter defensive forces on the way to its target – has diminished and that the chance of finding a needle in a haystack has increased.

Those naval officers who argue that only experience will determine the best tactics would have a stronger case if time was likely to be available for that purpose. Much will, in any case, depend on questions to which there is no certain answer. Will the Soviet Union consider it worth using nuclear submarines against merchant ships? Will the Allies be able to locate and destroy nuclear submarines? Will nuclear weapons be employed? If they are, naval war is likely to become a secondary issue, but the immediate results would probably favour the Soviet Union, if only because the Soviet navy is more extensively equipped for nuclear war than non-US NATO navies, but the political disadvantages – the risk of extension and escalation – are the main obstacle to an initial use of nuclear weapons by either side.

The chances of this kind of war, even if it remains conventional, are hard to assess not least because the size of the forces that might be engaged on each side is so uncertain. The general expectation is that the Soviet Union would start with more and better submarines than Nazi Germany against fewer NATO escorts than Britain alone could furnish in 1939, but estimates vary enormously with the assumptions made. Even the historical statistics are not foolproof. For instance, Nitze and Sullivan contrast 31 U-boats deployed in 1939 with 271 British surface warships assigned to Atlantic or Mediterranean commands.[21] Reference to Roskill, however, shows that the 39 U-boats deployed out of a total strength of 56 were all in the North Atlantic or the Narrow Seas, where, excluding those vessels assigned to fleet duties, a total of 60 British destroyers and 22 other escorts were available to deal with them, though not all were so deployed.[22] The initial basis of comparison is thus distorted by confusion about the sea areas involved and by the addition to the British side of the equation of numerous warships that had other tasks, were unsuited to hunting submarines or that themselves required protection against them.

Where the past thus betrays our faltering steps, no certainty can be expected from conjecture regarding the future. Nitze and Sullivan expect that 30–60 Soviet submarines would operate against trans-atlantic communications during the early phases of a major conventional war in Europe.[23] The Ministry of Defence are more precise and also more pessimistic: they put the figure at 83. They also credit NATO with only 94 surface escorts (including the French)[24] whereas Nitze and Sullivan can muster 146 destroyers and frigates without the French.[25] Any navalist worth his salt, of course, will deploy the entire Soviet inventory and disqualify half the allied fleets, but the Ministry of Defence have probably gone as far as is reasonable towards the worst case.

Adopting their figures gives approximate parity between Soviet submarines and their NATO surface hunters as opposed to the 1:2 ratio of 1939, a ratio which resulted in the loss of 114 merchant ships for the destruction of 9 U-boats during the first three months of the war.[26] Unfortunately this is a meaningless comparison. Aircraft, helicopters, attack submarines and improved detection must be added on one side of the equation; the true submarine, higher submerged speed, better weapons and aircraft on the other. Anyone lacking a printout from the computers at Byfleet is ill-advised to hazard an opinion. Nor can even those machines be expected to generate a single prediction from the variety of assumptions that must be fed into them.

Some general observations may nevertheless be permissible. Soviet submarines seem to be designed for nuclear war and armed for the battle of the first salvo. They are not ideal instruments for a protracted conventional war on trade. They would encounter more opposition on passage to the Atlantic than their German predecessors and, when they got there, be subject to a degree of airborne harassment unknown in 1939. In the altered balance between the surface and the depths, the Diesel submarines, so it is sometimes suggested, would be more vulnerable than the U-boats, the nuclear submarines less so.

The latter, of course, pose a serious problem at present, because neither British ships nor British aircraft yet have a weapon that is reasonably certain to sink them.[27] If war were to come in the near future, the Royal Navy might experience some difficulty in coping with any nuclear submarines that actually got into the Atlantic. Fortunately many of them are likely to have more important tasks than attacking merchant ships and their surface escorts: protecting Soviet strategic submarines and denying the Norwegian Sea to NATO, for instance. Similar considerations may also divert the equally formidable BACKFIRE bombers from shipping at sea to more lucrative targets on land.

Nevertheless, however much we reduce the extent of the likely Soviet deployment against transatlantic communications – and some published estimates do seem unrealistically alarmist – the NATO strategy for countering it is rather heavily dependent on geography. The Greenland–Iceland–United Kingdom Gap is to present a barrier even to submarines, although similar 'choke-points' were regularly penetrated by surface ships in previous wars. The fortunate interposition of the British Isles is to ensure that Soviet aircraft do not ravage the North Atlantic.[28] We must all hope that these shadowy admirals and air marshals are as potent as the legendary Generals Janvier et Février, because British warships and aircraft are not at present adequately armed for combat against Soviet submarines, aircraft or surface ships, the best of which could hope, in favourable circumstances, to out-range them, even if high claims are made for the ability of the British 'point-defence' system to destroy missiles despatched from an invulnerable distance. Naturally there are projects to remedy these deficiencies: TORNADO air defence aircraft; the STING RAY lightweight torpedo against submarines; SEA EAGLE and SUB-HARPOON against surface ships; a new heavyweight torpedo.[29] If time is granted, the position will be better soon. At present it is not good.

Of course, the Soviet Navy have their own weaknesses: short-service seamen; insufficient training at sea; excessive reliance on the first salvo. Their submarines are often less impressive on manoeuvres than in the pages of Jane's. Much Soviet matériel is on the verge of obsolescence. Numbers are their strongest point.

Confident prediction is impossible. Nobody knows when the decisive moment will come, if it comes at all, or what the balance will then be in the constant technological advance on both sides. How much of the United States Navy will be available; what Soviet naval priorities will be; or how ships, weapons, electronics and sailors never tested in combat will actually function in so conjectural a war: all these are unforeseeable. The sheer volume of analysis, human or computerised, devoted to extrapolating into a wartime situation the mathematical results of peacetime trials, exercises, speculations, intelligence and manoeuvres is impressive. The navies of the world have tried, harder than ever before, to discern the future. But they lack, as a necessary corrective, even the limited or the secondhand experience of contemporary soldiers and airmen, who do at least know what modern weapons – perhaps not quite the latest, but near enough – did when used on a substantial scale in 1973. Sailors can find little guidance in the isolated, poorly reported and unrepresentative instances of minor naval combat since 1945. Even their seagoing experience can not fill the gap: doing something under fire is not the same as doing it in other circumstances. Most naval officers and men today have never heard a shot fired in anger.

At sea the projection of statistical comparisons is even less reliable, as an indicator of future victory or defeat, than it is on land or in the air. Total numbers are important and some analysis of the impact on the Royal Navy of Mr Nott's latest plans will be attempted in a subsequent chapter. But all that is certain about the next war is that it will surprise the participants. An unforeseen political situation, an unexpected strategic initiative, a crucial technical failure, to say nothing of those deficiencies in training, professional skills or morale that reveal themselves only when action is engaged, could still exert an impact no less decisive than in 1939 or 1940 or 1941. All this applies to both sides.

The most that can be said is that, on the basis of the inadequate evidence available, it is easier to imagine circumstances in which the Northern Fleet could be repelled and an acceptable minimum of seaborne supplies could be brought across the Atlantic, than it is to envisage a successful defence of the Central Front against a Soviet offensive. Even Nitze and Sullivan, whose main purpose is to urge the case for greater allied naval preparations, consider that:

> If the conventional defense of NATO were successful for more than a month or so, then the West should be able to regain the use of essential sealanes at acceptable attrition levels . . .[30]

The global balance is more favourable to NATO at sea than on land; geography distances the Soviet fleets from one another and from their battle-grounds, as well as offering NATO a one-sided advantage in submarine detection; American reinforcement of the Atlantic could not be readily matched by Soviet and could tip the scale in the ocean as it could not on the continent. Nor is there, for the Soviet Union, enough advantage in the interdiction of maritime communications to warrant their risking their main naval strength in attempting it. A limited offensive is more likely. Of course, even if the surface ships and many of the most modern submarines and aircraft are withheld to guard the

Norwegian Sea, the approaches to Soviet bases and the seaborne nuclear striking force, there will be enough left to give serious trouble, particularly before the United States Navy are present in strength. The probable balance between the part of the Northern Fleet devoted to this task and the proportion of NATO naval strength available in the Atlantic is unpredictable, but the British share will be of greater relative importance than the contribution made by One British Corps to the defence of the Central Front, particularly during those first thirty dangerous days. Figures are not worth quoting without the elaborate assumptions on which they are precariously based, but it is worth mentioning that Nitze and Sullivan assumed that Britain would have more surface ships and attack-submarines in the Atlantic at the outset of war than the United States.[31]

What is more, if the Royal Navy and the Royal Air Force do not play this large part in bringing merchant ships safely to European waters, it is unlikely that anyone else would do it in their stead. That is one answer to our initial question: what could the Navy do?

Unfortunately the Atlantic battle would not be the whole story. The receiving ports in Europe, including the British Isles, are more vulnerable to even conventional air attack than shipping at sea, so much so that it is difficult to imagine the Soviet Union using BACKFIRES to attack merchant vessels. Mining is another danger and precautions against it are insufficient, little having been done since the Expenditure Committee reported that

> Soviet mine laying capability constituted a serious threat to UK reinforcement ports.[32]

The risk that ships might cross the ocean, yet find nowhere to unload in safety, cannot be excluded. Moreover, if the survival of the Central Front is the only criterion, the Soviet Union does not have to make seaborne reinforcement impossible: it would probably be enough to delay and reduce it. The estimate of thirty days as the period needed to blunt the Soviet submarine menace and to get more than half the ships sailed to their destinations is uncomfortably coincident with the maximum endurance of NATO ground forces.

A chain of assumptions, each possible on its own, yet improbable in combination, is thus required if we are to regard defeating Soviet interdiction of seaborne reinforcement for the Central Front as the main purpose of alliance naval war and as the contingency that both justifies the existence of naval forces and determines their characteristics.

The Soviet Union must allow the imminence of assault on the Central Front to become obvious far enough in advance to let the Allies decide on mobilisation and gather the necessary men, munitions and shipping before hostilities begin. To frustrate that reinforcement the Soviet Union must then choose, from the various options available to them, the difficult and uncertain course of attacking ships at sea. Allied armies must maintain a coherent defence long enough for the naval battle to be won and for a sufficient proportion of the transatlantic cargoes to be discharged in European mainland ports not destroyed or rendered inaccessible by enemy action. The rail and road communications of the NATO armies and air forces must not be disrupted. If all this can be accomplished without interruption by negotiation or nuclear escalation, the men and munitions reaching the front line must be enough to outweigh the reinforcements meanwhile received by the Soviet armies.

It could all just happen, but it is difficult to dissent from the view expressed by Field Marshal Lord Carver, speaking with the knowledge of high military office and the candour of retirement from it:

> Unless the reinforcements and supplies reach this side of the Atlantic before hostilities start . . . then I have not much hope, whether they come by air or sea, that they will be very relevant to the situation.[33]

But, if they must arrive before hostilities start, why are navies needed to protect their passage? Strictly speaking, the answer can only be that, without those navies, hostilities might start at sea rather than on land – and rather earlier. More fundamentally, it is the wrong question. Neither the value of navies, nor their function, depend on the ability to repel an assault on the Central Front.

For over thirty years the Central Front has dominated more than strategic thought. In that part of the popular imagination that is reluctantly conscious of the risk of war the Central Front ranks second only to the mushroom cloud. It has subsumed buried memories, ancient images, half-forgotten slogans. It is the blue line of the Vosges, the frontier on the Rhine, collective security. It is older still: the legions on the Wall. It is also seen, whatever NATO doctrine may say, as the terrible trip-wire, the field of Armageddon. Its political importance matches its symbolic significance. But, along that front no sea breezes blow. For the structure of navies and for their strategy its needs are subsidiary, not central.

Politically, the presence of allied navies in the Atlantic helps to maintain Western belief in the deterrent strength of the Central Front by encouraging the idea that it could be defended. Strategically, that presence makes it impossible for the Soviet Union merely to bypass the Central Front by severing communications between America and Europe. Only those navies, and their associated air-power, could offer the chance of continued resistance to any European countries or forces that survived the collapse of the Central Front.

These are all valid and valuable naval objectives. They do not add up, nor could they, to a naval guarantee of the survival of the Central Front. That is a matter for soldiers and airmen, perhaps also for politicians, all of whom will have to do unexpectedly well if a major attack on the Central Front is to leave the defending forces with a continuing need for seaborne supplies.

It was a mistake ever to have pretended otherwise. There were obvious political and diplomatic temptations in justifying naval forces in the Atlantic as an essential and effective contribution to the survival of the Central Front, but the flaws in that argument have undermined the cause it was intended to support: the need to maintain maritime communications. That could have been justified on its own merits and is now wrongly called in question, as subsequent chapters will seek to show. The damage already done is painfully obvious to every reader of Hansard and the British press. Yesterday's admirals gobbled an unripe scenario and the teeth of today's captains are set on edge.

Of course the Central Front is important. It may even be attacked. If it is, a brief campaign may end in negotiation or escalation, leaving little that is conventional for navies to do in a short war. None of this is certain and opinions differ about its probability, but it is possible. Bang or whimper? Perhaps, but those two options are neither the whole story nor the end of it.

7 Alliance Naval War II: choosing the threat

On the contrary, I was bound to assume and allow for all the worst contingencies.

Troubridge[1]

Choosing the threat to meet is not a notion which chimes well with the conventional wisdom. That demands preparation for the gravest threat indicated by the capabilities of the enemy and his presumed intentions. On this point, as on much else, the conventional wisdom is a trifle out of date. It made sense at the beginning of the century, when the gravest perceived threat seemed within Britain's power to meet. It made less in the thirties, when the obvious threat of simultaneous hostilities with Germany, Italy and Japan was admitted to be more than Britain could manage. It makes none today, when few pretend Britain could prevent, resist or even, in any nationally significant sense, survive a total nuclear war.

Super-Powers apart, most states do have to choose which threats they will attempt to meet. Some try to avoid the painful necessity by alliance or by espousing the concept of deterrence. This does no more than fudge the issue. NATO, no less than Britain, has chosen to surrender to the United States responsibility for the deterrence of total nuclear war, which remains an issue between the two Super-Powers and one likely to be decided in the light of what they perceive as their national interests. Collectively the Alliance lack even the restricted ability of Britain and France to meet the challenge of territorially limited nuclear war, but efforts to contrive a notional response threaten Britain's own freedom of manoeuvre. NATO has not tried to match the conventional strength of the Warsaw Pact, but has chosen a minimum defence as the condition of a deterrence that depends on a national decision in Washington. The

results are mixed. On the one hand, the existence of alliance helps to
deter war by increasing the effort required of an aggressor and the risk of
escalation. On the other hand, if deterrence fails, the dissipation of
British forces in an ineffective alliance defence might, as in 1940, leave
Britain worse off than she would have been without her continental
commitment. The necessary qualifications to this proposition have
been, and will be, separately considered. But neither alliance nor the
concept of deterrence have invalidated the need to choose with care the
threats to be met. One of the criteria ought to be the expected result.

The case for this test is even stronger when we turn from the idea of a
generalised menace – the power of a Soviet Union hostile to Britain and
her allies – to consider the particular ways in which this hostility might
find expression. Naturally the expected result cannot be the only
touchstone to determine the British reaction. Some threats would have
to be met even if resistance seemed hopeless: invasion of the homeland,
for instance. Others are too improbable, at present, to demand
preparations for a military response – an assisted coup d'état in
Britain – or too remote to receive one – intervention in Afghanistan.
Between these extremes lies a range of contingencies calling for choice:
of military response in the event; of specific preparation; of acceptance
as a factor influencing the peace-time size, structure and organisation of
the British armed forces.

In this middle range the predicted terminal situation should govern
the initial response and its preparation. Which is more likely to preserve
core values (those requiring defence against any odds): meeting the
particular threat in question or reserving one's strength for the next? If
the response to the threat is expected to be successful, then those
persuaded of the ultimate disadvantages of this undertaking must
assume the difficult burden of proof. But, if resistance is regarded as
gallant, honourable, but unavailing, then important arguments are
needed to justify its being attempted at all. Britain can no longer afford,
perhaps not even survive, such romantic luxuries as the Greek adventure
of 1941.

The strict logic of this analysis is naturally more applicable to France
than to Britain. France has accepted the NATO choice of threat –
assault on the Central Front – and has welcomed the efforts of her allies
to meet it, yet without committing her own forces to consequential
action. She supports the installation of American theatre nuclear
weapons – outside France. She has kept her options open: to reinforce
her allies or to reserve her strength for the defence of the homeland or
even to react to a different threat. She can suit her response to the

unfolding of events and is free to reach a national judgment of the predicted terminal situation.

The complex historical causes of a different British decision need not detain us: it was taken. The bulk of the British army and air force, with wives, families, barracks, civilian employees by the thousand, schools, clubs and canteens, is situated in Germany and committed to the difficult defence of the Central Front.[2] The reinforcements promised – and needed – in time of crisis would further denude the British Isles, while the tasks of the Royal Navy and the rest of the Royal Air Force have hitherto been to ensure the flow of men and munitions to Germany and to protect 'a forward base for operations in the Atlantic, a main base for operations in the Channel and the North Sea and a rear base for operations on the Continent'.[3] This trinitarian phrase, uninitiated British subjects may care to know, is intended to describe their country.

In these circumstances it must seem distinctly academic to suggest a British choice of the threat to meet. The action already taken, and promised, to implement earlier decisions has left little scope for second thoughts, for unforeseen contingencies or even for last-minute efforts to repair the consequences of a failed attempt to meet the chosen threat.

Neither in politics nor in strategy, however, are circumstances immutable. Some potential changes would be so drastic in their consequences that there is an understandable reluctance to accord them serious consideration before they are seen to be imminent: for instance, the advent in Britain of a Labour government able and willing to implement the declared policies of that party on Europe and nuclear weapons.[4] Others seem too speculative to permit firm conclusions: the apparent trend in Soviet strategic thought away from the automatism of escalation to total nuclear war towards acceptance of more limited forms of conflict. But there are also developments already established, if imperfectly acknowledged. The pressure exerted by a Conservative government on the defence budget has convinced even the most optimistic senior officers that they can no longer count on a political reprieve from their problems. The balance between the Services is already threatened and strategy is almost open to challenge.

To be fair, strategic thinking has evolved independently of financial pressures. The 1980 Statement on the Defence Estimates drew attention to a notable intellectual advance (compare the silence of the Statement for 1975):

over the last two decades the effort devoted to the air defence of Britain has been sharply reduced. This derived from strategic concepts which reasoned that we could not realistically hope to defend ourselves against a strategic nuclear strike, that hostilities in Europe would escalate to nuclear warfare almost immediately and that the need to defend against conventional air attack could accordingly be largely discounted. Now that the strategic situation has changed we must do what we can to improve our air defences, especially since the Warsaw Pact has dramatically improved its capability for conventional air attack.[5]

This was an example of choosing a threat which, in favourable circumstances, could be met, rather than the gravest threat, which could not.

The shift in emphasis thus implied was confirmed in June 1981, when *The Way Forward* struck an interesting balance between Defence of the Home Base ('we need to do more, not less, in this field')[6] and The British Contribution on the Continent of Europe ('it must be maintained').[7] A different note, however, was sounded concerning 'the future shape of Britain's maritime contribution'. In a phrase as ominous to those versed in bureaucratic parlance as any *Leitmotif* from *Götterdämmerung*: 'that such a contribution must continue, and on a major scale, is not in question'.[8]

Why did Britain's naval future receive such grudging acquiescence and that in the strange guise of 'the importance of maritime tasks to Alliance security'?[9]

The answer is not the simple one of 1911:

the Army and Navy representatives violently combated the other's views. Nothing was settled; but . . . taciturn by disposition, the Admiral simply could not express himself with the force and clarity of the General. Most of the politicians present were consequently more impressed with the General Staff point of view.[10]

Seventy years later the result was not attributable to any lack of eloquence but to the collapse of an unsound argument. The eleven detailed paragraphs devoted by *The Way Forward* to Maritime Tasks make no reference to, nor even hint at, nor have one single word about 'transatlantic reinforcement and resupply', on which, only two months earlier, 'the conventional defence of Central Europe depends crucially'.[11]

The disappearance of this argument will scarcely surprise readers of the previous chapter: it was belated, but necessary. It is also paradoxical.

The dawn of scepticism concerning the Central Front as the be-all and end-all of British strategy ought to increase the importance of the naval alternatives. Two have already been suggested: the need for navies to ensure that the Central Front cannot simply be by-passed; the need for navies if the Central Front collapses.

Each has its own validity, but both encounter conceptual and presentational obstacles. The threats to which these tasks are directed, though grave, are secondary: that is, dependent on the prior occurrence of other developments. In the first case, this would be a gradual, an imperceptible, a deniable process: the whittling away of allied naval strength in the Atlantic. The second depends on an assumption widely regarded as defeatist, repugnant, even inconceivable: the continuation of conventional war after the collapse of the Central Front. Neither threat will ever arise if there is truth in the belief (now even more prevalent than in 1914) that any war must be short. Preparation for Atlantic war entails competition for scarce resources and, without the scenario of seaborne reinforcement and resupply, implies incomplete confidence in existing defence policy. Institutional hostility is thus inevitable and is unlikely to be overcome before the evolution of British strategic thought has gone a good deal further – perhaps under political pressure – than the modest beginnings so far noted. Naturally, both these threats ought to be resisted if Britain is to survive as an independent state. They pose much the same demands as the less likely scenario for which the Royal Navy has hitherto been designed. As suggested in the previous chapter, more success might be expected for attempts to meet the second (if the first threat arises, it will be because the game has already been given away) than for corresponding efforts on the Central Front. Nevertheless, these threats are not now so obviously direct or imminent, given the present climate of political and strategic thought in Britain, as to constitute sole and sufficient justification for the correct response: the maintenance of a fleet in being.

The national arguments for this policy will be considered in subsequent chapters. So will the likely impact of a continuation, as indicated by foreseeable political developments, of that established trend: the contraction of Britain's defensive perimeter – geographically, qualitatively and in terms of commitments. Here we are concerned with alliance war, while not forgetting that alliances are supposed to serve the national interest, not vice versa. Do there now exist, in the context of the North Atlantic Alliance, other maritime threats? If so, which should be chosen as most requiring a prepared response?

Such questions require some consideration of likely Soviet intentions, a subject to which better qualified authors have devoted entire volumes. One possible view is that the Soviet Union consider Europe primarily in terms of their own defensive perimeter. A secure base is important in the contest for that global influence to which a Super-Power naturally aspires, but the Soviet Union lack the comfortable insulation provided for their rival by the Atlantic and Pacific oceans. As the Tsars did before them, the Soviet leaders have tried to create a glacis of their own, whenever opportunity offered. During the period of post-revolutionary weakness they lost some of the border territories of the old Russian Empire and their only successful venture was in Outer Mongolia. The favourable situation at the beginning and end of the Second World War enabled them to recover much of what had been lost, but the events of that war must have constituted a further incentive to turn to Soviet advantage the policy once applied against them: the *cordon sanitaire*. Poland, East Germany, Czechoslovakia, Hungary, Romania and Bulgaria provided not only a military glacis but a screen against political contagion.

It is interesting, however, to note the discrimination and caution with which this policy was pursued. Political rebuff in 1948 from Finland – *cet animal méchant qui se défend quand on l'attaque* – was not followed by military action, nor was it in Yugoslavia and Albania. The Soviet Union withdrew from Manchuria and North Korea and Austria. Probing of Iran and Turkey was discontinued when it encountered resistance. In Asia as in Europe Soviet frontiers were extended, a ring of satellites created, a few outposts entrusted to neutrals – when conditions were favourable and risks were low. Adventures were not numerous, mainly further afield, often undertaken by proxy and usually terminated if they ran into serious trouble – Cuba in 1962 or Egypt in 1973. On the perimeter firmness, when it seemed safe, has been blended with caution, when it did not. West Berlin is an interesting example of a coveted outpost that was repeatedly attempted by implied threats of military force. Although this coercive diplomacy often produced high levels of international tension, these were evidently regarded as acceptable because they could be, and were, carefully controlled. The efforts made were not successful, but they never led to open hostilities.

It is at least plausible to regard Soviet intervention in Afghanistan in December 1979 (itself only the culmination of a long process) as no more than the latest move in the established policy of consolidating the Soviet perimeter. Perhaps the local difficulties were under-estimated, but the larger risks seem to have been correctly assessed as low. These do, after all, vary with a factor of much importance in Soviet thinking: the general correlation of forces in the world.

None of this is intended to mitigate the danger to Britain and her allies inherent in Soviet policy, merely to emphasise its record of prudence, patience and opportunism. This record needs to be contrasted with the common Western interpretation of Soviet military doctrine as insisting that any war in Europe must be general and violent: nuclear as well as conventional, the flanks a mere adjunct to the Central Front, the navy only operating in support of the advancing armies. Possibly this is how the Soviet Union would fight if general war were, as they saw it, forced on them; certainly (or it would not be published) this is what they would like their enemies to believe; perhaps it represents a genuine military view of the best strategy to adopt in any event.

What people say, however, is often a less reliable guide to their future conduct than what they have been accustomed to do. In the last thirty-five years the Soviet armed forces have done less fighting than the British, much less than the American. Their rôle has been to support diplomacy by threats of force ranging from the latent to the explicit; to use force to prevent political change within the Soviet sphere of influence; to provide technical or logistic assistance outside that sphere to governments or organisations engaged in war, insurrection or repression. They were thus employed less often than the American armed forces;[12] no Soviet use of force in the period under review approached the scale and intensity of the Korean and Vietnamese wars; none has so far lasted as long as did Britain's Confrontation with Indonesia. The Soviet Union accept war as an instrument of policy, but have not so far employed it as openly as Britain and France at Suez in 1956.

This preference for the strategy of the indirect approach has hitherto proved remunerative. The Soviet Union now possess, to a greater extent than previously, the military capability to abandon this established policy and to stake their whole future on the success of a first strike or a deliberate assault on the Central Front. It is conceivable that they might so decide, but it does not seem very likely. It would be out of character for them even to attack the flanks of NATO as long as alliance solidarity persists.

It might be a different matter if war were to begin outside Europe, particularly if it did so in circumstances which diverted American forces and divided the United States from their European allies. Conflicting reactions within the Alliance to the 1973 war provided a small foretaste of how this could happen.

This could create one of those temporarily favourable situations which the Soviet Union have previously managed to exploit. Of course, the Politburo would then have a wide range of options. If we exclude the least rational (deliberately widening and formalising the war, at the risk of nuclear escalation, by a major offensive in Europe) and the most sensible (purely political exploitation of the split in the Alliance) we are left with the threat or use of military force to extract profit from a situation of momentary advantage. Possible Soviet objectives might extend from securing a promise of neutrality, with or without concrete pledges, through political changes in European countries and the lease of bases or facilities to outright territorial annexation. There are precedents for them all. Germany twice sought British neutrality; Imperial Germany demanded it of France in 1914 with the fortresses of Toul and Verdun as security; numerous governments have sought, and some obtained, political changes as the price of peace; the Soviet Union demanded bases and territory of Finland in 1939 and later annexed the Baltic States and occupied Eastern Poland.

Much would depend on the nature and intensity of the external crisis and on the international situation at the time. No general predictions are possible: only speculation about hypothetical scenarios. Suppose, for instance, that revolution in Saudi Arabia has disrupted oil supplies, precipitated American armed intervention, attracted a degree of Soviet support for the ensuing 'war of national liberation', evoked alarm, abstention and even anti-American attitudes from various European countries, diverted American armed forces and attention to the scene of conflict. Would American readiness, whatever it is now, to risk a strategic nuclear exchange in order to protect 'disloyal' Europeans against Soviet pressure be great? The Soviet Union might not think so.

A prudent Soviet government might nevertheless proceed step by withdrawable step, avoiding any direct challenge to American positions in Europe: no move against the Central Front, no confrontation with the Sixth Fleet (if that remained in the Mediterranean). Rocket-rattling would, ideally, be muted. On the other hand, naval deployments (with American carriers safely concentrated in the Indian Ocean) would be a particularly suitable means of reinforcing diplomatic and political pressure. The Northern and Baltic Fleets, together with their associated shore-based aircraft and amphibious forces, could, as they have done in the past, carry out threatening manoeuvres. They could go a long way towards actually initiating offensive operations, yet break off at the last moment if the risks seemed too great.

Of course, all this is extremely speculative. The initial scenario is plausible, but the use of the Soviet navy to exploit it in Europe demands many assumptions at variance with orthodox interpretations of Soviet policy and military doctrine. And yet, it would provide a rôle for those surface ships which Gorshkov persists in adding to his navy in spite of his repeated declarations that

> the main, most universal and effective kinds of forces of the fleet have become submarines and aircraft.[13]

It was not these kinds of forces which visibly, even ostentatiously, assembled off the Polish coast in August 1981 or, in earlier years, carried out amphibious landings close to the Norwegian border. It is not, perhaps, up to submarines and aircraft alone

> to solve the tasks connected with territorial changes[14]

Gorshkov may even have believed what he said:

> Ships that show up directly offshore constitute a credible threat of action. And if such a threat was great enough in the past, then today it has grown all out of proportion . . .
>
> In many cases, shows of force have made it possible to achieve political goals without resorting to armed combat but simply by applying pressure, using for this one's political might and the threat of initiating military action.[15]

Gorshkov may be wrong, but Soviet warships did 'show up directly' – on British television – off the coast of Poland in September 1981.

In the European context such notions are usually dismissed as fantasies. The reasons are less obvious than they used to be – and might become. Of course it would be risky for the Soviet Union to accompany demands for political concessions by the menacing concentration of a fleet, let alone to employ actual force. Even a distracted and alienated American president might not allow the absence of most of his navy to inhibit thoughts of escalation. But the risks of attacking the Central Front, which the conventional wisdom regards as a serious Soviet option, would be far higher. Of course a visible Soviet fleet might be attacked by aircraft and submarines. Which European government, one wonders, would give that order, if this meant the initiation of hostilities? Not many of them even have the equipment to tackle a Soviet surface fleet and the Americans, who do, might have neither the opportunity nor the inclination.

Some demands, moreover, might not seem intolerable: declarations of neutrality in the extra-European conflict, even the extension to monitoring installations and pre-positioning of the Scandinavian 'no foreign bases' policy. The Soviet Union might be initially less concerned with what was conceded than with the demoralisation produced by yielding anything under threat. They could afford to choose the countries to be tackled and the demands to be made in the light of political circumstances at the time: most European members of NATO (including Britain) contain minorities in favour of *some* concessions to the Soviet Union. But, if the Soviet Union were ready to run greater risks, or simply at a later stage, they could seek concessions of real military significance: a Soviet base on Svalbard or Bornholm, observation posts in Finmark, closing the Baltic to non-limitrophe warships, the demilitarisation of Iceland and the Faeroes. These are demands which might seem less intolerable than nuclear war, if this was the only alternative. If it were, would even the United States invoke it, say to defend the Keflavik base, against the wishes of the government concerned?

In a still worse case the Soviet Union, accepting general war as likely but anxious to defer and, if possible, avoid its nuclear escalation, might choose as their objective an actual extension of the perimeter. It is improbable that key points in NATO territory, even in outlying islands, could be occupied without fighting leading to general war, but the Soviet Union might be ready to run that risk while attempting to mitigate it by assurances concerning the limited and temporary character of their military measures. In some circumstances it could be a more advantageous and slightly less risky approach to war than attacking the Central Front. Why charge the wall if there is a chance of picking the lock of the postern?

The Northern Flank is naturally not the only region where the Soviet Union might be tempted to profit by American distraction and European disarray to seek inexpensive opportunities of extending their perimeter, but it is the area of most immediate concern to Britain and one particularly well suited to Soviet naval operations. In considering what the Soviet Union might do, it is as well to start with the extreme option: the invasion of Northern Norway. This does not seem the most likely course, but it would be the most dangerous and it is the possibility of such action that would provide the latent muscle for lesser threats in the same area.

Invasion seems improbable, because anything so blatant would invite a wider war and, even in conditions of Alliance disarray, carry a risk of American nuclear escalation. Admittedly this risk would be less than on the Central Front, for there are no Americans in Norway to suffer in the first assault. Indeed, if the Soviet Union actually intend to start a conventional war, Norway would arguably be the best place for them to do it. The chances of avoiding a nuclear response would be better and the conventional defences to be overcome far weaker. Militarily the advantages of success would be substantial. The radar chain in Northern Norway is a major NATO asset, not least for its surveillance of the Kola area. Its destruction and that of the northern Norwegian airfields would greatly improve the air defence of the Kola bases and of the Arctic sanctuary for Soviet ballistic missile submarines. If the Soviet Union could go further and themselves use the airfields (Bodö and Bardufoss are the most important) this would make much of the Norwegian Sea hazardous for Allied surface ships and aircraft; it would facilitate Soviet air, amphibious or naval operations against the Greenland–Iceland–United Kingdom Gap. Whether Soviet naval strategy is offensive or defensive, the elimination of allied radar and, more optimistically, the acquisition of Norwegian airfields and ports seems an obvious first step.

Politically, too, the move has its attractions. If represented from the start as a limited offensive, this could be the kind of lightning campaign, entailing relatively few casualties in a sparsely inhabited and lightly defended area, which NATO might prefer to terminate by negotiation rather than by nuclear response. Even an eventual Soviet withdrawal might have to be purchased by concessions and leave a deeply divided Alliance behind. Naturally it would be a high-risk operation of a kind that the Soviet leaders would scarcely contemplate unless they were ready for wider conventional war and prepared to accept the risk of nuclear escalation. This does not mean that it would only be launched as part of a wider and even more hazardous offensive, though it might be.

Militarily, the problems posed by an invasion of Northern Norway could vary considerably, for both sides. If this operation were to be deliberately selected by the Soviet Union, it would presumably include attacks by airborne troops on the Norwegian airfields and a border-crossing in the north as well as amphibious landings and air attacks on radar and other installations. The chances of a successful defence would thus depend on the availability of warning time and on allied ability and willingness to profit by it. The defence of radar and airfields against a full scale attack would demand not merely timely Norwegian mobilisation, but the arrival of substantial Allied reinforcements, including aircraft, before the outbreak of hostilities. If these rather steep conditions can not be met, even denying the enemy the use of the airfields might have to depend on a historically unreliable expedient: the timely execution of demolition plans. In Soviet hands those airfields could be exploited not only to protect the Kola bases and to provide air cover for Soviet surface ships, but also to interdict Allied airborne and seaborne reinforcement of Central Norway. This is, admittedly, a worst case. Orthodox opinion maintains that, even if these airfields were captured intact, they could still be attacked from the air and their use thus denied to the Soviet Union. This might prove an expensive second best.

Without attempting to examine every contingency, we may perhaps exclude the two extremes. If warning time is so long and the Allied response so energetic that sufficient forces can be deployed for the defence of Norway, then the Soviet Union would probably not attempt conventional invasion except, just conceivably, as part of a general offensive in Europe. If anything approaching a bolt from the blue could be achieved, it would be difficult for NATO to make any effective conventional response.

Complete surprise seems unlikely. Preparatory deployments, particularly of naval and air forces, would probably be detected (that Norwegian radar chain), but the political obstacles, as argued in an earlier chapter, would be even greater. Not only are the Politburo accustomed to proceed step by step, but they would have to reckon with the psychological impact of a massive surprise attack on the sensitive nerve of the American Pearl Harbor complex. It would at least impair the prospect of keeping hostilities conventional, let alone limited. This might not matter if Norway was the first objective in a deliberate war, let alone part of a general offensive. In other circumstances it would mean sacrificing the chance that a period of preliminary menace might secure concessions without resort to the risks of war. The quest for low-cost advantage, after all, is the basic motive that has been attributed to the Soviet leaders in order to explain why they might profit by Alliance disarray to bring pressure on Norway.

A surprise attack, therefore, seems less likely than one preceded by rising tension, by a propaganda campaign, by demands and threats. If these encountered Norwegian resistance, an attack might be launched after preparations to meet it had begun, but before these were sufficiently far advanced to constitute a convincing conventional deterrent.

Preparations against amphibious attack would be the easiest, both politically and logistically. Norwegian, British and American submarines could be deployed in the Norwegian Sea; shore-based aircraft and, in coastal waters, Norwegian missile-firing boats, brought to readiness. Some Allied aircraft could even be flown in to Norwegian airfields. None of these measures need arouse public alarm or opposition. But the maintenance of a substantial air effort, no less than the defence of the airfields and the strengthening of Norway's landward defences, would require steps that could not fail to be controversial as long as hostilities had not actually begun: Norwegian mobilisation, seaborne reinforcement and the politically difficult introduction of foreign troops into Norway.

Plans exist for such an operation and the NATO exercise TEAMWORK in the autumn of 1980 deployed 168 ships (47 of them British) for the landing of 6000 American, British and Dutch marines in Central Norway.[16] Even the very restrictive Norwegian policy on foreign bases permits a degree of pre-stocking in Central Norway for American, British and Canadian forces,[17] some of whom might thus come by air.

There are also many snags. Norway is only one of several possible destinations for the limited total of Allied troops available for immediate reinforcement overseas. The number actually sent would be unpredictably dependent on circumstances at the time, but could never be great enough to obviate the need for timely Norwegian mobilisation. Because most units have more than one potential rôle, complete pre-stocking has not been achieved (almost none for air force units) and most equipment would have to come by sea. Only the United States have sufficient specialised shipping for their own marines, but neither would necessarily be available in the situation so far envisaged. Other Allies, Britain in particular, would have to requisition merchant ships, perhaps even to empty them before they could be loaded with military stores, and would then need functioning ports in which to disembark them.

All this adds up to an unfortunate dilemma. Norway, with her small population, restricted defence expenditure, large area and strategic importance, is vulnerable to invasion. She needs rapid reinforcement in emergency. But the policies that have made this logistically difficult also make it unlikely that a Norwegian government would make an early, even a timely, request for reinforcements. Nor are her Allies well organised for a prompt response. If invasion is ever seriously threatened, there will have to be rather a long period of warning time and some smart decisions in more capitals than one, or reinforcements will arrive too late.

If they ever do. The Expenditure Committee of the House of Commons had little hope to offer:

We were left in absolutely no doubt by all the officers, British and Norwegian, to whom we spoke, that unless reinforcements arrived during the warning period of political tension, they would probably not get there at all.[18]

This is not an uncontested view. If warning time and the other commitments of the two sides permit, Allied plans for reinforcement of shore-based aircraft within striking distance should help to produce air superiority south of 64° North. Lack of suitable shipping might be a greater obstacle to seaborne reinforcement than hostile air attack. On the other hand, insofar as air support depends on the Strike Fleet Atlantic, there is nothing in the scanty particulars – so different from the voluminous reporting of a century ago – so far revealed of Exercise TEAMWORK 1980 to contradict this gloomy view. The numerically impressive armada then collected included only one carrier, the USS NIMITZ,[19] whereas Admiral Train had earlier argued that 'four carrier battle groups operating together' would be needed in the Norwegian Sea if the northern flank was endangered.[20] Admittedly Exercise MAGIC SWORD NORTH mustered two in 1981,[21] but the working hypothesis for Soviet initiation of an offensive against Norway has been the preoccupation of the United States Navy in distant seas. This assumption permits the reinforcement of the European naval resources of NATO by some American submarines, shore-based aircraft, even surface escorts, but the arrival of aircraft carriers – before the loss of the Norwegian airfields – demands a little bit of luck.

It is the vulnerability of these airfields that distinguishes the naval problem in the North and Norwegian Seas from that in the Atlantic. There the threat is predominantly from submarines. These must also be expected on the approaches to Norway, but, if the Norwegian airfields were in Soviet hands, Allied warships and their associated aircraft would also face a much greater weight of air attack. Even Soviet surface warships might be able to operate under shore-based fighter cover. The odds would be adverse for any Allied naval forces except submarines: in the absence of American carriers, probably prohibitively adverse.

In favourable conditions, of course, the use of those airfields might be retained by NATO, or at least denied to the enemy, for long enough to permit useful naval operations. Actual invasion of Norway is a scenario with many variables on which depend the tasks that might be required of the Navy: submarine attack on a Soviet amphibious task force; anti-submarine protection of reinforcing convoys; even strengthening the escort of any American carriers that happened to be available. But the crucial factors would be warning time, political decisions and the battle for the airfields and control of the air. These might not merely determine the outcome, but also the significance of any naval contribution.

It would nevertheless be wrong to make the facile assumption that any combination of circumstances which encourages the Soviet Union to launch an invasion at the moment of their choice would so reduce the chances of their defeat as to eliminate any useful, which means potentially successful, rôle for the Royal Navy. All the trumps do not have to be in the Soviet hand. It is quite conceivable that the politically, even the psychologically appropriate moment for invasion might be one in which Soviet airborne troops and long-range aircraft did not happen to be available in adequate strength. The need to over-fly Swedish territory might be considered an impediment. There could, in fact, be a choice between no invasion at all and one which relied predominantly on amphibious assault.

This, of course, is what the Germans successfully attempted in 1940. Then they received invaluable assistance from the British Admiralty, who chose the wrong threat to meet, diverted the Home Fleet and saddled its luckless commander with the nickname of 'Wrong Way Charlie'. Today the balance of forces is less favourable than it was then, but the Royal Navy, with the indispensable assistance of the Royal Air Force, could still make the passage of the Northern Fleet to the Norwegian coast distinctly hazardous, if prior planning had permitted an appropriate deployment. The most cursory study of the Norwegian campaign of 1940 is enough to dispose of the popular myth that the British are able, let alone specially able, to improvise effectively in the face of unforeseen emergencies.

The British rôle, if an invasion of Norway ever seemed likely, would be to bear the brunt of denying to the Soviet Union the economical option of a purely amphibious assault. This raising of the ante would increase the risks, for the Soviet Union, that a maximum effort might lead to nuclear escalation. A prudent Soviet government might thus prefer an expedient that would simplify their choices, yet complicate those of their opponents. Instead of deploying troops on the Norwegian border and stationing an airborne division in the Kola peninsula, they might order a naval manoeuvre. This would be no less visible, but it would be more ambiguous. Soviet mobilisation of airborne forces provoked an American nuclear alert in 1973, but the United States are the last country to over-react to the movement of warships. Besides, there are precedents. As early as 1968 Exercise sever featured a Soviet naval squadron sailing northwards along the Norwegian coast to carry out landing operations on the other side of the border, a procedure repeated by Exercise okean in 1970. Exercise vesna in 1975 included the defence of amphibious forces against naval attack and the as yet unnamed exercise of September 1981 in the Baltic again featured opposed landings.

The arrival, in peacetime, of a large Soviet amphibious force off the Norwegian coast would thus not be unduly provocative. Its passage would have been monitored but undisturbed and nobody would venture to attack it. The naval infantry, the tanks, the armoured personnel carriers aboard the IVAN ROGOV and other amphibious vessels would be there for the exercise. KIEV and MOSKVA would simply have their normal complement of aircraft and helicopters. KIROV would have come to show the flag. Menace would only scent the air when the Soviet Ambassador in Oslo started to talk to the Foreign Minister about those modifications in Norwegian policy which the Kremlin regarded as desirable.

Invasion from the sea is a threat often denigrated on the grounds that Soviet amphibious capability is inadequate. It may be, compared to what the British had in 1944 or the Americans have today. But it is a lot better than anything the Germans had in 1940, which was nil. They put ordinary soldiers into destroyers and merchant ships and took Norway. Comparisons based on Normandy or Iwo Jima are beside the point. The harbours, let alone the landing beaches, of Western democratic countries are not adequately defended, if they are defended at all, in time of peace. In 1914 or, more disgracefully, in 1939, the Germans could have strolled ashore at Scapa Flow. They only had to get there and, in the scenario sketched above, the Northern Fleet could easily reach the Norwegian coast.

The threat would be real but implicit. Soviet warships would be alarmingly visible on Norwegian television but outside Norwegian territorial waters. The threat might well be a bluff, but the Norwegians could reasonably expect Allied assistance in calling it. They would not want a nuclear ultimatum, even if Washington were prepared to extend one. As a response to actual invasion nuclear war is conceivable and might be a credible threat. As a counter to a Soviet request for concessions that some Norwegians might well consider tolerable, it would terrify them before it impressed the Russians. Mobilisation or a request for the despatch of foreign troops would be politically difficult decisions – easily depicted as premature and needlessly provocative. The kind of reassurance that would be wanted in Oslo – and that would create the least problems in other capitals – would be the matching presence of Allied warships.

Submarines would not do. They can alarm an adversary, particularly when their presence is suspected before their movements can be tracked, without encouraging anxious friends on shore. Declaring them would be counter-productive in naval terms and might be considered provocative in political. Aircraft could, without much departure from normal peacetime patterns, overfly the fleet as a discreet warning to the Soviet admiral. Some might even be specially transferred to Norwegian airfields for the purpose. But, without increasing activity to a provocative level, aircraft could not provide the kind of steady, permanently visible assurance of Allied support and resolution that might be needed for a week or more.

For that surface warships are required. It would not matter, in these circumstances, that NATO ships are usually out-ranged by their Soviet counterparts. Allied warships could arrive unchallenged and keep station close enough to cancel out such discrepancies, thus making the outcome of the battle of the first salvo an open question. Even the nuclear option, for which Soviet ships are better armed, would be ruled out by the shortness of the range. Similar tactics are employed by Russian ships when confronting American carriers. In this scenario the Soviet threat would receive a matching response: equally implicit, equally established by peacetime practice, equally sustainable and, above all, equally visible on Norwegian television.

This emphasis on political factors and on the simplistic reactions of public opinion may displease those readers who think such issues should be decided on military grounds alone. They are wrong. Nothing is more important to any government than the choice between war and peace, nor is there any question on which ordinary citizens have a better right to express their instinctive feelings. Enabling rulers to avoid a precipitate choice is not only an essential function of armed forces, but a prime justification, in the nuclear age, for the retention of conventional navies. Gaining time without tactical loss would be enough of a triumph, but nullifying a threat without resort to war is the most glorious victory now conceivable.

The consequences to Britain of failure to meet such threats require little emphasis. If Norway is lost to the Alliance, the value of NATO to Britain will be seriously diminished; if Norway is lost to the enemy, the left flank of Britain's forward defence will have been turned. Even in the first case there would also be repercussions in Iceland and Denmark and some risk that the Alliance would start unravelling. What may be less obvious is that there is a whole ladder of peacetime rungs, each a little less innocuous than the one before, that could lead up to those results: reductions in Allied capability to provide Norway with timely reinforcement or reassurance; diminished Norwegian readiness to receive or invoke it; withdrawal of NATO facilities in Norway; increasing neutralism in Norway; Norwegian departure from NATO; repercussions on other members of the Alliance. Although there is a British foot on the first rung already, the other steps will not necessarily be taken. Even if they are, any of them could be self-inflicted wounds rather than the results of direct Soviet pressure, but all of them are established objectives of Soviet policy. Naturally so. NATO needs Norway quite as much as Norway needs NATO.

What the Soviet Union might hope to gain in Norway is clear. That they would only attempt it if the risks were low is less certain, but is suggested by the pattern of previous Soviet policy. So is the idea that they might regard as a suitable opportunity some extra-European conflict that distracted the United States and divided the Alliance. This may never happen, but, if the Soviet Union do ever decide to apply serious pressure to Norway, their best tactics might be to present a choice between concessions and an invasion that could only be resisted by nuclear war. Whether this is only remotely hinted at during a long campaign of diplomatic attrition, or emphasised by naval manoeuvres or made the subject of actual threats, the task of the Alliance will be to offer Norway a third and more acceptable option: a reinforcement capability that might plausibly sustain a conventional defence and, so it may be hoped, deter a conventional attack.

In peacetime this demands resources, plans, preparations and manoeuvres; in time of crisis support that is prompt and visible but not provocative; in war assistance that offers some hope of proving effective. In NATO circles this kind of thing is known as flexible response. Naturally the Americans are best equipped to provide it, but, unless Soviet timing is inept or the Allies are lucky, the main burden is likely to fall on Britain and, more particularly, on the Royal Navy. British difficulties would increase with the degree of American distraction and with the magnitude of the Soviet effort and, in the case of an all-out, all-arms offensive, might well prove insuperable. At lower levels there would be, in the absence of further defence cuts, a fair chance. It seems a threat worth choosing: as likely, as imminent, as dangerous and as answerable as any other. Perhaps even more than most. And, if we do not choose it, there is no certainty that anyone else will be able or willing to replace us, let alone to remedy the consequences of our neglect.

Norway is only the most obvious target for Soviet operations of limited liability, but there is no need to multiply such hypothetical occasions for the application of Soviet naval force in the Treaty Area. It is of the nature of warships to be able to pose a threat in any sea they sail and there is no shortage either of vulnerable points or of causes of dispute: restrictions on fishing, access to oil rigs, navigational rules, controversial claims to territorial limits, intelligence gathering activities. In the last few months of 1981 a different turn of events in Poland could have added a new and dangerous complication: Soviet efforts to prevent the escape of refugees – in Polish ships or even in Western merchantmen – across the Baltic. This is a nightmare which might still materialise, bringing in its train a variety of threats, confrontations, even actual clashes – and a consequential Danish need for Allied naval reassurance.

The coastal states of the Mediterranean are, for the most part, so many powder-kegs and the Southern Flank of NATO altogether lacks two salient advantages of the Northern and Central regions: a clear boundary between East and West and a stable, if uneven, balance of forces. Which side of the line, for instance, is Yugoslavia? What political considerations are most important to Cyprus, Greece, Malta and Turkey? Who, and how, decides which islands or parts of the southern Mediterranean shore are hostile, friendly or neutral? On what forces, even American, can the Commander of the Sixth Fleet count in a crisis? The North and Centre might not be free from ambiguity in their response to extra-European hostilities, but in the South it is hard to devise any scenario to which the reactions of all concerned would be reliably predictable.

These uncertainties only increase the need for NATO to be capable of flexible response at sea. Any maritime threat which may emerge is unlikely to be as clear-cut as the crossing of a land frontier or to lend itself to easy resolution by the diplomacy of escalation. The spectre of nuclear war cannot be credibly evoked as an answer to menacing naval manoeuvres, interference with shipping at sea, violation of territorial waters or any of the other minor forms of maritime bullying that might initiate the process of coercive diplomacy. Assailants are more easily deterred and victims encouraged to resist by the ability to counter the first pressure, even to raise the ante, than by conjuring up the prospect of Armageddon, which is likely to terrify a small country before it impresses a Super-Power. Nor have the experiences of the Second World War encouraged the European members of NATO to regard eventual liberation as an acceptable alternative to immediate defence. A country that feels threatened by the Soviet Navy will expect the arrival of Allied warships. Politically it is as simple as that.

In naval terms, of course, it is more difficult to envisage the circumstances which would enable Britain, at a time of high international tension, to spare any warships to respond to a Soviet threat in the Mediterranean. That would be a job for others. The relevance of such contingencies is rather that they would further diminish the prospects of Britain receiving much Allied naval assistance in the North. When Admiral Train explained that 'our shortage of ships . . . compels us to make such accommodations as performing our missions sequentially rather than simultaneously', he added that this choice 'may be forced upon us by our adversaries', but hinted that the Mediterranean might have to come before the Norwegian Sea. Not that either will necessarily enjoy the first priority. The Admiral also pointed out that the 'swing strategy' (the transfer of American naval forces from the Pacific to the Atlantic) is no longer regarded as automatic even in the event of war.[22] One of his conclusions would have been less surprising had it emanated from any other American than the Supreme Allied Commander Atlantic:

> It can be argued that the NATO commitment is almost equally fulfilled by maintaining a high level maritime fighting capability in the Western Pacific or the Indian Ocean.[23]

Navies do exist to serve national purposes.

So do alliances. The time has not yet come to consider 'all the worst contingencies'. But one thing is worth repeating. Norway is the left flank of the British front line. If it is threatened when American forces are not available to assist in its defence, the Royal Navy and the Royal Air Force may have to bear the brunt. If the peacetime attrition of Britain's forces were to reach a point where this task became predictably impossible, when that flank seemed doomed to be turned, then it would be logical to consider withdrawing from the right flank – the Central Front – as well, thereby contracting Britain's defensive perimeter to what was actually held in 1940. Forward defence has to be feasible if it is to be preferred to guarding the coast and reviving the Counts of the Saxon Shore.

8 Alliance Naval War III: tasks and resources

> the plain question anyone judging military programmes must ask: how well can the United States expect to do in the most likely kind of war against the most likely opponent?
>
> Zumwalt[1]

Alliance, so the preceding chapters would suggest, may well provide both cause and context for the employment of the Navy. It is more difficult to argue that the existence of NATO does much to determine the size, composition or structure of the Navy. The Alliance is looser and vaguer at sea than it is on land. This difference has nothing to do with the Treaty itself. When a Libyan fighter fired a missile on 19 August 1981,[2] this was an armed attack over the Mediterranean on an aircraft of the United States, something which the Parties to the North Atlantic Treaty had bound themselves by Article 5 to consider as 'an attack against them all'.[3]

Nobody seems to have so regarded it at the time, nor is this surprising. On the Central Front the dry bones of the Treaty have been given flesh by the stationing of troops and aircraft; by the physical construction of elaborate, expensive and durable supporting facilities; by intricate arrangements for command, control, communications, surveillance, intelligence; by detailed planning; by a horde of dependent civilians. In Germany NATO is more than an alliance: it is a way of life. There is even a Protocol committing

> Her Majesty the Queen of the United Kingdom of Great Britain and Northern Ireland . . . to maintain on the mainland of Europe, including Germany, . . . four divisions and the Second Tactical Air Force, or such other forces as the Supreme Allied Commander Europe regards as having equivalent fighting capacity.[4]

There is no naval equivalent to this military incarnation of NATO, rooted as it is in German soil and enmeshed in a web of precise commitment. Major naval commands abound: more than for army and air force together.[5] But the admirals (including those on the staff) committed to NATO outnumber the ships:

> In peacetime, the Royal Navy provides a frigate or a destroyer for NATO's Standing Naval Force Atlantic and a mine countermeasures vessel for the Standing Naval Force Channel . . . A frigate is normally allocated to the NATO On-Call Force in the Mediterranean when it is activated.[6]

These token forces serve many useful purposes, but readiness for combat is not among them. In the NATO area, strategic submarines apart, only the Sixth Fleet might not need to redeploy for war. And that redeployment could follow different patterns, depending on the nature of the war, the forces available and the apparent intentions of the enemy.

To a considerable extent this strategic fluidity is inherent in the nature of navies, which do not occupy positions, whether they are awaiting attack or preparing to launch one. It is also the outcome of the curious political history of the last thirty years. This required British and American soldiers, each for different reasons, to be locked into the defence of Germany, but allowed the navies of both countries considerable freedom to roam the seas in furtherance of national interests. Oceanic cruising, though good for naval morale and recruiting, is no longer of great political or strategic consequence to Britain, but it has remained of the first importance for the United States. They have no intention of tying any defined proportion of their navy to the North Atlantic, but, without firm dispositions for the bulk of NATO naval forces, cut and dried plans for the employment of the remainder are scarcely conceivable. The safes of the Ministry of Defence hold such plans, in elaborate and probably over-optimistic detail, for the army and air force: the navy have alternatives. As one admiral put it: 'I know the name of every ship I shall have – if they are available.'

Enough of these alternatives have already been considered to illustrate the need for NATO to keep their naval options open. Unfortunately this strategic virtue is a distinct handicap when it comes to procurement. There is no ready-made matrix of forces in place and precise commitments to determine the size and characteristics of the British fleet or the tasks it should perform in war. Attempts to supply it are seldom convincing. On 6 June 1981, for instance, *The Economist* described the planned disposition of British naval forces in war as being:

1 INVINCIBLE class carrier and 14 escorts to join the Strike Fleet Atlantic;

1 INVINCIBLE and 4 escorts for the protection of merchant shipping on the northern transatlantic route;

4–6 escorts on the southern route;

8–12 escorts for anti-submarine warfare in the Channel;

7 escorts to protect reinforcements for Norway.

But suppose there are no American carriers and thus no Strike Fleet Atlantic? Suppose the struggle for Norway precedes, perhaps even replaces, the Battle of the Atlantic? Suppose it is the Sixth Fleet in the Mediterranean that seeks Allied reinforcement?

Generals can demand troops, and air marshals insist on planes, because the plans of the Supreme Allied Commander Europe require them and the matching contributions of Britain's Allies are there on the ground. His colleague in Norfolk, Virginia, is a less potent arbiter for the admirals, because his plans are as hypothetical as the forces he hopes to command – not for any lack of meticulous staff-work, but simply because naval forces are inherently mobile and not always available in the North Atlantic when they are wanted.

In practice, of course, British defence policy is determined by more considerations than NATO strategy, but it is often useful to argue that reductions in strength would upset plans, let down Allies and contravene commitments. This is easier for the Army and Air Force than it is for the Navy, whose largely autonomous development calls for an equal independence of explicit justification. Contributing to a nebulous NATO strategy is an insufficient answer to the question: what could the Navy do? Nor is it of much assistance in indicating what the Navy should be.

Part of the answer must be supplied by later consideration of the purely national functions of the Navy – in conventional conflict, that is. The significant task of British strategic submarines has already been established as national. In the Alliance context earlier arguments have suggested a number of different rôles for the Royal Navy (assisted, of course, by the Royal Air Force). These may conveniently be summarised in tabular form. See Table 1.

There must, in other words, be submarines to attack surface ships

TABLE 1   *Rôles for the Royal Navy in Alliance War*

Task	Objective	Commitment	Method	Remarks
1 Fleet in being	Countering a Soviet threat to sever transatlantic communications or otherwise exert maritime dominance	Encouraging and reinforcing US naval presence in the North Atlantic. Demonstrating NATO naval capacity	Balanced fleet with emphasis on anti-sub. warfare.	Continuing peacetime rôle
2 Resistance to coercive diplomacy	Visibly matching a visible threat	Probably without much American assistance but with some European	Surface ships	Most likely in Norway but possible anywhere in the NATO area, even off the Shetlands
3 Responding to the unforeseen threat at sea to the interests of a member of NATO	Breaking a blockade, protecting shipping or fishing or oil rigs, clearing a minefield or meeting any challenge short of outright war	Eventual assistance might be general, but the outcome, not least the balance between crisis and war, could depend on naval readiness	Balanced fleet	Unpredictable but possible
4 Protecting approaches to British ports	Repelling Soviet attacks on shipping	With RAF the sole burden	Anti-sub, Anti-air and anti-mine	Likely in any war except total nuclear
5 Protecting cross-Channel reinforcements	Repelling Soviet attacks on shipping	With some European assistance	As above (4), but also mine-laying	If the nature of any attack on the Central Front allows time to reinforce
6 Holding the Greenland–Iceland–United Kingdom Gap	Reinforcing islands and the gaps between them	With US and some European help, but possibly without much enthusiasm from the inhabitants	As above (4) and attack subs, amphibious landing	Difficult if Norway falls
7 Protecting transatlantic communications	Repelling Soviet attacks in Gap and ocean	With RAF main burden in Eastern Atlantic	Anti-sub and anti-air	Most likely in protracted war
8 Defence of Norway	Attacking Soviet amphibious forces, protecting re-	Extent of operations dependent on availability of	Attack submarines, anti-sub, anti-air	Warning time and air battle critical factors

TABLE 1 (*Contd.*)

Task	Objective	Commitment	Method	Remarks
	inforcements, aiding attack on Kola bases	US forces		
9 Defence of Danish Straits	In any foreseeable circumstances, only an exercise in damage-limitation	See extreme right hand column	Attack submarines and mining	Depends almost entirely on the non-naval aspects of this unlikely scenario
10 Offensive action not included above	Air strikes against shore or surface fleet	Reinforcing escort of US carriers	Anti-sub	Air strikes against the Kola bases would risk nuclear escalation

(and enemy submarines); surface ships to repel, with the aid of aircraft and helicopters, submarines and aircraft; surface ships to confront, in conditions of nominal peace, other surface ships; transports for troops and their equipment; aircraft to attack enemy surface ships beyond the range of our own and to repel enemy aircraft; submarines and aircraft to lay mines; specialised ships to hunt and sweep them. There may also be occasions when surface ships, though inadequately armed for this purpose, are compelled, perhaps because nothing else is available, to fight surface ships.

These are not the views of the Ministry of Defence. *The Way Forward*, for instance, devotes an entire page to 'Beyond the NATO Area', but has no room for the word 'Norway'. The Continent of Europe has contracted to 'the vital 65-kilometre sector assigned to' First British Corps. No objectives are suggested for maritime strategy,[7] but the Secretary of State for Defence, in his speech of 8 July 1981 in the House of Commons, gave first priority to 'the covering, as best we can, of the Greenland–Iceland–United Kingdom gap and other choke points against Soviet submarines'.[8] These may, the experience of previous wars notwithstanding, be valid tactical expedients, but they need to be set in the wider context of the presumed objectives, political as well as military, of both sides. Does it make even tactical sense to concentrate on the Greenland–Iceland–United Kingdom Gap without regard to the control of Norwegian airfields and harbours? Mr Heath was right when he said in the same debate:

we tend to give less attention to the basic strategy which our forces
should be adopting than to the particular problems which arise out of
the financial circumstances.[9]

The ears of admirals ought to be the first to burn. They have not
communicated the strategy to which they have devoted so much detailed
planning.

The result has been the customary bombination, in a strategic
vacuum, of arguments about matériel. Some of these have been quite
sensible. Mr Nott has correctly perceived the armament of the Royal
Navy as being even more inadequate today than it was in 1914 – mainly
defective shells and fire-control; or in 1939 – guns that jammed after the
first salvo or anti-aircraft weapons still the subject of debate. The
inelegant sentence – 'the balance of our investment between platforms
and weapons needs to be altered so as to maximise real combat
capability'[10] – can not, in itself, be seriously contested.

Some of the conclusions associated with ('drawn from' would be
going too far) this premise seem more questionable. There is the view
that aircraft and submarines (tanks, for that matter) are inherently
better platforms than surface warships. That depends on the task and
the strategic assumptions that govern it. These seem to be narrowing, in
the Ministry of Defence, to an armoured assault on One British Corps
and the attempted penetration of the Greenland–Iceland–United
Kingdom Gap by Soviet submarines. Either is quite conceivable, though
the link between them – seaborne reinforcement of the Central Front –
seems to have been abandoned. But there are other contingencies and
the need to get seaborne equipment to Norwegian airfields or surface
ships to a confrontation off the Norwegian coast seems no less plausible.
The case for putting all Britain's eggs in two baskets has yet to be
demonstrated.

Nevertheless the decision has been taken to cut the surface fleet. Three
carriers will be reduced to two and two amphibious ships to none. The
figures for escorts are more debatable. *The Way Forward* says from 59 to
50;[11] David Greenwood prefers 42;[12] a well-informed source suggests
37 or less. The differences depend on varying assumptions about the
utility of ships in reserve and the replacement of ageing ships. These
reductions will be offset (how far is a question only the Byfleet
computers could attempt to answer) by the introduction of better
weapons, but not by any important increase in the number of
submarines or of aircraft committed to maritime tasks. Not only did the
five extra nuclear attack submarines figure in existing plans, but three of

them, as David Greenwood points out,[13] will only replace vessels likely to be withdrawn from service by the end of the decade. Three additional NIMROD aircraft will be valuable, but scarcely a quantum jump in combat effectiveness.

By the logic of previous arguments these comparisons are beside the point. What matters is not whether the Navy is larger or smaller, stronger or weaker than it used to be, but whether it still matches Alliance requirements. This is a question on which *The Way Forward* [14] is as silent as its predecessor, the *Statement on the Defence Estimates 1981.*[15] Naturally it is a question more easily posed than answered. If we take, as an example, the defence of the Greenland–Iceland–United Kingdom Gap, we may safely assume that the naval staff, both in Whitehall and in Norfolk, Virginia, have done the necessary calculations. They will have figures, subject to all the inevitable margins of error, for the numbers of Soviet submarines attempting to penetrate the gap and for the numbers of surface ships, submarines, aircraft and helicopters needed to ensure a high rate of detection and destruction. They will have estimated how many Soviet submarines, in various scenarios, can nevertheless be expected to reach the Atlantic and what forces – and methods – will be required to deal with them there. Plans undoubtedly exist to cope with attack, by air or sea or both, on the detection systems, the airfields, the minefields, the harbours, the islands that make the Gap a choke-point.

All this, even with varying assumptions, must have produced at least a range of estimates as a basis for predicting the outcome. The Supreme Allied Commander Atlantic and the First Sea Lord could, if they wished, hazard an informed guess not only at the total air and naval strength needed by NATO for this task, but also at the size of the necessary British contribution.

There are many obvious reasons why they have not done so. Such estimates might not carry conviction without the reasoning on which they were based. If this were disclosed, it might reveal too much to the enemy. So might the estimates themselves. Any discrepancy between the estimates and what was apparently available might be damaging, either at home or abroad. Publication, even the effort to agree what should be published, would cross innumerable wires – naval, political, bureaucratic – both internationally and domestically. And to what purpose? Nothing good resulted from the decision of the NATO Council in 1952 that 96 divisions were needed for the defence of Europe – least of all, 96 divisions.

Not all these reasons are entirely valid. The penalties of disclosing information to the enemy are as often exaggerated as those of withholding it from the electorate are under-estimated. If the Royal Navy wish to continue, in the foreseeable climate of British public opinion, invoking the requirements of NATO, they will sooner rather than later find it necessary to specify, even to quantify, those requirements. This is not, at least in the case of the Greenland–Iceland–United Kingdom Gap, a task that can profitably be assumed by the amateur, who cannot expect to reach reliable conclusions without access to secret information. It is the admirals, if they wish to survive, who will have to stick their necks out.

Not every Alliance task presents such difficult problems. The scenario of the Northern Fleet exercising coercive diplomacy against Norway offers an easier example than most. If 30 Soviet ships (including transports and amphibious landing vessels) manoeuvre off the Norwegian coast, NATO would not have to match them one for one to provide a politically effective (and navally worrying) counter to this Soviet threat. Ten surface warships able to keep continuous station within a mile or so should be more than sufficient. This is a task tailor-made for the Standing Naval Force Atlantic, unless this has already been disbanded under a NATO Alert and provided all nine governments are ready to risk their ships in a hazardous confrontation. If they were, this would not only increase the political impact of the gesture, but would impose little strain on the British surface fleet – one ship immediately, perhaps a few more as reliefs if the encounter dragged on or other navies proved unable to relieve their own ships.

If Allied solidarity or readiness were inadequate and Britain had to play a major part in an ad hoc effort, the size of the British contribution would have to be greater: perhaps 6 ships off the Norwegian coast and as many again on stand-by. Allowing for those ships that are always temporarily unavailable when a crisis develops, even this minimum Soviet threat would take a large slice of the British surface fleet and some other tasks would inevitably be jeopardised unless the Norwegian confrontation had a happy issue.

This cannot be helped. If the United States Navy must resign themselves to the necessity of sequential rather than simultaneous operations, the Royal Navy cannot realistically expect the strength to cope with every threat at once. In the years to come, however, retention of the strength to meet any threats at all will increasingly require the Navy to demonstrate in detailed argument that some threats can be successfully countered by employing specified forces, whereas others cannot. This will not be easy. Admiral Zumwalt has recorded that 'it took the best part of half a year' for his staff to produce an assessment of the 'major types of non-strategic war scenarios' and their 'potential outcomes' on the basis of a comparison of American and Soviet naval capabilities. Unfortunately he adds: 'as far as I know, it is the only exhaustive military net assessment study ever done in this country'. He goes on to say that his attempt, with Congressional backing, to get it published was met by a demand for deletion of all 'references to adequate, marginal or inadequate capability; to superiority or inferiority to the Russians, and to the odds on winning the war'.[16]

What an analytically inclined admiral could not achieve in the open society of the United States is naturally an unreasonable proposition to advance in the cloistered stuffiness of Whitehall. There are perhaps only two arguments in its favour. Admiral Zumwalt's unconventional approach did help him to secure what he describes as 'the best naval budget' of his four years as Chief of Naval Operations and any future First Sea Lord will have a stronger incentive. Few Americans have to be convinced of the need for a navy, even if they disagree about its cost.

In Britain the case is different, not only among interested members of the public, who are increasingly coming to expect a fuller justification of the risks and burdens assigned to them, but also within those more influential circles with competing claims on national resources: politicians, officials, even soldiers and airmen. The frank exposition of naval problems would cause much extra work and vexation, but would at least permit a wider and more informed debate. Continued efforts to confine the discussion of naval planning to the Ministry of Defence, or to rely on the simplistic proposition that the magnitude of the threat demands maximum provision, can only result in the size and structure of the Navy being determined by the political judgments of small groups.

These judgments will seldom be reached on the basis of a predominantly strategic reasoning. David Greenwood's summary of the approach adopted by Mrs Thatcher's Conservative government is eminently fair:

When Mr. John Nott took up the defence portfolio in January 1981, the need for a thorough-going review of the defence effort was therefore self-evident. There was going to be less money for defence than the programme-in-being presupposed. To sustain that programme would, it had become apparent, require more money than had previously been supposed. And a new provision [TRIDENT] had been fed into the financial calculations.[17]

Of course, much rethinking had taken place behind the scenes: about matériel, tactics, logistics, even such important strategic contingencies as seaborne reinforcement and resupply of the Central Front or the defence of the British Isles against conventional air attack. Some sensible conclusions had been drawn and slotted into the general process of seeking greater cost-effectiveness, more bang for a given buck. But David Greenwood is equally fair in describing Mr Nott as 'running his merchant banker's eye over the defence business'.[18] Everything was questioned except the ultimate value of the product. 'Threats' exist and impose certain 'tasks' upon the armed forces, whose 'efforts' to perform them must be constrained by the 'resources' available. 'This means that the structure we set must be one which we can afford to sustain with modern weapons and equipment, and with proper war stocks.'[19] So far, so good. If 'which we can afford' is a political judgment, it is not one which any future government can be expected to consider unduly conservative. But 'effort' should be assessed by its predicted result as well as by its motive and its cost. This is where British defence policy, as expressed in a series of official publications and speeches, is deficient. Which British contributions to NATO 'efforts' to meet Soviet 'threats' can be expected to achieve success? Without an answer to that question a crucial element is missing from any future attempt to determine British defence priorities.

Such attempts will certainly be made. There is no reason to expect that the British economy will start to grow at a faster rate than the rise in the cost of sophisticated defence equipment. On the contrary, only better economic management and more luck will prevent the upward thrust of defence expenditure into the sagging belly of a stagnant economy becoming even more painful than it is already. There will be continuing pressure, manifesting itself in recurrent eruptions, to reduce the cost of this equipment: by downgrading its quality, or by reducing the quantity procured, or by altogether renouncing certain types of equipment, hence also certain strategic functions. This pressure may be expected without regard to political developments, at home or abroad, though these will naturally exert a significant influence on the nature of the response.

As for political developments, it is difficult to foresee the emergence of a British government more inclined to maintain or increase defence expenditure than Mrs Thatcher's. The likelihood is rather that any different government would want to reduce this spending. It is often assumed that such ambitions could be accommodated by abandoning the TRIDENT programme, thus leaving intact the remainder of Britain's defences, possibly even including POLARIS. This may be over-optimistic. In the first year of the next government, expenditure on TRIDENT will be a very small fraction of the defence budget. The penalties of cancellation might well exceed the immediate savings. A government that wanted a real reduction of defence expenditure, perhaps to help finance greatly increased spending elsewhere, would have to cut more widely.

More dramatic options – of a kind that might be considered by a government prepared to change the character of British defence and foreign policy – will be examined in a later chapter. The immediate point is that critical scrutiny of British force levels and defence expenditure must be expected to renew itself with every change of government, even within the conventional pattern of British politics. The need to provide a strategic justification will be a continuing one, but the nature of that justification should not be regarded as equally durable. It will probably require fairly frequent updating, even substantial revision. Obsolescence is as insidious, as easily overlooked and as damaging in an argument as in a weapon.

The obvious starting-point – the suitability of the post-Nott Navy for Alliance tasks – is thus only the first step in what should be a continuing process of analysis and exposition by the Ministry of Defence. Nobody else can do it properly – not until far more information is available – but they cannot afford to treat it as if they were painting the Forth Bridge, just changing the colour each time they start all over again. The external situation and the state of the art are in no less constant evolution than the British political scene.

Meanwhile the ten Alliance tasks suggested earlier in this chapter offer a basis for the kind of guesswork that is all an amateur can attempt at present.

The first three, for instance, might be grouped under the heading of Raising the Ante: fleet in being; resistance to coercive diplomacy; responding to the unforeseen. They have certain characteristics in common. In each case the assumption is that American naval assistance would be minimal. The Soviet Union could not expect to coerce Europe by demonstrating a threat to transatlantic communications if an American fleet was obviously ready to protect them. A second assumption is that the Soviet Union are trying it on. If they were bent on nuclear war, even general conventional war, they would start with a bang. Instead, intent on low-risk advantage, they are probing for resolution or its absence, placing a stake and watching whether it is covered. This assumption produces as its corollary the third character-istic: these are situations in which the degree of demonstrable European resolution will be equally interesting to the United States, whether this is measured by reaction to the actual course of events or by visible preparations to cope. It is not only because, in particular circumstances, the United States might be unable to help, that European navies must be ready to take the first strain. If they were not, the United States might not want to take even the second.

All this adds up to a requirement for a fleet that can risk a battle, even if it neither expects to fight one nor, without a good deal of luck, to win any battle that might be forced on it. This is not a need that can be readily quantified: the weight of the opposition is as unpredictable as the extent of Allied assistance. It calls for surface ships, with air and submarine backing, in sufficient numbers to be available; with endurance and sea-keeping qualities to sustain a confrontation – the Russians are good at sitting it out; with weapons that, given good tactics, could at least prevent them from being a push-over. At present, at a guess, the Royal Navy have enough for these tasks, but so barely enough as to make it certain, if any of these contingencies ever arise, that someone will face an agonising decision: whether to put the confrontation to the touch, 'to win or lose it all'.

There are ships to bluff it out and the resolution of their officers and men is not in question. But no naval staff could be blamed for wondering what would be left for other tasks if the bluff were called. It being inappropriate for elderly civilians to express any opinion on such matters, it may be better to quote the judgment of an Admiral of the Fleet on an even more hazardous encounter:

> I feel very strongly that we shall not be asking the personnel engaged to be taking any greater risks than the infantry and tank personnel are subjected to on every occasion on which an attack is delivered on land.[20]

When it comes to raising the ante, which is another name for conventional deterrence or avoiding nuclear war, the rôle of One British Corps and Royal Air Force (Germany) will be no less hazardous and they, too, will leave little for other tasks if their gamble fails. In naval confrontations of the kind envisaged the number of ships available will probably be less important than the readiness to risk them. On past form a resolute show of force may be enough to avert the need to use it. But some ships there must be, probably not much less than there are now.

The second category of Alliance tasks comes under the heading of Fighting Without Much American Help: protecting approaches to British ports; protecting cross-Channel reinforcements; holding the Greenland–Iceland–United Kingdom Gap; protecting transatlantic communications. The first two would, in any case, have to be attempted without direct American assistance, which might be slow to reach its full strength in the case of the last two.

On a snap judgment, success might be expected against Soviet submarines in the first two tasks, though the ability of the Royal Air Force to defend either ports or cross-Channel reinforcements against air attack could be decisively affected by developments in the continental battle. Defence against Soviet mining is another matter. In 1975 this was described as 'a serious threat' and NATO counter-measures as 'barely adequate'.[21] In 1975 Britain had 41 vessels available for this task, Belgium 30 and the Netherlands 43. In 1981 the figures were 33, 22 and 34, though the Netherlands Navy have a substantial building programme.[22] If the Soviet Union were to make a major effort at mine-laying, perhaps including the clandestine use of merchant ships and fishing vessels, to lay delayed action mines before the outbreak of hostilities, there could be considerable disruption of shipping movements to and from British ports, particularly if priority had to be given to ensuring the safe egress of strategic nuclear submarines.

Some American help is likely to be available, whatever the circumstances, for the next two tasks. Even if an extra-European crisis has pre-empted much of the surface fleet, there should still be submarines, land-based aircraft and some escorts in the North Atlantic. Whether there will be enough, with British assistance, to hold the Gap against Soviet submarines is beyond the scope of guesswork, but at least this task is directly relevant to the security of the United States and likely to be high on the list of American naval priorities. Without American carriers, however, the islands, their installations and any reinforcements despatched to them might be vulnerable to Soviet attack, particularly after the loss of the Norwegian airfields.

The protection of transatlantic communications was discussed at length in Chapter 6. All that need be added here is that, if the Soviet Union decide to deploy sufficient submarines to the North Atlantic before the outbreak of hostilities, their defeat would have to await the arrival of substantial American forces. There are not nearly enough British escorts to afford adequate protection right across the ocean.

These two tasks also figure in the last category of Alliance contingencies: Fighting With Full American Help. Then the prospects, in so far as such unprecedented warfare can be the subject of prediction on the basis of information that is not adequately available to anyone at all, should be reasonable – while the war remains conventional, which may not be long. The same caveat applies with even greater force to the other three tasks in this category: defending Norway, defence of the Danish

Straits and offensive action. The more effective the American carriers proved in strikes against the shore, particularly against the Kola bases, the greater would be the risk of nuclear escalation. In every case the major rôle of the Royal Navy would be to supplement American efforts, whether by strengthening the anti-submarine escort of American carriers or in other contributions to anti-submarine warfare. The chances of success are more dependent on the circumstances in which hostilities begin and on the way in which they develop than on numbers of ships and their characteristics. With warning time or surprise attack; Alliance unity and resolution or disarray; Atlantic First or other priorities for the United States; nuclear or conventional: these will be among the decisive factors. The size of the Royal Navy could also have some importance, but the scenarios are too variable to offer any basis for suggesting what the critical level might be.

No conclusions can properly be drawn from such rough-hewn guesswork, but a few impressions may be allowed to emerge. Nobody expects Britain, in the final decades of the twentieth century, to possess a worst-case navy – one able to withstand maximum Soviet pressure with minimum American help – but the emphasis in this and earlier chapters on the conditional character of the Navy's prospects of success may seem a trifle daunting. It is easy, but it would be mistaken, to underrate advantages that can only be secured in favourable circumstances. Admirals, no less than generals, need luck to succeed. In 1688 it was 'a Protestant wind' that won William of Orange the throne of England, but he needed a fleet, even an inferior fleet, to profit by it. Three centuries later we may have to place our main reliance on a fortunate combination of political factors, but enough contingencies have been analysed to suggest that the same condition could still apply. The situations in which the Navy could help to counter a threat are at least as plausible as those in which it could not.

On the other hand, there are too many variables in the NATO equation to permit any precision about the degree of security the Navy could offer to Britain, let alone about the resources required. The Navy, indeed Britain, can meet only a limited threat and, even for that, will usually require Allied assistance, which may, or may not, be adequately and promptly available. It is easier to argue that, because of the variety of the potential threats and the uncertainty of the Allied response, the Navy needs a flexible range of capabilities, than it is to specify the tolerable minimum in each. Enough deficiencies have already been noted to suggest that this minimum should be higher than the present level, but analysis so far has not met the requirement posed in Chapter 5.

No conventional Alliance contingency has been identified in which a plausible increase in British naval capability would offer such obvious prospects of assured success as to outweigh the sacrifice of the limited nuclear deterrent.

This is a heavily loaded formulation of the problem, but so, as previously argued, is the notion that sacrificing POLARIS or TRIDENT would result in any increase in expenditure on the rest of the Navy.

In the Alliance context the functions of the Navy, nuclear or conventional, are mainly to provide a measure of national insurance against limited threats in specific contingencies. The existence of this cover also increases the chances for the Alliance of avoiding nuclear war because it offers, in some circumstances but by no means in all, an extra option between submission and escalation. Both functions seem more important, because more plausible, than the ancillary contribution the Navy might make to the necessarily uncertain outcome of general conventional war.

Any larger rôle for the Navy would require radical changes, either in NATO strategy, or in Britain's relationship to NATO or in British defence policy.

9 On the Fringes of Alliance

The dragon-green, the luminous, the dark, the serpent-haunted sea.

Flecker[1]

Nothing is more habitual among writers on naval affairs, or has been more neglected in these pages, than their preoccupation with the perils of distant oceans.

A chilling picture materializes: The USSR today has the naval force and operating bases necessary to interdict every significant shipping lane in the North and South Atlantic Oceans, as well as all of those in the Caribbean Sea.[2]

The whole of the length of the Western sea-lanes can be effectively outflanked.[3]

The statistics of what is at risk in the South Atlantic, the Indian Ocean, the Arabian Sea and the Gulf are by now well known . . . Interdiction of these supply routes would quickly bring the industries of Western Europe and North America to a grinding halt . . . it can only be deterred or prevented by globally deployed sea power . . .[4]

the United Kingdom and other major countries must now shoulder responsibility for peacekeeping in an increasing proportion of the world oceans . . .[5]

There is no need to dispute the statistics of maritime trade, the figures of Soviet naval strength or the historical analogies that buttress these warnings and exhortations. A global campaign against Western shipping is not very likely, either in isolation or as part of a plausible scenario for general war, but it is sufficiently conceivable to make one wish it could receive the assured counter of a conventional naval response. On this issue, however, it is hard to disagree with the Ministry of Defence:

> That question [the global challenge to Western interests] must be considered, like the issues of out-of-area defence as a whole, with due respect for realities.[6]

These realities are that, as we have seen in previous chapters, the Royal Navy lack the resources and the assurance of adequate Allied support to guarantee the defence of Norway, the safe passage of British reinforcements to the continent or outlying islands of Europe, the maintenance of access to British ports or the arrival of transatlantic reinforcements and supplies. The chances of performing any of these tasks against maximum opposition depend on a degree of warning time that would permit a major concentration of NATO naval forces in the North Atlantic area. Readiness to disperse British forces, or to acquiesce in the dispersion of American, to more distant seas would demand a faith in the immunity of Europe difficult to reconcile with the existence of a general war on Western trade. Or else a very deficient sense of priorities. Naval defence, no less than charity, begins at home and, if there is to be general war, is likely to end there – for the Royal Navy.

Oceanic operations only make sense in other circumstances. Theoretically a limited war outside the Treaty Area could be one of them. Some contingencies have already been considered and it is as easy to imagine others as it is to guess at the kind of American pressure that might be applied, as it was over Vietnam, to secure a Union Jack (or a White Ensign) to wave alongside the Stars and Stripes.

Such pressure should be resisted. It is in just that contingency, as already argued, that a limited Soviet threat in Europe is most likely, a threat the Royal Navy could hope to counter. The strength needed for that useful, because possibly successful, task should not be dissipated in symbolic gestures. One distant ship, after all, needs two more to back it up, to say nothing of the demands of logistic support. Nor are there many contingencies nowadays in which a single ship would be more of an asset than a liability in the face of serious opposition.

If war, however limited, outside the Treaty Area should be excluded, what of the interventions of violent peace? It is hard to refuse cooperation to allies in such endeavours without forfeiting the prospect of their assistance in one's own and situations can be envisaged in which British national interests overseas might require naval support. Two tests suggest themselves. The first concerns the contingency in which an ally seeks British naval assistance. Can the use or threat of force be regarded as reliably limited, both in itself and in its predictable results?

> Coercive diplomacy is an alternative to war and, if it leads to war, we must not only hold that it has failed: we may even doubt whether it ever deserved the name. [7]

It would certainly not deserve British participation if that was the likely outcome.

The second test is the reasonable expectation of reward. Gratitude is not a very dependable sentiment in political affairs and is, in any case, more closely related to the need for a favour – and for its repetition – than to the effort of extending it. From October 1980, for instance, the Royal Navy long maintained two warships on patrol in the Gulf of Oman in response to 'the possibility of a threat to the free passage of merchant shipping in the area'. [8] The presence of these ships, which needed relief on the usual 3 to 1 basis as well as afloat support, had not been requested by the United States, which had already deployed a larger force, as did the French, also independently. Efforts to coordinate the operations, the rules of engagement, the command of these allied forces were more protracted than they were immediately efficacious. Admirals blamed these delays on the politicians and diplomats responded in kind. The motives of this concentration might be described as catalytic – on the basis that the presence of warships offered more options than their absence – or as expressive, because they manifested concern. The justification usually advanced is that nothing happened. So far, however, the diplomatic results have been less obvious than the maritime: in November 1981 *The Times* was able to record that

> HMS *Euryalus*, a Royal Navy frigate, yesterday rescued a cargo vessel carrying 240 tons of cow dung, towing it 70 miles into Muscat.

The ability to render naval services is probably less reliably productive of reciprocation when it is neither sought nor urgently needed. The principal beneficiary of this intervention was a necessitous rather than a profitable client: British self-esteem.

Not all overseas deployments need be so nugatory. There could be occasions when the United States would genuinely welcome, even solicit, the presence of British warships. Unfortunately these are likely to be of two kinds: those in which the existence of real opposition makes an extra anti-submarine escort desirable; and those in which British participation might help to assuage political doubts in the United States about the wisdom of undertaking the intervention at all. Either might, for other reasons, provide a valid, but scarcely an intrinsically desirable, motive for British decision-makers.

On the whole it does seem as if overseas intervention by the Royal Navy might more profitably be undertaken either in response to a genuinely perceived need of general importance or in pursuit of specific national interests. The mere demonstration of a capability or the hope of eliciting gratitude are unlikely to prove rewarding.

It is thus necessary to scrutinise with caution the latest statement of policy by the Ministry of Defence.

We intend to resume from 1982 onwards the practice of sending a substantial naval task group on long detachment for visits and exercises in the South Atlantic, Caribbean, Indian Ocean or further east. We intend to make particular use of the new carriers, with SEA HARRIERS and helicopters, in out-of-area deployment. We will coordinate all these deployments and exercises as fruitfully as possible with the United States and other allies, as well as with local countries with whom we have close defence relations.[9]

Some of the motives prompting this declaration of intent are thoroughly understandable. Cruising in tropical waters is better for recruiting and morale than an unbroken routine, with all its monotony and discomfort, of exercising in the North Atlantic and the Narrow Seas. There are still residual British interests and attachments overseas that can be nourished by an occasional showing of the flag. The simpler forms of training can as well be conducted in sunlit seas as amid the northern mists and gales.

The potential drawbacks are threefold. If trouble erupts in a distant ocean the presence of 'a substantial naval task group' may increase the political difficulty of avoiding a British involvement that may not be in British interests. If it is at home that danger threatens, the absence of so many warships will increase the warning time needed to permit the concentration of the British fleet. And, as suggested by the explicit reference to the rôle of 'the new carriers', the influence of this exotic environment could subtly, insidiously distort naval views of the most suitable structure and equipment for the fleet.

These dangers and the hypothetical objections they suggest are not insuperable. But they do demand a watchful eye, one animated by a sense of priorities as ruthless as Fisher's. 'The battle ground should be the drill ground': the words were Nelson's; the application was Fisher's; the relevance is not yet exhausted.[10]

None of these arguments is intended to suggest that there are no fruitful opportunities for the application of limited naval force. On the contrary, the author has previously insisted,[11] and still maintains, that a state of nominal peace offers more numerous and more advantageous occasions for the employment of navies than the desperate scenarios conjured up, nauseous ebullitions from the witches' cauldron, for the awful emergency of war: limited or general, conventional or nuclear. An eye to the main chance, the cost-effective venture, is urgently needed. But it must not become blurred by romantic illusions.

One of these is to suppose that the use or threat of limited naval force can be isolated, geographically or politically, from the main theatres of international rivalry. This is normally only possible for small powers not involved in the central balance, though repeated British naval deterrence of Guatemala shows how even a committed actor can occasionally exert an autonomous influence without wider repercussions. Significant interventions by a major navy usually occur in sensitive areas and often provoke as many international complications as they alleviate. They also attract rival navies to the scene – as did the largely innocent presence of British warships in the Bay of Bengal in 1971[12] – and pose at least the technical possibility of a sharper conflict. Naval deployments for limited purposes may well be preferred over even the threat of war, but they are neither easy to decide nor cost-free in their political consequences. Nevertheless, out of a sample of 131 exertions, great or small, of limited naval force since the Second World War as many as 68 can be said to have achieved their immediate purpose – not a bad success rate by ordinary diplomatic standards.

What may be more significant, in the Alliance context, is that only one of these successes resulted from a joint operation by two navies: the 1973 demonstration by Australia and New Zealand against French nuclear tests at Mururoa. In the other 67 incidents the assailant (the initiator of limited naval force) was a single nation, even if a handful of objectives independently attracted ships from more than one navy and one British squadron (in 1952) included a Canadian carrier. We have only the evidence of Soviet protests to support the theory that Anglo-American-French naval exercises off the Horn of Africa in 1978[13] represented an unsuccessful attempt at gunboat diplomacy and the record strongly suggests that this kind of activity is even more resistant to joint planning and coordinated action than the initial phase of naval warfare. Indeed, if we remember some of the salient characteristics of any exercise of limited naval force – the need for prompt decision, the element of risk, the inevitably controversial nature of any intervention, the crucial factor of naval availability – it may be doubted whether several governments could ever unite in a resolution that has so often proved beyond the grasp of one.[14]

Consider, for instance, a favourite scenario: the threat to oil supplies posed by the decision of the governments of producer states or by the danger of their overthrow. There are no foreseeable circumstances in which a decision to intervene, or its execution, would be easy or free from extensive risks. The American choice would be sufficiently agonising, but a timely Allied consensus on the correct response seems desirable rather than plausible.

Even in the NATO area there could be problems. Think of the Baltic, of Cyprus, of Gibraltar, of Libya, of Malta, of Northern Ireland, even of Norway. There, at least, would be a legal obligation to offset the misgivings of domestic opinion. Nucleus forces would exist, a command structure, perhaps even a plan. The unity of response and the promptness of action that must nevertheless be considered uncertain in home waters can only be regarded as the stuff of dreams in more distant seas.

Beyond the NATO area the active rôle of the Royal Navy in time of peace is twofold: ad hoc cooperation with the United States or any other ally thus disposed; and the protection of British national interests and aspirations.[15] Both are hypothetical contingencies unsuited to commitment before the crisis arises and its conflicting risks and opportunities can be assessed. The naval capacity to discharge such tasks would clearly enlarge British national options, but its maintenance can scarcely be represented as an obligation of Alliance.

In time of crisis, of course, it will be so represented, particularly by Americans, but also by some sections of opinion in this country. It is easy to argue that the kind of overseas threat – to trade, to navigation, to essential raw materials, to investments or to positions of influence – that might require a naval response would be a threat to the West as a whole. Europe, indeed Britain, would stand to lose as much as the United States, perhaps more, and should contribute accordingly to countering the danger.

In naval terms, of course, France, who will soon have as many surface warships as Britain but with a less urgent need for their presence in home waters, is the country best equipped to meet such a request. She has manifested considerable readiness not only for overseas deployments, but for the use of limited force, though latterly by airborne rather than seaborne intervention. Her naval presence of 1980–1 in the Gulf of Oman, with its backing of aircraft at adjacent bases, was stronger than the British, a point on which the British media have been curiously silent.[16]

Unfortunately the cherished independence of French policy makes cooperation with allies difficult and creates special obstacles to any kind of junior partnership in a joint operation. Nor, it must be admitted, do the many American virtues always include the tact and flexibility needed to charm susceptible allies into the illusion that they are being treated as equals. Logically France should be Europe's standard-bearer beyond the seas, but the obstacles are formidable: the French would reject any prior commitment, insist on their own judgment of the situation and expect an independent rôle, all of which the Americans would be reluctant to concede. They would accordingly prefer the more docile British, whose *amour propre* would, in any case, be pained if they lost the post of second fiddle.

Failing some major and unforeseeable change in political attitudes, we must thus expect recurrent demands for the overseas deployment of British warships, in the general Western interest but outside the NATO area. Whether or not it seems politically advantageous to comply, it will never be possible to do so without further reducing an already inadequate strength in home waters. In principle this is an argument for a larger navy, but it is hard to dissent from David Greenwood's judgment of the outlook of the most defence-minded government Britain can expect in the foreseeable future:

> provision for 'non-NATO commitments' is nominal in terms of manpower and money . . . it is clear that whatever extra-European dispositions the United Kingdom makes in future will be limited and will draw on force components which have their place in the programme for other reasons.[17]

This is not a satisfactory basis on which to envisage an active rôle for the Royal Navy outside the NATO area. If this rôle is needed, as some of Britain's Allies seem to think, they will have to play their part in reducing the risks to the home base of remoter deployments, risks that could even be significant to themselves, quite apart from their influence on British decisions. Unfortunately all the options are difficult: transferring this rôle to the French; enlarging the German Navy to the point at which it could deploy a substantial force in the North Sea; relieving

Britain of her continental commitment so that she could expand her navy and assume, with some degree of confidence, a dual responsibility. As it is, Britain's Allies are asking too much and, in naval terms, giving too little.

One of the more rational justifications for this curious British readiness to contemplate unreciprocated obligations to their Allies – the extra-European clients of the United States expect a stationed American fleet – is the British belief that they might need their back covered at home while pursuing national objectives overseas. This is valid – up to a point. If President Eisenhower, at a moment of maximum exasperation with Britain over Suez, could still react vigorously to Marshal Bulganin's threats of military intervention on 5 November 1956, future presidents are unlikely to leave unanswered any menace of similar magnitude. What is doubtful is whether the United States would assign extra warships to cover the British Isles, because part of the Royal Navy had been diverted to some dispute over the Falklands or Gibraltar. If the American president disapproved, as he might, of what Britain was doing, a degree of Soviet naval harassment, whether on the scene of distant operations or in home waters, might appear as a British problem that could usefully sharpen their sense of international realities.[18]

This is not an inevitable American reaction and it is as easy to invent cooperative scenarios as it is to devise those of internecine conflict. Support, however, cannot be taken for granted and the time to seek it, even on a conditional basis, may be when doing the Americans a favour. The North Atlantic Treaty, as its signatories have been severally and repeatedly pained to discover, has no clause about 'my ally, right or wrong'. It is a function of diplomacy (and one sadly neglected by the British, obsessed by their slogan of 'on its merits') to ensure that every extended 'quo' attracts at least the promise of a 'quid'.

Precautions are needed to preserve the possibility of naval intervention in support of national interests, because this practice is neither reliably avoidable nor assured of Allied sympathy. It is wrong to regard it as the result of deliberate British choice. Since 1945, for instance, Britain has been the victim (not the first to use or threaten limited naval force) in one third of the incidents in which she has been involved. Of the remainder, in which she did take the naval initiative, many could be considered, even by third parties, as featuring Britain in a politically responsive rôle. A British decision to renounce limited naval force as an instrument of policy would not, of itself, end the practice. It might not even attract enough imitators to relieve the Royal Navy of their responsibility for defensive measures in time of nominal peace. Indeed, one of the new trends of gunboat diplomacy that emerged during the seventies was Britain's growing international prominence as a victim: a natural rôle for a country whose naval strength has declined more rapidly than her overseas interests.

A second common misconception concerns the part played by the Soviet Union. Only two incidents since 1945 have involved Britain with the Soviet Union, both indirectly and by no more than implication. Admittedly the Red Fleet have manifested a flattering interest in the manoeuvres of the Royal Navy. On one occasion this interest, in the opinion of American commentators, may have had a political motive.

> about ten Soviet ships and an equal number of submarines exercised in Icelandic waters in May 1973, in the midst of the 'cod war' between Britain and Iceland . . . Moscow probably intended the exercises to signal Iceland that it did not have to face Britain alone and to show Britain that it might have to contend with a super-power.[19]

Whether or not this interpretation of Soviet intentions is correct, it was not so perceived in London at the time. British experience of gunboat diplomacy has so far been one of conflicts that may impinge on the central balance of power, but do not directly derive from it. Those involved have more often been allies or neutrals than enemies. For Britain, the exercise of limited naval force has not been an anti-Soviet activity. Even outside the Treaty Area this may prove less true in future, as Soviet warships extend their invigilation of Western naval movements, but in the past it has acted, and may continue to act, as a disincentive to American support. In Washington actions unrelated to the Soviet Union are easily regarded as frivolous. In other Allied capitals there is a general absence of enthusiasm for any activities not directly conducive to European tranquillity.

Such activities are unfortunately conceivable. British freedom of choice is constrained by too many obligations, interests and potential sources of conflict beyond the seas. Anguilla, Belize, Cyprus, Diego Garcia, Eire, Falklands, Gibraltar, Hong Kong: it would not be difficult to exhaust the alphabet or to devise scenarios in which problems arose that warships could help to solve. There has, of course, been a considerable contraction in British overseas responsibilities and scope exists for its continuation. Many years, however, must elapse before Britain attains a comfortably insular outlook and finally pays off the death duties of her imperial past.

Even then, as long as seaborne imports remain a condition of British survival, there will be an occasional need for warships to protect them and the maritime trade they generate. The relevant menace is not that of general war or the unlikely bogey of global interdiction in time of peace. No foreseeable Royal Navy could meet such threats. But warships could help to counter the side-effects of local wars: break a blockade, escort merchantmen, rescue British subjects. They could provide the appropriate response to an unfriendly threat or use of limited naval force. They could offer an effective deterrent to, or defence against, seaborne terrorism or piracy. This ancient practice is now enjoying a revival in the congenial environment of international rivalry, particularly in those seas that wash the shores of South East Asia. Pirates are no longer *hostes humani generis* but, as long as they only prey on others, potential instruments of political purposes.

Political purposes: that phrase sets the bounds for British naval activity on the fringes of Alliance. In any particular encounter, of course, the prospects of success are crucial. The oceans are not a suitable theatre for sacrifice, which, if it must be incurred at all, should be reserved for the Narrow Seas. Too great an oceanic commitment would be undesirable, because Britain would then be increasing her vulnerability nearer home, both navally and politically, by serving purposes that might not be those best suited to her own survival. The absence of any capability at all might, paradoxically, have similar effects, by forcing Britain to depend, in small issues as in great, on American goodwill. The ideal course would be to maximise British naval strength and to minimise her obligations to employ it. Considerable advance is possible in both directions without any risk of creating surplus capacity. In the real world neither objective is attainable, but it will continue to be true that:

The opportune presence of a British ship of war may avert a disaster which can only be remedied later at much inconvenience and considerable sacrifice.[20]

10 If Alliance Fails

> Every treaty has the significance only of a constatation of a
> definite position in European affairs. The reserve rebus sic
> stantibus is always silently understood.
>
> Bismarck[1]

There are three ways in which the Alliance could fail Britain: by defeat,
by disintegration or by major divergence.

A major war in Europe would be a defeat irrespective of the outcome,
for the purpose of NATO has been to prevent war rather than to win it.
Some kinds of defeat might, however, be survivable. Total nuclear war,
to which any major war might escalate, is naturally not among them.
That would be a final defeat for Britain, to whom it would be irrelevant
which Super-Power secured nominal victory.

Limited nuclear war might, in certain circumstances, offer Britain a
chance of survival, but in a new and harsher world. That, too, would be a
defeat and Britain's ability to recover from it would depend on
unpredictable factors: how the nuclear exchange ended; the extent of the
damage, whether nuclear or conventional, to the British Isles; fall-out
from the European mainland; the probably traumatic political repercussions at home and abroad. The survival of NATO in its present form
seems most improbable and rather optimistic assumptions are needed to
support the idea that Britain might still be able and willing to maintain
her independence, whether as the Atlantic bridgehead of a rump
Alliance or in neutralist isolation. At best the situation might not differ
greatly from some of the other contingencies to be considered in this
chapter; at worst it could be beyond present imagination or useful naval
planning. The unpredictable consequences of limited nuclear war will
not, therefore, receive separate treatment, but their milder variants
should be borne in mind as extreme cases of lesser reverses.

These all presuppose a double failure by NATO: the outbreak of conventional war in Europe followed by defeat. Neither is inevitable, but even in combination they are conceivable and could face Britain with the need to maintain her independence either in continuing conventional war or in a state of more than usually nominal and precarious peace. This is naturally not a probable contingency. It does not seem particularly likely that either Super-Power would accept defeat in conventional war without resorting to the use of nuclear weapons, unless both recognised each other's political objectives as limited. The difficulty of achieving such recognition would naturally increase with the geographical extension of the conflict, with its duration and with the intensity of any fighting between the conventional forces of the Super-Powers themselves. Conventional war is hardest to imagine as global and protracted (the oceanic war on trade, for instance): easiest as a localised campaign that culminates in an offer of terms before the exchange of nuclear threats has reached actual explosion.

Nevertheless conventional war is worth considering, because even an initial defeat for NATO would leave Britain with more options than nuclear war, which offers only the single chance of excluding the British Isles from the nuclear battlefield of a territorially limited war. One of these options has already been discussed: maintaining Britain, with American support, as an island of resistance in protracted conventional war after much of Western Europe had been overrun by Soviet armies. This is not an option which would necessarily be adopted.

If it were, the scenario would be discouraging, but not hopeless, and it is talked about, discreetly of course, in the United States. There is no point in analysing all the possible permutations of such a disaster – Soviet objectives, the limits of their advance, the extent of continuing resistance on the mainland. Three factors are obvious: the British losses to be expected in the initial fighting would leave the air and ground defence of the British Isles heavily dependent on American help; the Royal Navy would be needed, as previously argued, to ensure that this help could be maintained; naval efforts would be the principal British contribution to continuing war, apart from the provision of their territory as an advanced American base, and thus a major constituent of any British claim to some say in the political and strategic direction of that war.

In naval terms this is essentially a different, possibly more plausible scenario for the conventionally accepted task of protecting, in the Eastern Atlantic, seaborne reinforcement and resupply. British ports would be more vulnerable if the Low Countries had fallen and possession of Norwegian airfields and harbours would significantly augment the Soviet challenge both to barrier operations in the Greenland–Iceland–United Kingdom Gap and to those in the Eastern Atlantic. The western ports of the British Isles, the Biscayan ports of France and those of the Iberian peninsula might be the only practicable destinations for transatlantic ships. Provided some American carriers were available, protection of this use of the sea would still be a useful, albeit difficult, task for the Navy in – not the worst case, for that is nuclear war – but in the next worst contingency for the Alliance as a whole.

Other forms of defeat – and most of Britain's wars have begun with them – might be more limited, yet create naval and political problems of greater complexity. The northern flank of NATO has already been considered, but a Soviet invasion of Turkey or Greece would present a painful dilemma. The obligations of Alliance, to say nothing of existing contingency plans, might seem to call for the despatch of disposable British forces to the southern flank, but the national interest would probably be better served by a precautionary reinforcement of Norway. Not only is that the crucial sector, but it is the one where the timely deployment of relatively small forces might make a significant difference to the outcome. British involvement in the Eastern Mediterranean, on the other hand, could only weaken the direct defence of the British Isles without, in all probability, achieving anything of importance to the Alliance.

Any Soviet offensive in Europe would mean that NATO had already lost its principal raison d'être: the deterrence of war. In the new situation thus created, Britain would have to reassess what the Alliance could still contribute to British survival. That would be a major political decision of grand strategy. It would inevitably be influenced by the actual circumstances at the time and by the apparent intentions of both allies and enemies. It ought not to be left to foreign NATO commanders or determined merely by staff plans devised to strengthen Allied solidarity in time of peace. Exercise ANVIL EXPRESS 1980, which deployed 3000 Allied troops to Turkish Thrace, served that purpose well, but would be of questionable value to Britain as a response to a Soviet offensive against the southern flank.[2] That would be an occasion for strict application of Article 5 of the North Atlantic Treaty:

> The Parties agree . . . that, if such an armed attack occurs, each of them . . . will assist the Party or Parties so attacked by taking forthwith, individually and in concert with the other Parties, *such action as it deems necessary*, including the use of armed force, to

restore and maintain the security of *the North Atlantic area* [my italics].[3]

This is especially relevant for the Navy, which is not anchored in Germany, or anywhere else.

It goes without saying that Britain would not be the only member of the Alliance with reason to rethink her policy in the event of a localised or limited Soviet offensive. The United States would have to decide whether or not to use or threaten the use of nuclear weapons. European members would have to choose between strengthening their own defences and attempting reinforcement of the Ally attacked. Even the attitude of the victim is not, in every case, entirely predictable. Some of the other members might even be tempted, depending on where and how hostilities began, to adopt a neutral or non-belligerent posture. The mutual loyalty between the northern and southern wings of the Alliance is less than fanatical.

The likelihood of an uncertain and divergent Allied response would be increased if the Soviet Union accompanied their offensive by a statement of limited political objectives and were able to bring a local campaign to a swift and successful conclusion. Resistance to Soviet armies still advancing on a broad front would be one thing. Counter-attacking a Soviet Union that had halted its localised incursion and even offered to withdraw in return for concessions might be quite another.

None of these contingencies is inevitable. They are not even suggested as particularly probable, but no amount of military planning or integrated command structures will ever remove the possibility of an unexpected political response when crisis strikes somebody else. Moreover, it has throughout been assumed that Soviet military initiatives in Europe are most likely, perhaps even only likely, when the Alliance is already in some disarray. If this disunity is confirmed, even accentuated, by the nature of the Allied response, the consequences could be profound.

Most Europeans, including the British, would probably not want the United States to react to a limited Soviet offensive by starting a nuclear war. Nevertheless, if such an offensive could not be successfully countered either conventionally or by threats of escalation, there would be considerable disillusionment with the whole concept of NATO. The Alliance is both a bluff and a paradox. If the bluff is called, a full response would be catastrophic to all concerned. Everybody would prefer a lesser response, but, if that fails, the bluff will no longer hold. Peace at the price of minor concessions might well be the attainable and desirable solution, but it would leave the Alliance bedraggled. Some members could certainly be expected to seek alternative solutions to their security problems and, casting their glances around Europe, could find examples ranging from France to Finland.

These are risks which suggest two special functions for the Royal Navy. The first, when circumstances permit this to be done without detriment to the defence of the British Isles, is to offer a more acceptable, perhaps even a more convincing response than threats of nuclear escalation. Norway is an example already argued in more than one mode. The second, which will be further considered, is to provide Britain with an extra card to play if Alliance solidarity, and thus the effectiveness of the NATO bluff, is seriously impaired.

This unfortunate situation could have other causes than defeat and might as easily develop in the absence of Soviet belligerence in Europe as because of it. Indeed, Moscow and East Berlin are probably the only capitals where the persistence of Soviet hostility is not recognised as the necessary cement of NATO. After more than thirty years there is little risk of a Russian leader reading Aesop's *Fables* and concluding that sustained sunshine might tempt Western travellers to remove their cloak, but the possibility exists.

It should not be exaggerated. There does, admittedly, survive in Western Europe a persistent optimism about the prospects for change in Soviet policy; a recurrent tendency to imagine that change is already occurring; and an underlying readiness to respond to change. The long-standing Soviet proposal to abolish both NATO and the Warsaw Pact still attracts surprising sympathy – not least from the British Labour party – in spite of the one-sided advantage it would confer on the Soviet Union. Politically, Western Europe often seems as vulnerable to a Soviet 'peace offensive' as, militarily, it is to armed attack. It would be easy to regard the ingrained caution of the Soviet leaders as offering the most assured defence against either.

It would be easy, but it would also be misleading. European eagerness to draw optimistic conclusions from Moscow's occasional intimations of benevolence exercises more influence on popular sentiment than it does on official decisions. Most Western leaders and their advisers have been fairly cautious themselves. It would take a Soviet concession of considerable substance to impress them. This is just the kind of unilateral move which, for understandable reasons of domestic and imperial policy, the Soviet leaders would find peculiarly difficult. Collectively, NATO may never manage to match the Soviet military threat, but the Alliance has so far proved remarkably resistant to Soviet blandishment. The era of détente, for instance, offered repeated opportunities for imaginative ventures by particular Allies. These annoyed the less enterprising, but nothing of importance was conceded – or achieved. Whenever they were united, which was surprisingly often, members of NATO proved as grudgingly conservative as any Russian.

The danger is that NATO might not remain united. The risk is twofold: divergent national interests and ideological disaffection. On the first count the last decade has already seen threats, and sometimes action, to cut American, Canadian and other troops in Germany; to reduce British contributions; to eliminate bases in Greece, Iceland and Turkey; to withdraw Greece from NATO; to refuse nuclear weapons in a number of countries; to deny arms or facilities to Allies. On the second, there is growing opposition to preparations for the use of nuclear weapons and a certain reluctance, which may or may not be increasing, to accept the basic concepts of Soviet hostility and Western solidarity.

Both strains on the unity of the Alliance are exacerbated by an underlying conflict between American and European attitudes: between priority for the global struggle and the idea of peace in one continent; between theatre nuclear war and *aut Armageddon aut nihil*; between the notion that he who pays the piper should call the tune and the belief that influence should be proportional to risk. There is even an atavistic faith, scarcely justified by the historical record, in the superior political wisdom and diplomatic ability of Europeans, a group seldom defined with agreed precision.

In more practical terms, there are potential political combinations in Belgium, Britain, Denmark, Greece, Iceland, Italy, Portugal and Turkey that could significantly reduce the commitments and contributions of those countries to NATO. If that happened, it could, in some cases, also have repercussions on the attitude of the remaining members. Neither the causes nor the effects are inevitable. The Alliance has survived a great deal: the partial disengagement of France; revolutions in several member states; conflicts between them; communist participation in some governments.

Nevertheless, if Mr Benn or someone of similar persuasion became British Prime Minister, the impact could be considerable. British demands for the withdrawal of American nuclear weapons would find a ready echo in other countries, but would be much resented in the United States. Serious reductions in defence expenditure, an option more widely favoured in the British Labour party, would call in question not merely the size of the British contribution to NATO, but its structure.

With relations further bedevilled by simultaneous British disengagement from the Community, the prospects for a smooth adjustment of NATO strategy and of the nature of British participation would be poor. Mutual recrimination could easily encourage neutralist tendencies in the Labour party and alienate Britain from the Alliance.[4]

This is an extreme and perhaps an unlikely case, but the protracted European consensus of support for the Alliance is everywhere exposed to the workings of a political dissent that is becoming more contagious. This is only incidentally concerned with strategy or international relations, although opposition to nuclear weapons and a degree of hostility towards the United States are significant elements. What actually happens will largely be determined by economic, social and political developments within the various countries of Europe. Some of these may be as irrelevant to any argument advanced in this book as the peculiar sequence of parochial events in 1981 that diminished the likelihood of a Bennite air-burst over Brussels.[5] NATO attracts dissent less in its own right than as a feature of the established order. Both may well survive, but both must expect to be on the defensive and, if it ever seems too difficult to protect a double position, the supporters of the established order will know which to sacrifice. NATO is far from doomed, but its internal vulnerability demands some contingency planning, not least from its British enemies – and friends.

Disintegration is perhaps a less immediate danger than divergence. The first is the foreseeable consequence of conceivable change. The second is the predictable result of failure to correct existing trends. Some of these have already been indicated: Europeans are concerned with their own continent, Americans with the world. The Korean War and the Cuban Missile Crisis were partial exceptions to the rule that extra-European conflicts tend to divide the Alliance, but the rule would probably apply to American intervention in Latin America, Africa or even the Middle East. Much the same can, as indicated in the previous chapter, be said of some conceivable British interventions. Nor is the Treaty Area itself immune: Suez, Algeria, Israel (1967 and 1973), Cyprus, Iceland (1958–9 and 1972–6) were all productive of inter-Allied friction and no amount of oil would lubricate some of the rough edges still remaining in the Mediterranean – rather the reverse. A still worse case, for Britain, might be the coincidence of major trouble in Ulster with the installation of another Irish Catholic in the White House. Patrolling for gun-runners would no longer be such an unobtrusive operation for the Royal Navy.

A deeper, if less headline-catching, source of divergence is the running debate over NATO strategy. This has never been – and can never be – primarily technical, always more a matter of reconciling conflicting political requirements, of which process both forward defence and flexible response are outstanding examples. The present compromise is out-of-date, militarily unsound and politically unstable, but the obstacles to agreement on any alternative are daunting. Even such apparently technical expedients as standardisation, specialisation, interoperability, common procurement, pre-stocking are constantly exposed to political objections, many of them soundly based on valid conceptions of national interest. Some of these, of course, are less fundamental: the petty mines, for instance, that sank the Anglo-Dutch frigate.[6] Perhaps the two most obvious, even inevitable, sources of future divergence are nuclear policy and the nature of the British contribution to NATO. Both are liable to engage sections of public opinion otherwise uninterested in military affairs.

The nuclear dilemma has existed for at least twenty years: how to make the American deterrent credible to the Europeans without so terrifying both them and the Americans that it ceases to be credible to the Russians. That dilemma made an early contribution both to France's partial disengagement from NATO and to the maintenance of British and French nuclear forces. It also fuelled political dissent throughout Western Europe. Recent attempts to resolve this dilemma through the concept of theatre nuclear weapons have been, and predictably will be, counter-productive. Those discerning no option worse than nuclear war will reject them, because they appear to make this disaster more likely. Others will object, as did the French Prime Minister, because they reduce – at least in European eyes – the efficacy of the threat.

> L'Europe peut très bien n'être, pour les Etats Unis, qu'un barreau de l'échelle de la violence et non l'une des fins suprêmes de leur défense. Eventualité inacceptable pour des Français.

Those words will find wider echoes in Europe, and in France, than his next sentence, however persuasive it may appear.

> Eventualité qui devrait faire réfléchir les Européens à la perspective d'un ensemble politique disposant d'une défense autonome.[7]

Nuclear policy can be expected to divide the Europeans among themselves as well as from the United States. The British contribution to

NATO is a source of dispute of which the origins are essentially parochial, but which could nevertheless have wide-ranging repercussions. Only the British – and by no means all of them – see any need for change: the rest of the Alliance are broadly content with things as they are, at most wishing for more and better of the same.

The problem is simple and has already been adequately discussed. It can be stated as a prediction: any future British government can be expected to seek economies in defence expenditure. The extent of the cuts, their motive and their distribution will depend on the composition of the government concerned, but there is probably no party or coalition that would not at least consider reducing the continental commitment. The Conservatives did in 1981, even if they then rejected the idea, and might do so again if the cost of Trident escalates as expected. Not only does the continental commitment account for 41 per cent of the defence budget,[8] but its unpopularity springs from a chauvinism that cuts across party lines. It is a focus for the belief that Britain is contributing more than her fair share; bearing a burden that rightfully belongs to richer Germans; losing her independence; needlessly exposing herself to danger. These are not very generous sentiments, but they are more attuned to the late-twentieth-century public mood than the counter-arguments: the need to retain European goodwill; the uncertainty of Allied replacements for any British forces withdrawn; the dangers of weakening Allied solidarity in Soviet eyes.

It was significant that Mr Callaghan, a defence-minded politician of experience and responsibility, but with a shrewd eye for the commanding heights of the middle ground, should have publicly advocated halving the British Army of the Rhine.[9] A future government might well prefer to scrap TRIDENT, but, as already argued, this would not bring the immediate savings they will probably want. It was under a right-wing Conservative administration that a Committee of the House of Commons concluded:

> if the money earmarked for the purchase of the TRIDENT system was not devoted to that purpose, there could be no guarantee that it would be available to be spent on other *defence* projects.[10]

No great leftward shift need be assumed to justify an amendment of the concluding phrase: 'no guarantee that this would be the only cut in defence spending'.

This is not the moment to consider the strategic arguments – predictably popular among naval officers – for reducing Britain's continental commitment. These will not decide the issue. Warranted or not, it is a likely threat to the existing pattern of Alliance solidarity. It could be survived – Allied reactions to French disengagement in 1966 offer an encouraging precedent which Britain's Allies are now materially better equipped to follow. Politically it could precipitate a generally damaging chain-reaction. It is rather more likely to leave NATO intact, but less credible, both politically and militarily, to the Soviet Union. It is most likely to diminish any readiness that may now exist among Britain's Allies to assist her in matters not directly involving their own vital interests.

Alliance solidarity is menaced, not by those bogies of American professors, 'Finlandisation' or 'Hollanditis',[11] but by the old-fashioned diseases of all alliances: conflicting national interests and divergent political developments. It should be no surprise, even in a chapter entitled 'If Alliance Fails', to discover that some of the germs are British. Their origin increases their virulence and the need for British precautions.

For naval purposes it does not greatly matter whether the Alliance has been defeated, has come apart in Britain's hands or has been deserted by Britain; whether the national purpose is to pursue an existing policy with less help or to embark on a new one with next to none. Whatever the causes, the results will be similar: greater vulnerability to threats that must be met with less resources. Unfortunately this prediction depends on two variables, each covering a considerable spectrum: the nature of the threat and the state of the Alliance. A non-Soviet threat against Britain alone might attract negligible Allied support even today: for instance, against the Falkland Isles. On the other hand, an Alliance that had successfully adapted itself to partial British disengagement might offer an unimpaired deterrent to, or defence against, a general Soviet assault on Western Europe. Darker scenarios might suggest another Suez as the by-product of alienating Allies or another 1940 as the result of Alliance defeat or disintegration. The consequences of a failure of Alliance are as unpredictable as its causes. The critical risk for Britain, however, would be isolated exposure to a Soviet threat: whether of coercive diplomacy while Britain was conducting an unsupported defence of Gibraltar or of invasion while the remnants of Alliance conventional forces were holding the Pyrenees.

Neither contingency, one hopes, is at all probable, but some degree of isolated exposure does seem a likely consequence of any failure of Alliance. As British decisions may not suffice to prevent failure, there is a case for a measure of insurance.

So what could the Navy do to provide it? Their first contribution should be the maintenance of their submarine launched ballistic missiles. However Alliance fails, one result seems obvious: diminished Soviet expectation that attacking the British Isles would lead to American nuclear retaliation against Soviet territory. This does not mean that there would necessarily be a greater incentive to launch such an attack. Some forms of Alliance failure, particularly those resulting from British disengagement, might even make Britain a less important objective, both politically and militarily, for the Soviet Union. But, insofar as there was still a threat to be deterred, more of the burden would fall on the Royal Navy. The cessation of American support would naturally make it difficult to maintain technical credibility, but, if this could be achieved, the political problems would actually be eased by the attainment of a British monopoly of nuclear weapons in the British Isles.

Whatever the circumstances, of course, it would still be a limited deterrent. It is often argued, for instance, that a British government would not dare respond to a crippling, but limited, attack for fear of provoking obliteration by a second salvo. After the failure of Alliance that objection might seem even more daunting in London. In the Kremlin, however, the reasoning could still appear hazardous. Who could be sure what the handful of Britons concerned, all under emotional stress, would deduce from the inevitably inadequate information at their disposal? Would they even recognise that the attack had been limited? Would control be retained, and by whom? The Soviet leaders might hope that limiting the scale of their attack would reduce the risk to Moscow: they could scarcely expect to eliminate it.

A nuclear attack resembles an assassination: always possible to those prepared to run sufficient risk. All the Royal Navy can do is to ensure that the hazards are high.

Conventional attacks, as already indicated, are another matter. At any foreseeable level, these would not be instantaneous in their impact. They would leave open the hope that defence would ultimately prevail, that reinforcements would arrive, that resistance could be prolonged until counter-attack became possible. A necessarily suicidal nuclear attack on Moscow would not be a credible response to conventional bombing, to interdiction of seaborne trade, even to invasion. In such circumstances any British government would be expected, in Moscow, to wait for the last gasp before playing the death card. Threats might be made, but it is doubtful whether they would be believed. Spasm is a less plausible response to attrition, however dangerous, than it is to sudden and overwhelming devastation.

Conventional attack, therefore, would at least initially have to be met by conventional means. The defence of seaborne trade has already been discussed and aerial bombing (even conventionally tipped missiles from across the Straits of Dover) would not be the responsibility of the Navy, even though either might prove the misfortune of inadequately defended ships. Invasion is a more controversial problem.

Except for some months in 1940 this is a contingency which has traditionally preoccupied Britain's military leadership only when it was least likely, before and during the First World War, for instance.[12] In 1939 it was not seriously considered by anyone except Admiral Raeder, who ordered a preliminary study as early as 15 November.[13] It is a little disconcerting, therefore, to discover that neither the Army nor the Navy now regard invasion as deserving even a contingency plan. It has not featured in any of the numerous naval exercises, some of them apparently based on scenarios of equal extravagance, during the last few years. This neglect is based on two rather different arguments: the soldiers expect war to begin in Germany, to develop rapidly to negotiation or nuclear exchange and to be short. Naval forecasts are vaguer, but envisage protracted maritime conflict as the alternative to an abrupt nuclear decision. Neither regard the Russians as able, or inclined, to invade the British Isles. They may be right. Between the apocalyptic scenario, in which there is no need to conquer what can so easily be destroyed, and the optimistic, in which Soviet inability to mount an Operation Overlord against an island bristling with American reinforcements removes all cause for apprehension, there is little middle ground to warrant any preparations. There may nevertheless be some. The Germans finally decided against the invasion they had contemplated in 1940 because, apart from their other preoccupations, they had no hope of superiority at sea and had failed to achieve it in the air. One can imagine circumstances in which the Russians might be more fortunate.

Very much, of course, must go wrong for Britain, both politically and militarily, before the Soviet Union can seriously contemplate conquest by invasion. There is a strong temptation to echo Captain Liddell Hart, who declared, for once in tune with official thought, in July 1939: 'England . . . is . . . more secure than ever before against invasion.'[14] Nevertheless it is disquieting that Britain should be so dependent on her Allies for defence against a threat which may be unlikely, but which would also be fundamental. In previous wars the ability of the Royal Navy to prevent invasion was always regarded as a necessary condition for sending troops abroad and, in 1940, when everything did go wrong for Britain, the Royal Navy and the Royal Air Force successfully met an unforeseen challenge.

It is doubtful whether they could repeat that performance now. If the opposite shores of the North Sea, to say nothing of the English Channel, were in enemy hands, the Royal Navy could not be sure of defeating a Soviet amphibious force without more air cover than a Royal Air Force depleted by losses in Germany might be able to provide. The problem of detection, which so exercised past strategists, is less difficult today. If the NATO bluff succeeds, of course, none of these perils will ever arise. If failure leads to nuclear war, invasion will be the least of our worries. In other circumstances Britain will still need help to provide an effective back-stop: not much of the Army may remain in the British Isles.

It may be unreasonable to expect that British defence policy should, at present, make express provision for the worst conventional case: resisting a major invasion with minimum Allied help. The converse argument is stronger. Nothing should be done now, by way of reducing or transforming the Navy, which would rule out the possibility of preparations for that task, should altered circumstances later make this more obviously desirable. The threat of invasion, after all, could take several forms and have more than one purpose. If the Central Front had collapsed, a large raid might seem a sufficiently alarming prospect, if there were no Navy to tackle it at sea, to influence political decisions. The loss of the Shetlands would do more military damage than that of the Channel Islands in 1940 and might be a particularly effective instrument of coercive diplomacy against a neutralist Britain. Amphibious operations do not have to attempt total conquest to exert their impact and, the smaller their scale, the easier they would be to launch.

The value of the Navy would not be confined to its ability to meet and, if possible, deter such limited attacks – the most likely variety. Even in the worst of situations a fleet in being can raise the price of an enemy offensive and, in some cases, increase, perhaps create, the inclination of allies to render assistance. The risk that the Royal Navy, if supported only by a depleted Royal Air Force, could not resist a maximum Soviet effort by air and sea should not be allowed to obscure their real utility even in so desperate an emergency. Mahan's favourite quotation from Nelson (it appears in various forms) is still relevant:

> by the time they have beaten me soundly, they will do England no more harm this year.[15]

In the more conditional wording appropriate to the late twentieth century, one thing the Royal Navy can do is to make the price of their destruction so high that a prudent Soviet admiral, conscious that he has still to encounter the United States Navy, will not attempt it.

In lesser contingencies the concept of raising the ante is equally applicable and often more hopeful. There is no need to rehearse all the ways, many of them touched on already, in which Britain might be attacked in war or threatened in peace. Few countries have more maritime pressure points and most of these would become more vulnerable if Alliance failed. At the red end of the spectrum General Whiteley has pointed out that 'within the range of Soviet-based air cover . . . amphibious operations are possible against . . . the Shetlands'.[16] If Norway had been lost, of course, the possibility would be even more obvious: Bergen is no further from the islands than the Royal Air Force base at Lossiemouth. At a much lower level Soviet warships might escort a fishing fleet defying restrictions in Britain's 200 mile zone. The existence of Alliance and the credibility of the NATO bluff have hitherto provided Britain with a political shield against limited war and coercive diplomacy. If that shield were ever to be lost, in whole or in part, the first response to a threat could no longer be a communiqué from Brussels or a statement from the White House. British words, which have long ceased to carry intrinsic conviction, would have to be backed by the movement of British warships.

This would be considerably less impressive than the deployment, in 1904, of the Channel Fleet in ominous escort of the erring Admiral Rozhestvensky,[17] but the Royal Navy could at least unmistakeably raise the stakes without necessarily precipitating a showdown – or being sure of victory if one occurred.

By one of history's frequent ironies, the rôle of the Royal Navy, at least in the special circumstances envisaged in this chapter, has come to resemble that devised for his own use by their most dangerous, because ultimately most destructive, enemy, Gross Admiral von Tirpitz: that of the Risikflotte.

The essence of that theory [the 'risk theory' put forward by Tirpitz in 1900] was that as the German Navy could not be made strong enough for a reasonable chance of victory against every opponent, it should be made so strong that its destruction would cost even the strongest sea power such heavy losses, endangering its supremacy vis à vis third navies, that the mere thought of that risk would act as a deterrent against attack. In other words, unable to provide the objects to be protected – the German oversea communications and interests – with an adequate *direct* military protection against the overwhelming sea power of Great Britain, Tirpitz fell back upon the idea of safeguarding them *indirectly* by developing the German Navy into a 'risk factor' which, so he hoped, would prevent the war politically, which he could not hope to win *militarily*.[18]

That deterrent did not work, primarily because neither the strength of the German Navy nor the character of German policy was perceived by the adversary as essentially defensive. This would be less of a problem for Britain. Nevertheless, in the altered world of the late twentieth century, it is not suggested that the Royal Navy could either deter war or, in most circumstances, fight it successfully. But, if Alliance fails, the Royal Navy could be so employed as to create, for the Northern Fleet, a risk that would provide a useful deterrent, perhaps even an effective counter, to certain classes of operation and of threat. More cannot, in the present decayed state of the nation, be demanded.

11 Doing Without a Navy

> If you open that Pandora's Box you never know what Trojan 'orses will jump out.
>
> Ernest Bevin[1]

The master question of this book has so far received an equivocating answer. What the Navy could do depends on the circumstances in which they are required to do it. There is no scenario today as simple and straightforward as that which seemed so obvious in 1914: battle with the High Seas Fleet. Different kinds of war could impose very various demands. Of them all only the task of nuclear deterrence offers the Royal Navy, in the special conditions that might make it relevant, some prospect of unaided success. The remainder depend on support from the Royal Air Force, sometimes from the Army as well; often on the cooperation of allies; nearly always on the inability or disinclination of the enemy to apply his maximum strength. Many assumptions, none of them certain, are needed to support any prediction of a significant contribution by the Royal Navy to meaningful victory. There are several plausible scenarios in which the Navy could not hope to prevent defeat and, in some conceptions of the short war, the Navy might not even be needed.

Similar doubts, of course, could be formulated about the wartime rôle of Britain's other armed forces but, as already explained, the continental commitment gives them a protective screen against their critics.

Lesser conflicts and the exigencies of violent peace admittedly offer more scope for those functions which warships are particularly fitted to discharge, but such contingencies are highly scenario-dependent. They lack the actuality of Ulster. In war and peace alike the threats which the Navy might encounter, no less than the action required to meet them, are necessarily conjectural. This is not for want of precedent – even in the last thirty-five years the Royal Navy have found much employment[2] – but for lack of any conspicuous exploit which the image-makers could label as successful, significant and contemporary. Suez was significant, but scarcely a success; the achievements of Confrontation with Indonesia belong to a forgotten era; irreverent youth remembers the Royal Navy for Anguilla and Iceland.

History being out of date and most personal memories unhelpful, the case for the Navy tends to rely rather heavily on hypothetical contingencies of an unwelcome character. Nobody cares for this kind of foresight, unless accompanied by the prescription of swift and painless remedies. Unfortunately all that is on offer is a typical insurance policy: limited cover and the small print bristling with exclusion clauses. The premium increases annually without abatement by any no-claim bonus and the declining sense of security enjoyed by the public rests ever more precariously on the classical syllogism of Tong So. This ancient Chinese 'averter of calamities' and legendary father of insurance was reproached, as often as Her Majesty's Government, for his real inability to provide his clients with immunity, for which they made him regular payments, from fire and the disasters of life.

To this narrow-minded taunt the really impartial would reply that, if *some* among those who sought Tong's aid might occasionally experience fire or fatal injury, *all* those who stubbornly refused to do so inevitably did.[3]

Scepticism concerning the value of Britain's naval insurance has many different causes and assumes various forms. Some need not be treated here.

Many experts, for instance, criticise the ships, the weapons, the electronic equipment, the entire matériel of the Royal Navy. On several points of important detail, some of which have already been mentioned in passing, they have a case. So have those who concentrate on tactics, who deplore, for instance, the apparent reluctance to accept the historically established validity of escorted convoys in preference to such dubious concepts as protected sea lanes or anti-submarine barriers. Exercise OCEAN SAFARI 81 appeared to support their arguments.[4]

Those who castigate the administration of the Navy can evoke the echoes of many centuries, but with modern advantages. Certainly the time nowadays taken to conceive, design, build and deploy not merely a new ship, but a new weapon or radar set, is surprising. HMS WARRIOR, the world's first iron-hulled, ocean-going iron-clad, needed only three years before she joined the fleet in October 1861. HMS DREADNOUGHT, equally revolutionary, completed an even shorter gestation in December 1906. The still-faster tempo of the Second World War (destroyers built in fifteen months) had the spur of necessity, but the ten year delays now customary do seem excessive. They are less apparent in the Soviet Union.

There are important respects in which the Royal Navy could be improved and proposals have often been aired for doing so without any major increase in expenditure. Even if all or any of these ideas could be shown to be both sound and feasible – a task which will not be attempted here – their adoption would not greatly alter the present argument. A more efficient British navy would still be subject to the constraints imposed by relative numbers, by dependence on allies, by an unpredictable strategic situation which others would determine. The chances of success in particular types of conflict might be improved, but there would be no general transformation of the naval scene. Nor would the class of critics now under consideration be appeased.

These are not the pacifists. Replacement of the Navy by a Greenpeace coastguard is not, to adapt a convenient phrase of Dan Smith's, on the political agenda at present. He himself favours, with some left-wing support, disengagement from NATO and believes that a policy of defensive deterrence 'centred on the ability to resist aggression rather than the ability to retaliate' would make 'an ocean-going navy' irrelevant.[5] Correlli Barnett, a distinguished military historian who starts from the same widely shared premise that Britain cannot indefinitely afford to maintain balanced forces on the present scale, reaches a similar conclusion through very different arguments.

> we again have to consider . . . what roles we could reduce or scrap with the least political and strategic damage to NATO . . . the least such damage would result from a drastic curtailing of the Royal Navy's high seas role . . . [in order to] give clear overriding priority to the land/air defence of Western Europe (in which that of the United Kingdom is now subsumed).[6]

In less extreme form both points of view (each including the renunciation of TRIDENT and, in some cases, of POLARIS as well) command the support of minorities enjoying some influence. Politically, of course, they differ considerably: the first regarding membership of NATO as aggravating Britain's exposure to the risk of war; the second pinning all hope of British security to maintenance of the NATO bluff. They may be contrasted with a third, more diffuse group of critics, whose various proposals are not so much intended to reduce the Navy as to transform its character: expanding the nuclear deterrent at the expense of conventional forces; replacing surface ships by greater numbers of submarines and aircraft; contracting the perimeter of naval operations; preferring many cheap, simple ships to fewer of the highest quality.

No serious proposal now current envisages doing without a navy altogether, but the ideas thus briefly cited would eliminate or reduce some of the naval rôles now accepted, whether in the interests of economy or in order to concentrate available resources on other strategic tasks. Table 2 offers a summary analysis intended to bring out the implications for naval strategy rather than to do full justice to ideas which even their authors have not always elaborated in much detail. The notion that TRIDENT might be sacrificed in order to maintain the rest of the Navy at no less than its present strength has not been included. It has already been adequately discussed.

TABLE 2 *Alternative Futures for the Navy*

	Proposal	Governing principle	Roles reduced or enlarged	Comments
1	Reduce high-seas rôle	Limited conventional defence of British Isles only and without Allied assistance	Everything would be excluded except countering threats within the 200 mile zone	No deterrent to any kind of nuclear threat, inability to resist distant blockade or, without increase in air force, invasion. No defence of overseas interests
2	Reduce high-seas rôle	Reinforce NATO bluff and rely on it	Presumably some capability would be retained to protect access to British ports and cross-Channel reinforcements. Otherwise as above	Complete dependence on USA for deterrence of nuclear threats and for most forms of defence in protracted war or against low-level threats overseas
3	Contracting perimeter	Economy in ships and men	Reduced contribution to Atlantic war or out-of-area operations. Enhancement in Western approaches	Implies a greater Allied contribution to NATO naval operations and less British ability to assist Norway or other Allies

TABLE 2 (*Contd.*)

Proposal	Governing principle	Roles reduced or enlarged	Comments
4 Eliminating surface ships	Assumption that submarines and aircraft can operate unaided	Presumably a glorified coastguard would be kept for fishery protection etc. but amphibious operations and resisting coercive diplomacy out	Even if the assumption is right, this is a policy for high intensity conflict only
5 Cheap, simple ships	High-intensity naval war is improbable and unrewarding	This would eliminate most chances of resisting any maximum Soviet naval effort. If numbers increased as much as quality declined, there would be more capability for most low-level conflicts	If it is certain that there exists no middle option between nuclear war and violent peace, this might be sensible, but the Navy would find second-class ships demoralising. Sometimes combined with renunciation of nuclear deterrent
6 Concentrating on the nuclear deterrent	Conventional war at sea improbable	Depending on how far it went, this policy would progressively erode capabilities for the more sophisticated forms of conventional conflict	Even if combined, as logically it should be, with no. 5, this would focus on the single contingency of territorially limited nuclear war as the only alternative to low-level conflict

Naturally each of these encapsulated ideas could be qualified, expanded or presented in a more attractive guise. It would be grossly unfair to assess their merits without the fuller treatment which others, one hopes, will accord them. Nevertheless, it may plausibly be suggested that two comments are likely to survive even an extended advocacy.

The first is that the general tendency, differing only in degree from one to another, of all these proposals is to narrow the range and flexibility of Britain's strategic options. There is no need to specify the particular threats which could no longer be met in each of the six cases considered above. These should be obvious to readers who have followed the earlier argument and who may well be surfeited by conjecture. Moreover, it would be a tedious process to balance existing chances, in favourable circumstances only, of meeting some hypothetical threat – to the Falkland Islands, for instance – against the degree of hopelessness implied by the renunciation of an ocean-going navy or a decision to concentrate on the nuclear deterrent. A simpler test is the extent to which all these proposals, except no. 3, rest on rather narrow assumptions. Of course it is an established principle of gambling that betting on a single number, if it turns up, brings a greater reward than trying to spread one's money over every red possibility. Even in preparations for armed conflict, which so often assumes unexpected forms, the idea is not necessarily reprehensible. The case for choosing the threat to meet has already been argued, as have the insuperable obstacles to being strong enough for every threat. It is not the act of choosing that is open to question, but the nature of the choice.

Some of these proposals are the result of polarised thinking. Either deterrence focussed on the Central Front succeeds and peace is maintained or war is nuclear, total and short; either submarines and aircraft sink everything they can or there is no naval confrontation; either Britain threatens a nuclear strike or she leaves the seas for others to contest. Low-level threats, probing, coercive diplomacy, limited war and protracted war are not considered. It is all or nothing; the Soviet Union is Britain's only opponent; and flexible response can be confined to the Central Front.

Contracting the naval perimeter (which does not exclude support for American naval operations in the Eastern Atlantic) is less a change of strategy than an adjustment to predictably reduced resources, another slice off the existing salami. It might become inevitable in one form or another.

The two remaining proposals have interesting premises, but the acceptability of their consequences has yet to be demonstrated. The idea that British disengagement from NATO – which could happen, in greater or lesser degree, for more than one reason – might actually reduce certain kinds of threat to Britain is not wholly absurd. It merely requires a number of rather unreliable assumptions about the likely repercussions abroad. Even if these proved as favourable to Britain as they were to France – surely the most that could be expected – it is hard to see how Britain could preserve much sense of security without an ocean-going navy. This might not be needed, given a strong enough air force, for the deterrence of invasion, but the interdiction of Britain's seaborne trade is not an option that should be at the unfettered discretion of the Soviet Union or of any other, perhaps even a lesser naval power. If the objective is an independent foreign policy, not just a change of patron, then some of the savings on the continental commitment ought to be devoted to a stronger navy.

As for cheaper and simpler ships, these are obviously desirable and many ingenious proposals have been made for building them. Some progress ought to be possible in this direction, but it is a path to be followed with caution and with full awareness of the risks and penalties involved. Otherwise British naval officers might find themselves compelled to cultivate a Spanish irony.

It is well known that we fight in God's cause. So when we meet the English, God will surely arrange matters so that we can grapple and board them, either by sending some strange freak of the weather or, more likely, just by depriving the English of their wits . . . But unless God helps us by a miracle the English, who have faster and handier ships than ours, and many more long-range guns, and who know their advantage just as well as we do, will never close with us at all, but stand aloof and knock us to pieces with their culverins, without our being able to do them any serious harm.[7]

There are situations – a Norwegian scenario has already been suggested – in which superior ships can be outfaced.[8] Nor do simpler and cheaper ships, particularly if they can be deployed in larger numbers, have to be inferior even in combat. Missile-firing patrol craft can sometimes prove formidable opponents to larger and costlier warships. Unfortunately sophistication is often the necessary price of versatility. If economy in construction is to be pursued without requiring future British captains to sail 'in the confident hope of a miracle',[9] a very clear conception will be needed of the strategic rôle of their ships and of the tactics they and their enemies are expected to employ. This conception had also better be right.

In the Second World War simple ships, corvettes for instance, were successfully employed to defend convoys against submarines, themselves rather simple in those days. But different and more complex ships had to be used for other tasks. In a much smaller navy such multiplicity is not easily achieved. Of course simplification, unlike some proposals, is actually intended to arrest the shrinking of the Navy, but the effort would be counter-productive if the price had again to be a narrowing of strategic options.

Britain's Naval Future

This is a process – and the second major comment applies to existing trends as well as to the proposals outlined above – which exposes more than one flank. Concentrating one's capability on a limited range of conflicts may not only tempt an opponent to choose other varieties. It may also prove incompatible with altered political purposes at home. The contraction of naval tasks and resources could ultimately tend towards doing without a navy altogether.

This is not an immediate danger. Nobody of any influence in Britain now intends it or even seriously contemplates it. The risk seems too remote to warrant any analysis of the form it might take or of its consequences. Naval shrinkage, after all, has been going on for more than thirty-five years. Compensation, in the medical sense of adjustment and adaptation, has been good. So it could be to a ceremonial squadron and a coastguard fleet.

The risk remains. If the process continues – and some of the proposals mentioned would impart a sharp acceleration – it might reach a critical point. Water, after all, can undergo prolonged cooling without perceptible change until it suddenly turns to ice. There are, in most organisations, limits to contraction, whether of size or functions. Beyond these the muscles no longer support the limbs; the school cannot sustain a sixth form; the business ceases to justify its overheads; the battalion has to be broken up and its survivors distributed as reinforcements to other units. A gradual process may culminate in a sudden collapse.

An obvious catalyst, in the case of the Navy, could be the advent of a new government and their discovery that the Navy had become either too small, or else functionally too specialised, to serve an altered political purpose. Logically, for instance, a government bent on renunciation of nuclear weapons and disengagement from NATO should have more need of a navy, not less. But, if that navy had been run down after withdrawal from the Eastern Atlantic or been reshaped around the nuclear deterrent or contained only submarines or could only operate against submarines, it might not fit the new strategy. In such a situation – and this scenario is available in more than one colour – voices would not be lacking, nor would all of them belong to politicians, to suggest that resources could be better devoted to the army and air force than to refashioning a new navy. It is not only the enemy who may demand flexibility of response.

It is, of course, this flexibility, against different opponents, in high-intensity conflict or in low, in home waters or in distant seas, in war or in violent peace, that is both the justification for the Navy and the main source of loss to Britain's defence if the Navy were to disappear. Two important qualifications are nevertheless required to this claim.

The first is that flexibility is not a naval monopoly. Armies, particularly when transported and supplied by air, have given notable proofs of their ability to engage in combat at many levels and in very various circumstances. Air forces often find this more difficult. The United States, for instance, have made much use of land-based combat aircraft in the last thirty-five years, but nearly always at high levels of conflict. For coercive diplomacy they and others have usually preferred naval forces. Overseas intervention is a task for which enterprising airmen are prepared to compete, even if they still have a formidable hurdle to overcome:

> During the October 1973 Arab–Israeli war it took six tons of jet fuel to airlift every ton of cargo to Tel Aviv.[10]

The second qualification is that the inherent advantage in flexibility enjoyed by the Navy has been much eroded by the sacrifice of various capabilities – notably strike carriers and amphibious landing craft – and is further threatened, from within as well as from without. Specialisation in particular functions – anti-submarine warfare, for instance – tends to produce ships of diminished adaptability to other tasks. This is not a problem admitting of any easy solution, but it does demand a steadfast resistance to the seductions of the single scenario. The damage done by the concept of protecting the seaborne reinforcement of the Central Front has already been discussed, but the moral can be extended. If only one kind of threat exists, whatever that may be, counter-measures can probably be devised, whether or not they are actually the most efficacious, that do not require the use of the Navy. And the threat itself may be judged, by political fiat, no longer worthy of consideration: territorially limited nuclear war, for instance, or protracted conventional war.

The raison d'être of the Navy is to meet a range of risks at sea, preferably without escalation and, in some cases, probably. Naturally it is necessary to choose, in peacetime preparation and planning, those threats which seem plausible and susceptible of successful response. 'But something must be left to chance.'[11] If either the tasks or the capabilities of the Navy are too narrowly conceived, whether as the result of rigidity in strategic thought or in response to the exigencies of an ephemeral political combination, it might not be only the unforeseen confrontation at sea that decided the issue. The Naval Staff could do as much as political upheaval to bring on that distant, improbable, but not altogether inconceivable climax of British decline: doing without a navy.

12 Towards an Uncertain Horizon

> Every naval project which takes account neither of the foreign relations of a great nation, nor of the material limit fixed by its resources, rests upon a weak and unstable base. Foreign policy and strategy are bound together by an indestructible link.
>
> Darrieus

> Whoever writes on strategy and tactics ought not in his theories to neglect the point of view of his own people. He should give us a national strategy, a national tactics.
>
> Von der Goltz[1]

Eleven chapters have ranged widely in their efforts to give the central issue of Britain's naval future its necessary political, economic and strategic dimensions. Change has been allowed for, but only as a plausible modification of existing patterns and trends. Revolutionary transformation has not been considered, either in the nature and purposes of governments or in the resources and technology at their disposal. Even the future has not been imagined beyond a misty horizon perhaps some ten years away. This is as far ahead as practical men are prepared to look.

In a world of accelerating change much can happen during a decade. Between 1970 and 1980, for instance, Britain's share of world shipbuilding fell from 6 per cent to 1.8 per cent; of world merchant shipping from 11 per cent to 6 per cent. It is hard to believe that the corresponding figures for 1950 were 38 per cent and 30 per cent.[2] The traditional roots of the Royal Navy are shrivelling fast and the process is not fully compensated by the maintenance of a medium-sized fishing industry[3] or the expansion of pleasure boating, even by exploits of Elizabethan daring. The British maritime drive no longer has that compelling characteristic of commercial success to which Mahan ascribed such importance in explaining the reasons for British naval predominance. If the Navy are to maintain even their diminished place, the reasons must be more explicitly strategic, which means political. Sea power, in the full sense of the word, is no longer attainable.

Britain's naval decline, in somewhat superfluous answer to the question posed in Chapter 1, is not reversible, not in the time-scale of this book. Whether it can be arrested depends on the character of the prospectus. The electorate must be offered something for their money. This means a naval strategy expounded in terms of its expected results, which should be plausible, but encouraging. This strategy and naval preparations for its execution must reflect existing foreign policy, but be capable of adaptation to likely changes in the international situation or in political attitudes at home. The interested public realise that, with resources on the present scale, the Navy cannot do everything: what they want to be told are the useful results the Navy could actually achieve. This might at least sustain the present flow of money: protestations of impotence in the face of an exaggerated threat will not increase supplies, but breed defeatism.

Such medicine, as readers of this book will have observed, is more easily prescribed than dispensed. Before attempting even the first, a further word about the needs of the patient may be in order. His outstanding symptom is alienation. This condition should not, of course, be exaggerated by elderly persons in nostalgic mood. There never was a time – not even in 1940 – when the British people had complete confidence in their leaders, armed forces, police, institutions or allies. There has seldom been a period when they had so little confidence in themselves as they have today. This unhappy state of affairs has many causes, but one of them is arguably a deficiency of communication between rulers and ruled. Paradoxically, but predictably, this has been aggravated by the growth of the mass media. They provide information, criticism and innuendo on a scale never previously attained and quite unmatched by the authorities. These seem to be withdrawing ever further into Olympian heights of distance, discretion, security and non-accountability. Cursing the Treasury was never very profitable, but it was a healthier outlet for indignation than blaming everything on the Community or the International Monetary Fund. Before the First World War Beresford could rage against the Admiralty and command a sympathetic hearing from civilians who knew precisely whom he was attacking and why.[4] Nowadays there is little chance of finding anyone in

Piccadilly who knows the name of the First Sea Lord. It is all the fault of something called NATO or perhaps of President Reagan. 'We' and 'They' have never been further apart.

The politically conscious in Britain today fall into three classes. The majority are mainly aware of government as something that makes their existence more difficult, though they distinguish between greater and lesser evils. A substantial minority are more active – academics, analysts, media-men, party-workers, politicians – the onlookers who, though they may not see all of the game, have most to say about it, predominantly committed and critical. Finally there are the mandarins, political or official, service or civilian, to whom inside information is a badge to be displayed for the status it confers, but an asset not to be dissipated without the expectation of advantage.

This is often too narrowly conceived. A century ago, for instance, the Royal Navy had become concerned, not only by the declining ratio of their advantage over the French, but by an inadequate ascendancy in popular esteem over the Army. The reaction was vigorous and disseminated.

One of the revolutionary steps the Sea Lords of the Admiralty had taken in their campaign, was to encourage the appointment of naval correspondents, and even to allow them on board during manoeuvres. The 1888 manoeuvres provided these correspondents with a golden opportunity to prove themselves, and they were all given column after column . . . The whole nation identified itself with this game of mock-warfare as if it were a new form of sport put on for its benefit . . . For the following year the Naval Estimates were substantially increased.

Of course admirals were admirals in those days. Which of them would now venture to bombard Liverpool with blank ammunition, to crown offshore appearances by levying mock fines on the municipalities of Aberdeen, Edinburgh, Glasgow, Grimsby and Hull, or to tell the press that 'the English Ministry had been impeached for high treason, and the Sea Lords of the Admiralty shot by an indignant people'?[5]

Such flamboyant frankness would be refreshing today, but no longer enough. Indeed, nothing will restore that remarkable combination of popular enthusiasm, a crusading press and outspoken admirals, which characterised the early years of the century, when

it was a brave candidate for parliamentary election who did not say 'yes' to the Navy League's standard question of whether he was for the maritime supremacy of Great Britain.[6]

Seventy rather unfortunate years and two world wars have left the British people weary, disillusioned and a trifle cynical. They are no longer persuaded of the possibility of national greatness, nor are they attracted by any of the corporate substitutes devised by their leaders: Commonwealth, Special Relationship, Community or NATO. They would rather be left in insular peace. They are not reluctant to defend themselves, nor indifferent to allies, but they need convincing that defence is practicable and allies worth more than the trouble they always cause. It was strategically quixotic of the British people to have been happier in the summer of 1940 than either before or since, but that emotional experience has not entirely lost its political significance.

It is not altogether to the credit of the British people that their patriotism tends to be atavistic, nor that insularity and chauvinism are so easily tapped by the demagogues of Left and Right. Even those mandarins willing to accept this analysis may well be reinforced in their conviction that the gentlemen in Whitehall, particularly the uniformed gentlemen, know best. Right or wrong, however, the people possess, and occasionally exercise, the power of saying no. The strategist, who has also to be something of a politician, will thus 'neglect the point of view of his own people' at his peril – and theirs.

Let us start with a few propositions, all of them already argued.

For Britain defence is about survival. Greater prizes are not meaningful if they are merely collective, not attainable if they are national and, in any case, not the object of popular aspiration.

Only some threats to survival are insurable and there are limits, politically narrower than they are economically, to the premium that can be demanded, a premium unlikely to be increased in real terms.

This premium will not long suffice for all the four types of cover now maintained: the nuclear deterrent, the air defence of the British Isles, the continental commitment and the Navy.

Salami-slicing has gone as far as it can and probably a good deal further. Something must now be sacrificed to preserve the efficacy of the rest.

No further cuts, which are probably inevitable, can be made without consequential changes in strategy.

Any decision will be political and influenced by the international environment, the party struggle in Britain and a question without a certain answer: what will the British people accept with least reluctance?

Nevertheless it is the duty of strategists to offer options and to bear in mind the processes that will determine the ultimate choice. Without a strategy defence is wasted effort.

The fundamental choice, there is no getting away from it, is between a collective and a national strategy. There are many ways of expressing the dilemma. Does one rely on the vast spectrum of graduated nuclear deterrence at the disposal of Washington or take out limited national insurance against the one contingency an American president might be unwilling to cover? Is the Central Front, as Alliance mythology suggests, the only target for Soviet attack? If so, can failure of the NATO bluff lead to anything but short war? Are British troops in Germany an essential condition of the NATO bluff? If that bluff is either unlikely to be called or, contrariwise, unlikely to survive a call, could British resources be better employed elsewhere? Which allies are more of an asset than a liability to British survival? What, in a variety of contingencies, could the Navy usefully do, whether for NATO or for Britain?

Two extreme views are possible. Britain might regard herself as no more than a component of an Alliance dedicated to bluffing the enemy out of war. If that bluff failed, there would be few choices left for Britain, but her chances of survival might be less unfavourable with a navy than without one. Or Britain might adopt a French position: support without irrevocable commitment, alliance while it seemed advantageous, independence if it did not.

The British choice, such is the British temperament, is likely to be an unsatisfactory compromise. It is worth considering what this might be, bearing in mind that the interaction of defence and foreign policy exacts a price in one currency for any benefit sought in the other.

Obviously there is no point in attempting the ideal approach: a general policy, a foreign policy, a strategy and forces to fit it. Nobody in the real world has any intention of going back to the drawing board and starting again. The most that can be considered is the modification of what now exists and even that would scarcely be feasible if financial stringency and other non-strategic pressures were not already in operation to enforce the need for future change. The practical way to tackle the problem must be to start with the four pillars of existing defence policy and to consider how these might most plausibly be adapted to support, at less cost, a coherent strategy.

The nuclear deterrent is the most vulnerable. Unless the Conservatives win the next election, TRIDENT will probably be cancelled – almost certainly for the wrong reasons – and POLARIS will be lucky to last as long as the submarines that now house it. This will not improve the international situation, increase Britain's influence or provide more money for the armed forces. Any savings – and even these will depend on the date and circumstances of the cancellation – will probably be frittered away on whatever will o' the wisp the Treasury is then pursuing. If both TRIDENT and POLARIS go and Britain is subsequently threatened by territorially limited nuclear war, the chance to escape the worst consequences of that catastrophe will have been lost. If the decision has to be taken, then, for the reasons argued in Chapter 5, something might be saved if it were combined with a request for the withdrawal of land-based American nuclear weapons from the British Isles.

On the whole the strategic arguments now favour persistence in the TRIDENT project, but thirty-five years of needless nuclear obfuscation have left the Ministry of Defence with little credibility on this subject and it is probably too late for such reasoning, even if frankly attempted, to exercise much influence. Nevertheless, neither TRIDENT nor POLARIS could ever constitute more than a limited deterrent applicable to a single contingency. Retention would not enhance British ability to meet a conventional threat nor disappearance reduce it. At worst one option would have gone; others would remain.

The air defence of the British Isles – and of ships in the surrounding seas – is a different matter. It is almost unbelievable that anyone could ever have objected to its obvious necessity. They did – and for two wrong reasons. The first was the assumption that any war must be nuclear, brutish and short. The second was the wholly deplorable notion that 'offensive' action – strategic bombing, tactical bombing, 'tank-busting', ground support of troops – was somehow superior to 'defensive' – protecting the homeland, its maritime perimeter and its essential seaborne communications. There are signs – already noted – that sanity is at last returning, even if it still has a long way to go. All that need be said here – this book is about the Navy – is that reinforcement of the Royal Air Force in the British Isles is highly desirable.

That leaves two pillars: the continental commitment and the Navy. These tend to be competitive rather than complementary, more so than in the past. The Army is too solidly ensconced in Germany to constitute 'a projectile to be fired by the Navy'; the circumstances in which it can be supported – or evacuated – by the Navy are implausible; the strategic assumptions of the two Services are fundamentally conflicting.

That is not the fault of either generals or admirals, but is simply one reflection of the politico-strategic dilemma created by the development of nuclear weapons. These have compelled even practical men to realise that conflict could reach a level at which war would no longer offer any of the participants the prospect of securing advantage or abating loss. It can no longer, therefore, be regarded as axiomatic that belligerents will employ the maximum force of which they are capable. In the case of the Super-Powers this would be literally self-defeating.

Various conclusions can be drawn from this premise and from thirty-six years of abstention from the use of nuclear weapons. Two are worth considering: one that the risk of total nuclear war only imposes a kind of ceiling, however ill-defined, on the persistent tendency of states to employ the maximum force at their disposal; the other that this risk provides a protective umbrella encouraging states to regard limited force, itself an equally imprecise concept, as adequate for the pursuit of their political purposes.

In the first view the fear of total nuclear war is all that prevents the exercise of maximum force. NATO exists to maintain this fear by visible preparations to raise the level of any conflict to a point at which the danger would become fully credible. As the use of maximum force suggests the main forces of the enemy as the obvious objective, this points to the Central Front, to the probable employment of nuclear weapons and to a very short war terminated by negotiation or disastrous escalation.

This is essentially a military argument from capability and can easily be supported by analysis of the structure of the Soviet armed forces and their published writings. Political considerations, as already argued, detract from the inevitability of this scenario and make it impossible to rule out the contingency of protracted conventional war. But these considerations – basically Soviet insistence that war should serve a political purpose and their traditional caution – are also objections to the concept of maximum force. There is very little evidence that only the existence of NATO and the nuclear deterrent have preserved Western Europe from Soviet invasion. The argument from Soviet practice, the best basis for guessing at Soviet intentions, is that they have always been much more interested in opportunities that are potentially profitable precisely because they are limited. They could thus regard the balance of terror as a political umbrella rather than a military ceiling, reasoning that, in the words of Lt.-Colonel Bondarenko:

new possibilities of waging armed struggle have arisen not in spite of, but because of the nuclear missile weapons.[7]

Neither view, of course, can safely be neglected. Soviet invasion of Western Europe may be politically implausible but, as writers on military affairs are never tired of repeating, intentions can alter faster than capabilities. Defence against a maximum assault on the Central Front, a matter for soldiers and airmen, is no less desirable, particularly for those directly concerned, than against those lesser, if more probable threats, for which a naval response, often with the assistance of the other two services, is indicated. Both should be covered, but not necessarily by Britain. What, after all, is the point of an alliance if it does not permit the application of that principle so dear to Soviet economists: the division of labour? Those predominantly naval tasks of most direct concern to Britain and best adapted to her resources and traditions should fall to her share; the defence of the Central Front, for equivalent reasons, to that of her continental Allies.

Britain cannot do both. The comparative economic statistics for 1976, which have not improved in subsequent years, are clear enough.

Gross National Product in Million Dollars[8]

United States	–	1,698,060
Soviet Union	–	708,170
Japan	–	533,140
Germany	–	457,540
France	–	346,730
Britain	–	225,150

On this basis it is anomalous that Britain should have spent more, in 1981, on defence than either France or Germany and twice as much as Japan.[9] What is even odder is that some 42 per cent of this expenditure should be devoted to the defence of Germany.[10]

Equity, of course, is not a strategic argument, though it has considerable political appeal, and it may be as well to strike a rough strategic balance before tackling the many extraneous considerations – as thickly encrusted as they are around the nuclear deterrent – which have attached themselves to the continental commitment. One difference is immediately obvious. If POLARIS and TRIDENT have a valid strategic function – and this is admittedly debatable – it is one which can only be discharged by a force under British control. The military purposes of the British Army of the Rhine and of Royal Air Force Germany could equally well be met by soldiers and airmen furnished by other Allies. To the extent that British forces withdrawn from Germany were replaced, some funds might be provided, without detriment to the defence of the Central Front, to maintain or even increase the strength of the Royal Navy and of that portion of the Royal Air Force based in the British Isles.

There is no point in exploring all the possible permutations of a change: how many might be withdrawn, what proportion should be retained under arms in the British Isles, what provision should be made for the despatch of reinforcements to Germany in emergency. But the ratio between the cost of the continental commitment and its contribution to NATO strength is worth remarking. The former, as already noted, accounts for 42 per cent of the British defence budget. Even local expenditure in Germany in 1981/82 was nearly three times that on POLARIS[11] and, if the TRIDENT programme goes ahead, the total cost of the nuclear deterrent, even in the years of peak expenditure, is not expected to exceed one fifth of the total cost of the continental commitment. On the other hand, Britain supplies only about 10 per cent of NATO's fighting soldiers and combat aircraft on the Central Front as opposed to 70 per cent of the naval forces assigned to the Eastern Atlantic. Numerically, at least, the continental commitment is not a particularly cost-effective contribution to NATO. Nor, as long as financial stringency (to say nothing of the demands of Ulster) imposes crippling restrictions on equipment, training and war stocks, can quality, with all due apologies to British soldiers and airmen, be said to offer full compensation for quantitative deficiencies. Insofar as withdrawals from Germany were reflected in financial savings available for the Navy and for home-based air defence – a premise which would encounter formidable institutional opposition stemming from the principle of equal shares for the three Services – Britain might stand to gain more than NATO would lose, even without compensating efforts by the other Allies.

Nevertheless the key military questions must be: would British forces withdrawn from the Central Front be replaced by other Allies and how much would it matter if they were not? To both the answers are highly speculative.

Belgium, Canada, France, Germany, the Netherlands and the United States could, collectively, replace any British forces withdrawn and experience little economic or military strain in doing so, but they would all have political objections. Whether these could be overcome depends on when the withdrawal takes place, on the international situation at that time and on the way the withdrawal is presented. The outcome is uncertain.

If British reductions were not matched by Allied increases, two consequences would be foreseeable. The first would be that the British move might break the log-jam in the unending talks at Vienna on mutual and balanced force reductions and lead to some Soviet withdrawals. This is equally uncertain, even unlikely, but not inconceivable. If it happened, any adverse results would at least be mitigated. If it did not, the damage is a little hard to assess. The true nature of the conventional balance on the Central Front has always been disputed. Most analysts regard it as favouring the Soviet Union, some considering that Soviet advantage would permit a successful surprise attack, even an assault after mutual reinforcement. Others contend that the margin of superiority is insufficient to offer assured prospects for any kind of offensive. Few, in all probability, would argue that the military balance would be decisively swayed by a reduction of up to 10 per cent in NATO strength.

This reasoning is very widely challenged on political grounds. The conventional defence of the Central Front, so it is contended, is not a self-sufficient military objective: merely a threshold needed to lend credibility, and acceptance, to the nuclear deterrent. Both depend on a visible commitment, by most of the Allies, of forces on the ground. The defection of one would be, not compensated, but followed by others and lead to the disintegration of the Alliance. This is perhaps more of an objection to total than to partial British withdrawal from Germany. Several Allies have made partial reductions without disaster and the decline in the military effectiveness, during the Vietnam War, of the United States Seventh Army was perhaps more of a military temptation to the Soviet Union than anything to be expected from Britain. But the Americans do tend to exaggerate their own contribution to meeting the threat to Europe, just as they underestimate their contribution to creating that threat. They would be especially influenced by any reduction in another 'off-shore' contingent. The halving of the British continental commitment, as suggested by Mr Callaghan,[12] could have political repercussions out of proportion to its limited military significance. The delicate adjustments and the fine tolerances the Allies expect from the inner workings of NATO are sometimes difficult to reconcile with the image of robust solidarity they hope to present in Moscow.

Nevertheless, the argument that the health of the Alliance is too fragile to survive change does constitute an objection to be taken seriously. This does not apply to the rag-bag of dire warnings about the impact on British prestige, influence and bargaining strength of any withdrawal from Germany. The relationship between power and effective influence is complex, and linkage, as stronger governments have discovered to their cost, is a concept requiring great skill in its application. But one principle is sufficiently obvious. The potential influence of a military force is proportional to its freedom of manoeuvre and declines, rather than increases, when that force is committed to positional defence. What Britain can grant or withold is more reliably productive of reward than what she has already given away.

Another argument equally undeserving of consideration, though dear to the more deeply conservative members of the British Labour party, is that the British Army of the Rhine is needed to reassure the peoples of both Western and Eastern Europe by keeping a check on the Germans. Apart from being a military nonsense – there are eight German tanks for every British one and the conventional defence of the Central Front is nonexistent if it is not predominantly German – this view altogether fails to recognise the number of European capitals, even Moscow, where German policy now commands more confidence and respect than British.

There is really only one argument against a reduction in the British continental commitment: it might impair the self-confidence of Britain's Allies; weaken Allied solidarity; set off a chain-reaction; erode the NATO bluff. This may well be an exaggerated apprehension: compounded of British self-esteem, of contempt for foreigners, of instinctive conservatism and of institutional loyalty to a system that preserves the traditional balance between the three Services.

It cannot be disregarded, but it needs to be weighed against the alternatives. Some of these do not really exist – the supposedly painless options: maintaining all the four pillars of defence policy at their present strength or sacrificing only the nuclear deterrent to support the other three. Each of the pillars is already flawed and there is no way of preventing the deficiencies from getting steadily worse without regular and substantial increases in the real total of the defence budget. For defence to stand still would require a faster acceleration of expenditure than is at all likely to be seen as economically bearable. The illusory nature and inadequate extent of the savings to be expected from scrapping the nuclear deterrent have already been argued.

To be sure of battle-worthy conventional forces in the nineties, Britain needs to decide whether these are most required in, over and around her islands or in Germany. That is where 80 per cent of the money goes, now split about equally between home and away.[13] Tipping the balance decisively to one side or the other would make financial sense and, depending on the assumptions, even strategic. Continued salami-slicing would progressively reduce the effectiveness of the British contribution to every aspect of Alliance defence, eventually replacing strategy by tokenism. It would arouse less opposition than any other course – until some impertinent infant announced that the Emperor had no clothes. A progressive diversion of expenditure from the Navy to the Army and Air Force in Germany is probably essential if the continental commitment is to be maintained at its present numerical strength and made lastingly battle-worthy. This would be satisfactory to many of Britain's Allies and help to sustain the NATO bluff on the Central Front at the expense of maritime communications, of the Northern Flank and of the capacity to respond flexibly to any kind of amphibious or maritime threat. It would be a better course than salami-slicing, but it would be contrary to all the arguments hitherto advanced in favour of choosing those threats which are likely, which might be successfully met and which are directed to core-values. What is more serious, for these arguments could be mistaken, is that British options in foreign policy would shrink in step with the growing ratio of her total military strength physically committed in Germany. Soldiers abroad are hostages to the Alliance in a way that ships at sea are not.

A case thus exists, on both political and strategic grounds, for arguing that the British contribution to NATO should progressively be re-aligned, away from territorial defence of the Central Front and towards air and naval defence of maritime communications and, with military assistance, the defence of Norway and the islands of the North Atlantic. This would be a major change in British defence policy with reper-cussions far beyond the future of the Navy. Nevertheless, as that is the restricted subject of this book, a glance at the purely naval implications is in order.

These are unlikely to include much in the way of naval expansion. Political pressures will maintain, if they do not actually lower, the ceiling on total defence expenditure; institutional pressures will limit the extent to which the Army's share can be reduced and the Navy's increased. It would be wishful thinking to hope for more than the maintenance of existing naval strength, with a gradually increasing share of the defence budget to meet the ever-growing costs of keeping naval equipment up to date.

Some shift in emphasis, however, seems indicated. The present preoccupation with anti-submarine warfare in the Eastern Atlantic has reflected a dubious strategy of protecting reinforcement and resupply for the Central Front. The suggested re-orientation would imply greater concern for the Northern Flank, for amphibious operations, for defence against air attack and even for the possibility of confrontation with surface ships. It would be absurd to describe Soviet submarines as yesterday's threat, but, on the graph of Soviet naval strength, the rising curve of major surface vessels crossed that of submarines (rallying after a long decline) in 1978 and continues to climb above it.

Professor Bellany, who produced the graph, draws the inference:

> that the Soviet Union wishes to have a navy that can have a political-strategic function outside the central balance.[14]

It all depends whether the word 'outside' is given a political or a geographical significance. Admiral Wegener, for instance, argued plausibly that:

> the maritime presence of the Soviets can command only as much political credit as corresponds to its prospects of conversion into sea power in case of war. Where chances of conversion are good, or it can be assumed that they will grow, political credit is justified. In other areas of the world, where conversion can be ruled out, i.e., where Soviet forces in presence would disappear at the very outbreak of war, it is definitely not justified.[15]

The oceans that wash the shores of the Third World are likely to fall in the second category: the Baltic, Barents, Black and Norwegian Seas in the first. Politically as well as strategically the Norwegian Sea seems a suitable theatre for the kind of navy that Gorshkov envisaged as early as 1967:

> By a well-balanced fleet we mean a fleet which, both in composition and armament, is able to complete the missions assigned to it in rocket-nuclear war and in wars without nuclear weapons, and also to guarantee state interests on the sea in peace-time.[16]

A more maritime alignment of British strategy would be consonant with British foreign policy, which sees NATO as an alliance intended to prevent war rather than to win it. Because the British contribution to NATO would then be more directly related to national defence, as the German contribution already is, support for the Alliance in Britain would be fortified. Such a change would also lead to a defence posture more easily adapted to any modified foreign policy that might emerge in response to the kind of developments considered in Chapter 10. Even if no change in foreign policy is contemplated, a predominantly maritime strategy would give a British government more control over their own forces and thus more political freedom of manoeuvre in a crisis. General agreement on policy is not always reflected in immediate reactions to emergency and the added flexibility could offer Britain an advantage that might literally be vital.

As always there would be a price to pay. To begin with, any withdrawal from Germany, however partial, gradual and skilfully presented, would exacerbate existing strains and stresses within the Alliance. It would involve an element of risk, the kind of risk accepted by the patient who prefers a surgical operation to the insidious, and not immediately dangerous, worsening of his chronic complaint.

It is never an easy choice and it would be foolish to deny the seduction of arguments either for salami-slicing or for staking Britain's future on the Central Front and the NATO bluff. The contention here advanced has been that the first would so reduce what the Navy could do as eventually to call in question its continued utility, while the second would not only impair flexible response, but deprive Britain of even her limited national insurance against a failure of Alliance. No suggestion has been made that the Navy, or any foreseeable navy, could protect Britain against every threat to her survival, only that there is a reasonable chance of success in certain specified, limited, but not improbable contingencies. These claims are now for others to debate.

The final choice, which may not be many years away, will naturally not be made on strategic grounds alone. Nothing can prevent a major part being played by sentiment, nostalgia, tradition, vested interests, political prejudice, 'fate, chance, Kings and desperate men'. To say nothing of administrative inertia and public apathy. But the purpose of this book, however imperfectly discharged, has been to argue that Britain's naval future depends on the ability to predict a naval contribution to British survival; and that this demands a strategy at once plausible, adaptable and conformable to British policies, present and future.

Foreseeable policies are likely to have NATO as their core, but Alliance is one thing and contribution to the Central Front quite another. Half the members of NATO do not make it. Of course, in the ample days when British soldiers defended a dozen countries in various continents and British ships sailed every ocean, this was the appropriate gesture of a Great Power. For an embarrassed nation it is becoming an anachronism and the principal impediment to Britain's naval future. Not that the future of the Navy really matters. Defence is about survival, which depends on having options. If these are wider, as here suggested, in the Narrow Seas than on the North German Plain, then the Navy is a necessary instrument. If not, perhaps not. It is the nation that counts, not the Navy, not the balance of the Services, not the Alliance.

Palmerston is still right and his words apply at home as they do abroad:

> We have no eternal allies, and we have no perpetual enemies. Our interests are eternal and perpetual, and those interests it is our duty to follow.[17]

Not least, if that way survival lies, at sea.

Notes and References

Preface

1. Admiral of the Fleet Lord Chatfield, quoted in Captain John Litchfield, article on Admiral of the Fleet Sir Dudley Pound in *Naval Review*, vol. 69, no. 3, (July 1981) by kind permission of the Editor of the *Naval Review*.
2. *Statement on the Defence Estimates 1982*, Cmnd 8529–I (HMSO, 1982) p. 17.
3. Hansard, vol. 26, no. 144, Thursday, 1 July 1982 and vol. 27, no. 147, Tuesday, 6 July 1982.

Introduction

1. Minister of Defence, *Defence: Outline of Future Policy, April 1957*, Cmnd 124 (HMSO) p. 4.
2. Letter to the Editor from Mr Correlli Barnett, *The Times*, 22 December 1980.
3. Quoted in Michael Howard, *The Continental Commitment* (Temple Smith, 1972) p. 106.
4. Labour Party Defence Study Group, *Sense About Defence* (Quartet Books, 1977).
5. Admiral Browning, *John Maynard Keynes – Two Memoirs* (Rupert Hart-Davis, 1949) p. 13.
6. Sir Julian Corbett, *Some Principles of Maritime Strategy* ed. Bryan Ranft (1911; Conway Maritime Press, 1972).
7. Reported in *The Times*, 7 April 1981.

Chapter 1: The Trident and its Passing

1. Quoted in Garrett Mattingly, *The Defeat of the Spanish Armada* (Jonathan Cape, 1959) p. 83.
2. H. J. Mackinder, *Britain and the British Seas* (William Heinemann, 1902) pp. 9–10.
3. Paul M. Kennedy, *The Rise and Fall of British Naval Mastery* (Allen Lane, 1976) p. 24. In writing this chapter I am much indebted to that admirable book.
4. Ibid., p. 24.

5. A. L. Rowse, *The England of Elizabeth* (Macmillan, 1951) pp. 110–11.
6. Arthur Bryant, *Samuel Pepys: The Years of Peril* (Collins, 1949) p. 131.
7. Mackinder, op. cit., p. 24n.
8. An interesting defence of Dartmouth's conduct will be found in Edward B. Powley, *The English Navy in the Revolution of 1688* (Cambridge University Press, 1928) who attributes Dartmouth's inaction to repeated bad luck with winds and tides. There is room for more than one opinion, but it is intriguing that this vindication of an unlucky admiral has a preface by Jellicoe.
9. Captain A. T. Mahan, *The Influence of Sea Power Upon History 1660–1783* (1890; Boston: Little, Brown, 1940) p. 225.
10. Percy A. Scholes, *The Oxford Companion to Music* (OUP, 1938) p. 47 and pp. 818–19. Marder has a delightful story of Beatty ordering the band to play this tune as a distinguished German visitor left Beatty's flagship at the Spithead Review immediately preceding the war of 1914 (Arthur J. Marder, *From the Dreadnought to Scapa Flow, Vol I: The Road to War 1904–1914* (OUP, 1961) p. 423n).
11. James Boswell, *Life of Johnson*, 10 April 1778.
12. Captain A. T. Mahan, *The Influence of Sea Power Upon The French Revolution and Empire 1793–1812*, vol. ii (Sampson, Low, Marston, Searle & Rivington, 1892) p. 118.
13. Mahan, *Influence of Sea Power on French Revolution*, vol. i, p. 70.
14. Mahan, *Influence of Sea Power on French Revolution*, vol. ii, p. 18.
15. Mahan, *Influence of Sea Power on French Revolution*, vol. i, p. 327.
16. Wellington's comment on Waterloo, quoted in Elizabeth Longford, *Wellington: The Years of the Sword* (Weidenfeld & Nicolson, 1969) p. 489.
17. Kennedy, op. cit., p. 173.
18. Richard Hough, *Admirals in Collision* (Hamish Hamilton, 1959) *passim*.
19. H. J. Mackinder, 'The Geographical Pivot of History', *Geographical Journal*, xxiii (April 1904) no. 4.
20. Kennedy, op. cit., p. 206.
21. Mahan, *Influence of Sea Power on French Revolution*, vol. ii, p. 217.
22. Ibid., p. 141.
23. John Terraine, *To Win A War* (Sidgwick & Jackson, 1978) pp. 19–20.
24. John Winton, *The Forgotten Fleet* (Michael Joseph, 1969) *passim*. See also Peter C. Smith, *Task Force 57* (William Kimber, 1969) and Captain S. W. Roskill, *The War at Sea 1939–45*, vol. iii, Part ii (HMSO, 1961).
25. Prof. Ambrose in Lt.-Com. F. C. Rouse (ed.), *To Use the Sea* (2nd edn), *Readings in Seapower and Maritime Affairs* (Annapolis: Naval Institute Press, 1977) p. 18.
26. William R. Braisted, 'On the American Red and Red-Orange Plans 1919–1939', in Gerald Jordan (ed.), *Naval Warfare in the Twentieth Century* (Croom Helm, 1977).
27. C. J. Bartlett, *The Long Retreat: A Short History of British Defence Policy 1945–1970* (Macmillan, 1972) p. 114.
28. Ibid., p. 140.
29. International Institute for Strategic Studies, *The Military Balance 1977–78*, 1977 *passim*.
30. Quoted in Marder, op. cit., p. 4.

Chapter 2: The Causes of our Present Discontents

1. Quoted in Arthur Bryant, *Samuel Pepys: The Years of Peril* (Collins, 1949) p. 150.
2. Paul M. Kennedy, *The Rise and Fall of British Naval Mastery* (Allen Lane, 1976) p. 341.
3. Ibid., p. 342.
4. Central Statistical Office, *National Income & Expenditure 1967–77* (HMSO, 1978) table 9.4, pp. 67–71.
5. Captain A. T. Mahan, *The Influence of Sea Power Upon History* (1890; Boston: Little, Brown, 1940) p. 67.
6. *National Income & Expenditure 1967–77*, table 9.3, p. 66.
7. *Statement on the Defence Estimates, February 1979*, Cmnd 7474 (HMSO) p. 15.
8. Mahan, op. cit., p. 67.
9. Estimates of the ratio differ a little, but this period did produce a record level of peacetime spending.
10. Marder, *From the Dreadnought to Scapa Flow, vol. I, The Road to War 1904–1914* (OUP, 1961) *passim*.
11. Ursula K. Hicks, *British Public Finances* (OUP, 1954) p. 14.
12. Marder, op. cit., pp. 44 and 59.
13. *Jane's Fighting Ships* (Macdonald & Jane's, 1981–82).
14. Quoted in Captain A. T. Mahan, *The Influence of Sea Power Upon the French Revolution and Empire*, vol. II (Sampson, Low, Marston, Searle & Rivington, 1992) p. 358.
15. Ibid., p. 18.
16. Correlli Barnett, *The Collapse of British Power* (Methuen, 1972) p. 113.
17. 1976 figures, *World Bank Atlas* (1978).
18. International Institute for Strategic Studies (IISS), *The Military Balance 1977–78*, p. 88.
19. IISS, *The Military Balance 1981–82*, p. 112.
20. IISS, *The Military Balance 1978–79*, pp. 88–9.
21. Barnett, op. cit., p. 476.
22. *National Income & Expenditure 1967–77*, table 9.3, p. 66.
23. On being told, for the second time, by the Treasury that his views were 'rubbish'. R. F. Harrod, *The Life of John Maynard Keynes* (Macmillan, 1951) p. 201.
24. Joan Mitchell, *Crisis in Britain 1951* (Secker & Warburg, 1963), a perceptive book on which this section of the argument draws heavily.
25. Ibid., p. 271.

Chapter 3: The Relevance of Sea-Power

1. Herbert Rosinski, in B. Mitchell Simpson III (ed.), *The Development of Naval Thought* (Newport, Rhode Island: Naval War College Press, 1977) p. vii.
2. Captain S. W. Roskill, *The Strategy of Sea Power* (Collins, 1962) p. 15.

3. Sir Julian Corbett, *Some Principles of Maritime Strategy* (1911; Conway Maritime Press, 1972) p. 90.
4. Quoted in James A. Nathan and James K. Oliver, *The Future of United States Naval Power* (Indiana University Press, 1979) p. 41.
5. Captain A. T. Mahan, *The Influence of Sea Power Upon History* (1890; Boston: Little, Brown, 1940) p. 138.
6. Corbett, op. cit., p. 264.
7. Ibid., pp. 272–3.
8. Francis Bacon, *Essays* (1625; Everyman edition, J. M. Dent, 1906) p. 96.
9. As Admiral Holloway put it in 1970: 'a sea denial capability requires a much smaller investment than the sea control capability required to defend against it'. Quoted in Nathan, op. cit., p. 94.
10. Ibid., p. 48.
11. Johan Jørgen Holst, in *Power at Sea, II: Super Powers and Navies*, Adelphi Paper No. 123 (IISS, 1976).
12. Michael K. MccGwire, 'Advocacy of Seapower in an Internal Debate', *Admiral Gorshkov on Navies in War and Peace* (Arlington, Virginia: Center for Naval Analyses, 1974) p. 49.
13. Admiral Sir James Eberle, 'Designing a Modern Navy: A Workshop Discussion' in Adelphi Paper, op. cit.
14. Harold Brown, Secretary of Defense, Annual Report Fiscal Year 1979 (Washington DC: Department of Defense, 2 February 1978) p. 92.
15. S. G. Gorshkov, Admiral of the Fleet, *The Sea Power of the State* (Russian, 1976; English trans., Pergamon, 1979) pp. ix, 221 and 217.

Chapter 4: Contingencies of Conflict

1. Grant Hugo, *Britain in Tomorrow's World* (Chatto & Windus, 1969) p. 227.
2. IISS, *The Military Balance 1979–80*, 1979, p. 3.
3. Ibid., p. 80.
4. 'Der Krieg nicht bloss ein politischer Akt, sondern ein wahres politisches Instrument ist, eine Fortsetzung des politischen Verkehrs, ein Durchführen desselben mit anderen Mitteln.' ('War is not merely a political act, but a true political instrument, a continuation of political dealings, their implementation by other means.') Carl von Clausewitz, *Vom Kriege*, I (erläutert durch W. von Scherff, Berlin, 1880) ch. 1, section 24, p. 16.

   Clausewitz gave various expression, in different sections of *Vom Kriege* (*On War*) to his conception of the relationship between war and politics. Sometimes he emphasised that war was part of the political process, at others the need for political objectives to determine the conduct of war. What is missing from his pages is the idea of war as a catastrophe to be avoided.
5. A recent writer has given this scenario somewhat extreme expression. 'By about 1982 it is expected that, by using only about a quarter of its total ICBMs in a surprise attack, the Soviet Union would be able to destroy all but a few of the American ICBMs, plus all SLBMs at [*sic*] port and heavy bombers that have been unable to fly from their bases.' Lawrence Freedman, *Britain and Nuclear Weapons* (Macmillan, 1980) p. 106.

6. Dr Kissinger has argued that the notional third option of an American 'launch on warning' could not be adopted unless authority to do so had been delegated in advance and that such delegation would be highly undesirable. Speech of 1 September 1979, *Survival*, November/December 1979.

7. John Erickson and E. J. Feuchtwanger (eds), *Soviet Military Power and Performance* (Macmillan, 1979) p. 34.

8. The Office of Technology Assessment reported that a Soviet counterforce attack on US ICBM silos would cause at least 1 million immediate deaths and up to 20 million within 30 days. 'Quite optimistic assumptions' were needed for estimates below 8 million. The American riposte against Soviet missiles was expected to produce between 4 and 28 million deaths. Office of Technology Assessment, Congress of the United States *The Effects of Nuclear War* (Croom Helm, 1980) pp. 10, 84, 86 and 91.

9. Facilities for command, control, communication and intelligence are all more vulnerable than the weapons themselves and would probably suffer severely in any counterforce attack. See Desmond Ball in *Can Nuclear War Be Controlled?* Adelphi Paper No. 169 (IISS, 1981).

10. Henry Kissinger, *Nuclear Weapons and Foreign Policy* (Harper & Row, 1957) p. 244.

11. Kissinger, Speech of 1 September 1979, *Survival*, November/December 1979.

12. *Statement on the Defence Estimates 1980*, vol. I, Cmnd 7826 (HMSO) p. 28.

13. Article 6 of the North Atlantic Treaty of 4 April 1949.

14. *The Times*, October 1980, *passim*.

15. *Statement on the Defence Estimates 1980*, vol. I, p. 39.

16. Article 1 commits the Parties 'to settle any international dispute in which they may be involved by peaceful means' and 'to refrain . . . from the threat or use of force'. Article 6 obliges the Parties to regard an armed attack 'on the Algerian Departments of France' as 'an attack against them all', an obligation only cancelled on 3 July 1962.

17. Preamble of the North Atlantic Treaty.

18. *Statement on the Defence Estimates 1956*, Cmnd 9691 (HMSO).

19. Roy Fullick and Geoffrey Powell, *Suez: The Double War* (Hamish Hamilton, 1979) pp. 36 and 50.

Chapter 5: The Limited Deterrent

1. Hilaire Belloc, *Complete Verse* (Gerald Duckworth, 1970) p. 184.

2. Margaret Gowing, *Independence and Deterrence: Britain and Atomic Energy 1945–1952, Vol I: Policy Making* (Macmillan, 1974) p. 255.

3. Ibid., p. 164.

4. Ibid., p. 218.

5. *Statement on the Defence Estimates 1966: Part I, The Defence Review*, Cmnd 2901 (HMSO).

6. *Statement on the Defence Estimates 1970: Part I, The Defence Review*, Cmnd 4290 (HMSO, 1970).

7. *Supplementary Statement on Defence Policy 1970*, Cmnd 4521 (HMSO).

8. *Statement on the Defence Estimates 1971*, Cmnd 4592 (HMSO).

9. *Statement on the Defence Estimates 1975*, Cmnd 5976 (HMSO).
10. *Statement on the Defence Estimates 1979*, Cmnd 7474 (HMSO).
11. *Statement on the Defence Estimates 1980*, Cmnd 7826–1 and 1981, Cmnd 8212–1 (HMSO).
12. Ibid., (1980) p. 12.
13. Ibid., p. 12.
14. Ibid., (1981) p. 11.
15. Ibid., p. 12.
16. Ibid., pp. 13–14.
17. Ibid., pp. 11–12 and Mr Pym's speech of 24 January 1980, *Survival*, July/August 1980, p. 180.
18. Robert S. McNamara, *The Essence of Security* (Hodder & Stoughton, 1968) p. 60.
19. E. P. Thompson and Dan Smith, *Protest and Survive* (Penguin, 1980) p. 19.
20. Francis Pym, 'The Future United Kingdom Strategic Nuclear Deterrent Force', Defence Open Government Document 80/23 (Ministry of Defence, July 1980). For some reason the Ministry seem to have wanted to keep this notable light under a bushel. It was not printed and published in the usual way as a White Paper. In February 1982 copies were no longer available; the Cambridge University Library did not have one and only the kindness of the Ministry of Defence Library produced a photostat.
21. An example of the kind of undertaking on offer was given by President Brezhnev on 2 November 1981:

    I can also say with all responsibility that the Soviet Union will under no circumstances use the nuclear weapon against states which have re-nounced its production and acquisition and do not have it on their territory. We are ready to give contractual assurances of it to any country without a single exception . . . Quoted in *Survival*, January/February 1982, p. 33.

    President Brezhnev may well have meant what he said, but his offer would have been no more convincing if it had been made by the British Prime Minister or the Archbishop of Canterbury. A 'scrap of paper' is not reliably fireproof in the hands of any human being.
22. Anyone who considers, as one very eminent critic did, this comment to be unfairly dismissive, should read the excellent speech of 16 October 1981 by Mr McGeorge Bundy, *Survival*, January/February 1982. This is one of many opinions to the effect that the NATO decision to deploy intermediate-range missiles in Europe was not so much a logical military response to the perceived threat of the SS 20 as a political reaction to Allied apprehensions that were incorrectly diagnosed.
23. *Statement on the Defence Estimates 1980*, p. 9.
24. *Statement on the Defence Estimates 1981*, p. 15.
25. Ibid., p. 15; 'the use of mobile launchers would not change it [vulnerability to surprise attack] in Britain's circumstances of a small territory within a very short flight time of Soviet land-based and sea-based missiles', Pym, 'The Future United Kingdom Strategic Nuclear Deterrent Force', p. 11.
26. This argument has been again criticised as unfair. So it is if British rationalisations about the supposed increase in the Soviet threat resulting

from the installation of SS 20 missiles are accepted at their face-value. The argument is a subjective interpretation of human motives and not a proposition ever likely to receive documentary confirmation.

27. *Statement on the Defence Estimates 1981*, p. 66.
28. Ibid., p. 66.
29. Ian Smart, *Future Conditional: The Prospect for Anglo-French Nuclear Cooperation*, Adelphi Paper No. 78 (IISS, 1971) p. 19.
30. Ibid., p. 19.
31. *The Defence Review 1966*, Cmnd 2901 (HMSO) p. 10.
32. *Statement on the Defence Estimates 1981*, p. 66.
33. Ibid., p. 52.
34. *Statement on the Defence Estimates 1981: Part 2, Defence Statistics*, Cmnd 8212–II, p. 22.
35. David Greenwood, 'British Defence Budgets for the 1980s: Some Cost Analyses and Attributions' (unpublished, 1980).
36. *Statement on the Defence Estimates 1981: Part I*, pp. 14–15.
37. Mr Nott, quoted in *The Times*, 12 March 1982.
38. David Greenwood, *The Polaris Successor System: At What Cost? Aberdeen Studies in Defence Economics*, no. 16, Spring 1980.
39. *Statement on the Defence Estimates 1980: Part I*, p. 84.
40. Central Statistical Office, *National Income and Expenditure 1967–77* (HMSO, 1978) p. 66.
41. *The Times*, 24 February 1982.
42. Mr Nott, Hansard, vol. 5, no. 106, Tuesday, 19 May 1981 (HMSO) col. 167.
43. Mr Nott, Hansard, vol. 5, no. 107, Wednesday, 20 May 1981, col. 372.
44. Michael Howard, *The Continental Commitment* (Temple Smith, 1972) p. 109.
45. Labour Party Defence Study Group, *Sense About Defence* (Quartet Books, 1977). See also the expanded version: Mary Kaldor, Dan Smith and Steve Vines, *Democratic Socialism and the Cost of Defence* (Croom Helm, 1979).
46. *The Times*, 23 May 1981.
47. Peter Nailor and Jonathan Alford, *The Future of Britain's Deterrent Force*, Adelphi Paper No. 156 (IISS, 1980); Lawrence Freedman, *Britain and Nuclear Weapons* (Macmillan, 1980); David Greenwood, *The Polaris Successor System: At What Cost?* Ian Smart, *The Future of the British Nuclear Deterrent: Technical, Economic and Strategic Issues* (RIIA, 1977); William Rodgers, 'Yes to Cruise, No to Trident' *RUSI Journal*, March 1981.
48. Prime Minister, *The British Strategic Nuclear Force July 1980* (exchange of letters), Cmnd 7979 (HMSO, 1980).
49. The British nuclear deterrent originally consisted of a free-falling bomb to be dropped from manned aircraft, the V-bombers. In 1962 ability to penetrate Soviet defences was enhanced by the introduction of BLUE STEEL, which allowed bombs to be released at a distance of 200 miles from their target. All these were British developments and the deterrent could then be regarded as fully independent. As early as 1957, however, the decision had been taken that reliable delivery would henceforth require missiles rather than manned aircraft and the BLUE STREAK project, a missile based on American designs, was adopted. This was cancelled, for technical reasons, in

1960, when the British government announced their intention of replacing it with an air-launched missile purchased from the United States: SKYBOLT. When this was cancelled by the United States government in 1962, the British government arranged to buy American POLARIS-submarine-launched ballistic missiles, fit them with British warheads and install them in British-built submarines. This arrangement was reached with some difficulty and gave rise to considerable controversy at home and abroad, but was continued by successor governments and the 4 strategic submarines were all operational by 1971. See Andrew J. Pierre, *Nuclear Politics* (OUP, 1972).

50. A partial exception is the argument that 'the size of the Trident submarine tends to be a disadvantage as far as nonacoustic detection is concerned, since most nonacoustic signatures are aggravated by increased body size'. Paul H. Nitze and Leonard J. Sullivan *Securing the Seas* (Boulder, Colorado: Westview Press, 1979) p. 259.

51. James McConnell, *The Interacting Evolution of Soviet and American Military Doctrines* (Alexandria, Virginia: Center for Naval Analyses, 1980).

52. Gowing, op. cit., p. 185.

53. Nigel Lawson, *Financial Statement and Budget Report 1979–80* (HMSO, 1979) p. 11.

Chapter 6: Alliance Naval War I

1. Mr J. Enoch Powell, MP, Hansard, vol. 8, no. 137, Wednesday, 8 July 1981 (HMSO) col. 299.

2. 'an armed attack on one or more of the Parties is deemed to include an armed attack; . . . on the forces, vessels or aircraft of any of the Parties, when in or over . . . the Mediterranean Sea . . .', Article II of the London Protocol to the North Atlantic Treaty of 22 October 1951.

3. Vice-Admiral Ronald J. Hays, USN, 'Sea Power and World Affairs', in Captain John Moore, P. N., (ed.), *Jane's 1981–82 Naval Annual* (Jane's, 1981).

4. *Statement on the Defence Estimates 1980*, vol. I, Cmnd 7826–I (HMSO) p. 27.

5. *Statement on the Defence Estimates 1981*, vol. I, Cmnd 8212–I (HMSO) p. 25.

6. Ibid., p. 21.

7. For a useful exposition see Robert Lucas Fischer, *Defending the Central Front: The Balance of Forces*, Adelphi Paper No. 127 (IISS, 1976).

8. The House of Representatives Subcommittee on NATO Standardization, Interoperability and Preparedness, quoted in Kenneth A. Myers (ed.), *NATO the Next Thirty Years* (Croom Helm, 1980) p. 296.

9. Mr Nott, Hansard, vol. 8, no. 137, Wednesday, 8 July 1981, col. 278.

10. 'we can not rule out the possibility that the powerful Pact forces already positioned in Eastern Europe would attack without reinforcement, and with little tactical warning', Harold Brown, Secretary of Defense, *Annual Report Fiscal Year 1979* (Washington DC: Department of Defense, 1978) p. 6.

    There is informed British support for the view that such an attack could break through allied defences in six days.

    General Robert Close, in a plausible analysis marred only by the absence of any allowance for Soviet errors or mishaps, has argued that complete surprise could be achieved and could result in Soviet forces reaching the Rhine in 48 hours. Close, *Europe Without Defense* (Pergamon, 1979) pp. 153–98.

11. 'In all of Gorshkov's writings, only one direct reference is made to interdiction of the sea lines of communication as a *contemporary* mission of the Soviet Navy', John G. Hibbits 'Admiral Gorshkov's Writings: Twenty Years of Naval Thought' in Paul I. Murphy (ed.), *Naval Power in Soviet Policy*, (Washington DC: US Govt Printing Office, 1978) p. 8.

On the other hand Admiral Swarztrauber has quoted the *Soviet Military Encyclopaedia* (1976) to support the proposition that 'disrupting enemy ocean and sea communications' now ranks third among the tasks of the Soviet Navy. Rear Admiral Sayre A. Swarztrauber, 'The Potential Battle of the Atlantic', *United States Naval Institute Proceedings*, May 1979.

12. Arthur J. Marder, *From the Dreadnought to Scapa Flow, Vol. I: The Road to War 1904–1914* (OUP, 1961) p. 26.

13. Admiral of the Fleet S. G. Gorshkov, *The Sea Power of the State* (Russian 1976; English trans., Pergamon, 1979) p. 244.

14. Mr Nott, Hansard, op. cit., col. 278.

15. Expenditure Committee, *Sixth Report, Session 1976–77: Reserves and Reinforcements* (HMSO, 1977) p. x.

16. Ibid., p. xvii.

17. Paul H. Nitze and Leonard Sullivan Jr., *Securing the Seas: The Soviet Naval Challenge and Western Alliance Options* (Boulder, Colorado: Westview Press, 1979).

18. Ibid., p. 18.

19. Ibid., p. 204.

20. Carl von Clausewitz, *On War* (English trans. ed. Anatol Rapoport) (Penguin, 1968) p. 399.

21. Nitze and Sullivan, op. cit., p. 339.

22. Captain S. W. Roskill, *The War at Sea 1939–1945*, vol. I (HMSO, 1954) pp. 59 and 583–4.

23. Nitze and Sullivan, op. cit., p. 111.

24. *Statement on the Defence Estimates 1981*, vol. I, p. 19.

25. Nitze and Sullivan, op. cit., p. 201.

26. Roskill, op. cit., p. 106.

27. House of Commons Defence Committee, *Third Report, Sting Ray Lightweight Torpedo*, no. 218 (HMSO, May 1981). Rear Admiral Murphy told the Committee: 'The homing torpedo is the only conventional weapon apart from mines that has any reasonable chance of inflicting lethal damage on a modern nuclear submarine' p. 29.

28. Some estimates of Soviet aerial activity seem exaggerated. Mr Duffy, a former Minister for the Navy, told the House of Commons: 'There are 40 to 50 naval BACKFIRES in the Northern and Baltic Fleets, all armed with PGM and anti-ship missiles. With air refuelling their range could extend from the Kola to well south of the Azores. It is estimated that they are capable of sinking 20 to 40 ships per day, compared with the two, three or four per day sunk by the U-boats in the Second World War.' Hansard, 19 June 1980, col. 1801.

29. Secretary of State for Defence, *The United Kingdom Defence Programme: The Way Forward*, Cmnd 8288 (HMSO, June 1981) *passim*.
30. Nitze and Sullivan, op. cit., p. 431.
31. Ibid., Table 8–1, p. 201.
32. Expenditure Committee, op. cit., p. xix.
33. Lord Carver, Hansard, House of Lords, vol. 423, no. 121, Monday, 20 July 1981, col. 59.

Chapter 7: Alliance Naval War II

1. Rear Admiral Ernest Troubridge, from his statement at his court martial, quoted in Redmond McLaughlin, *The Escape of the Goeben* (Seeley Service, 1974) p. 128.
2. Anyone regarding as churlish this reference to wives, families and creature comforts should consider the reasons given by Field Marshal Lord Montgomery for deciding that wives and families 'were not allowed to live in the area of divisions that had an operational role in repelling invasion'. Montgomery, *Memoirs* (Collins, 1958) pp. 72–3. Disregard of this principle had an important influence on Britain's failure to honour her treaty obligations after the Turkish invasion of Cyprus in 1974.
3. This conception of their country seems to have a peculiar fascination for the Ministry of Defence. It appears in embryo in the *Statement on the Defence Estimates 1975* (Cmnd 5976 (HMSO) p. 10) where efforts to preserve the 'security of the United Kingdom' are justified on the grounds that 'without this no contribution to the security of our allies and no reinforcement of our forward-based forces would be possible'. The words quoted in the text come from the 1980 *Statement* (Cmnd 7826–I, p. 32), are mentioned with approval in 1981 (Cmnd 8212–I, p. 27) and are paraphrased in *The Way Forward* (Cmnd 8288, p. 5).
4. Anyone who thinks that the Labour Party are only concerned with the Common Market should read an interesting Fabian pamphlet by Robin Cook (an intelligent and defence-oriented member of the Labour Left): 'the way forward [how politicians reveal themselves by the coincidence of their clichés] to a better defence policy would seem to rest with some form of partial disengagement from NATO'. Robin Cook and Dan Smith, *What Future in NATO?*, Fabian Research Series 337 (1978) p. 27.
5. *Statement on the Defence Estimates 1980*, p. 34.
6. *The Way Forward*, p. 5.
7. Ibid., p. 6.
8. Ibid., p. 8.
9. Ibid., p. 8.
10. Arthur J. Marder, *From the Dreadnought to Scapa Flow, vol. I* (OUP, 1961) p. 245.
11. *Statement on the Defence Estimates 1981*, p. 25.
12. Adopting a generous measure Kaplan identified 190 occasions between June 1944 and August 1979 when Soviet armed forces were employed in support of foreign policy. During the shorter period from January 1946 to December 1975 and excluding the wars in Korea and Indo-China he

identified 215 similar incidents for the US armed forces. Stephen S. Kaplan, *Diplomacy of Power* (Washington DC: The Brookings Institution, 1981) and Barry M. Blechman and Stephen S. Kaplan, *Force Without War* (The Brookings Institution, 1978).

13. Admiral of the Fleet S. G. Gorshkov, *The Sea Power of the State* (Russian 1976; English trans., Pergamon, 1979) p. 184.
14. 'Today, a fleet operating against the shore is able not only to solve the tasks connected with territorial changes . . . '. Ibid., p. 221.
15. Gorshkov, quoted in Bradford Dismukes and James McConnell, *Soviet Naval Diplomacy* (Pergamon, 1979) p. 302.
16. Desmond Wettern, 'Teamwork '80', *Navy International*, December 1980.
17. Johan Jørgen Holst, 'Norwegian Security Policy and Peace in Northern Europe', *The World Today*, January 1981.
18. House of Commons, *Sixth Report from the Expenditure Committee: Session 1976–7*, HC 393 (HMSO, 1977) pp. xxii–xxiii.
19. Wettern, op. cit.
20. Admiral Harry D. Train II, USN, 'Preserving the Atlantic Alliance', *United States Naval Institute Proceedings*, vol. 107, January 1981.
21. Ministry of Defence News Release 36/81, 19 August 1981.
22. Train, op. cit. This was not the first time the Admiral had suggested that the Mediterranean might receive priority. See the report, in *Navy International*, September 1980, of the Admiral's speech of 15 July 1980.
    Interestingly enough, reconsideration of the 'swing strategy' was one of the principal recommendations made by Nitze and Sullivan (on the grounds that carriers would be more useful in the Pacific) and this in spite of their repeated emphasis on the importance of the likely battle for the Norwegian Sea. Preference for the Pacific has deep roots in even the most NATO-minded of Americans. Paul H. Nitze and Leonard Sullivan Jr., *Securing the Seas* (Boulder, Colorado: Westview Press, 1979).
23. Admiral Harry D. Train II, USN, 'NATO – Global Outlook', *Navy International*, January 1981.

Chapter 8: Alliance Naval War III

1. Admiral Elmo R. Zumwalt Jr., *On Watch* (New York: Quadrangle, 1976) p. 461.
2. *Guardian*, 20 August 1981.
3. See Article 5 of the North Atlantic Treaty of 4 April 1949 and Article II of the London Protocol of 22 October 1951.
4. Article VI of Protocol II of the Paris Agreements of 23 October 1954.
5. *Statement on the Defence Estimates 1980*, vol. I, Cmnd 7826–I (HMSO) chart on pp. 20–1 – 11 naval commands to 9 army and air force.
6. Ibid., p. 29.
7. The United Kingdom Defence Programme, *The Way Forward*, Cmnd 8288 (HMSO, June 1981).
8. Mr Nott, Hansard, vol. 8, no. 137, Wednesday, 8 July 1981, col. 278.
9. Ibid., col. 293.
10. *The Way Forward*, p. 4.

11. Ibid., p. 10.
12. David Greenwood, *Reshaping Britain's Defences: An Evaluation of Mr. Nott's Way Forward for the United Kingdom, Aberdeen Studies in Defence Economics*, no. 19, Summer 1981, p. 43.
13. Ibid., p. 45.
14. *The Way Forward*, p. 4.
15. *Statement on the Defence Estimates 1981*, vol. I, Cmnd 8212–I.
16. Zumwalt, op. cit., pp. 462–4.
17. Greenwood, op. cit., p. 16.
18. Ibid., p. 19.
19. *The Way Forward*, p. 4.
20. Admiral of the Fleet Sir Roger Keyes on the projected attack against Zeebrugge, quoted in Arthur J. Marder, *From the Dreadnought to Scapa Flow, Vol. V: Victory and Aftermath* (OUP, 1970) p. 48.
21. Attributed to Ministry of Defence in House of Commons, *Sixth Report from the Expenditure Committee*, Session 1976–7 (HMSO, 1977) p. xix.
22. See *Statement on the Defence Estimates 1975*, Cmnd 5976, p. 97; and *1981*, Cmnd 8212–I, p. 75; IISS, *The Military Balance 1974–5*; and *1981–2*.

Chapter 9: On the Fringes of Alliance

1. James Elroy Flecker, 'The Gates of Damascus' in Sir John Squire (ed.), The Collected Poems of James Elroy Flecker (Martin Secker, 1935) p. 153.
2. Rear Admiral Robert J. Hanks, *The Unnoticed Challenge: Soviet Maritime Strategy and the Global Choke Points* (Cambridge, Mass.: Institute for. Foreign Policy Analysis, 1980) p. 23.
3. Captain John Moore, *Seapower and Politics* (Weidenfeld & Nicolson, 1979) p. 173.
4. Admiral of the Fleet Lord Hill-Norton, letter in *The Times* of 9 January 1981.
5. Statement of 11 June 1981 by the Greenwich Forum.
6. *Statement on the Defence Estimates 1981* Cmnd 8212–I HMSO p. 30.
7. James Cable, *Gunboat Diplomacy 1919–1979* (Macmillan, 1981) p. 38.
8. *Statement on Defence Estimates 1981*, p. 32.
9. Secretary of State for Defence, *The United Kingdom Defence Programme: The Way Forward* Cmnd 8288 (HMSO, June 1981) p. 11.
10. Paul M. Kennedy, *The Rise and Fall of British Naval Mastery* (Allen Lane, 1976) p. 217. Admiral of the Fleet Lord Fisher, as First Sea Lord, concentrated his efforts on preparing the Royal Navy to fight the Germans in the North Sea. It is only fair to point out that most naval exercises already take place in the Treaty Area.
11. See Cable, op. cit.
12. Bradford Dismukes and James McConnell, *Soviet Naval Diplomacy* (Pergamon, 1979) pp. 178–80.
13. For this and other examples see Cable, op. cit.
14. Various critics have suggested Anglo-French cooperation over Suez in 1956 and Commonwealth cooperation over Confrontation from 1963 to 1966 as exceptions, but these were wars and, in both cases, our American Allies were distinctly unhelpful.

15. For the distinction between these two concepts see Grant Hugo, *Britain in Tomorrow's World* (Chatto & Windus, 1969).
16. The French fleet in the Indian Ocean was maintained, during the three years 1979–81, at a level of 10 surface warships with several auxiliaries and landing-craft and was supported by one or two maritime patrol aircraft based at Djibuti. It was reinforced in October 1980 by a minesweeping force. See *Le Dossier du Mois*, April 1979 and *Le Monde*, 1 February, 15 February, 14 October and 30 October 1980.
17. David Greenwood, *Reshaping Britain's Defences: An Evaluation of Mr. Nott's Way Forward for the United Kingdom* (Aberdeen: Centre for Defence Studies, 1981) p. 49.
18. There were two threats: a proposal that Soviet (and American) forces should intervene directly in Egypt and a message to Eden that mentioned 'rocket technique' and declared 'we are filled with determination to use force to crush the aggressors'. Eisenhower immediately announced American opposition to the first, but left the second unanswered until after the ceasefire at Suez. 'Eisenhower evidently was not averse to letting the Russian threat add to the pressures pushing Eden and Mollet towards a cease-fire.' Kennett Love, *Suez: The Twice-Fought War* (Longman, 1969) p. 615.
19. Stephen S. Kaplan, *Diplomacy of Power* (Washington DC: Brookings Institution, 1981) p. 135.
20. A Foreign Office argument of 1907 against Fisher's policy of sacrificing oceanic deployment to the strengthening of the battle-fleet in the North Sea – quoted in Arthur J. Marder, *From the Dreadnought to Scapa Flow*, vol. *I* (OUP, 1961) ch. 4.

Chapter 10: If Alliance Fails

1. Quoted in E. H. Carr, *The Twenty Years' Crisis* (Macmillan, 1940) p. 234. '*Rebus sic stantibus*' is legal shorthand for the doctrine that the obligations of a treaty are binding in international law as long as the conditions prevailing at the time of the conclusion of the treaty continue, and no longer.
2. Ministry of Defence News Release 43/80 of 2 September 1980.
3. North Atlantic Treaty of 4 April 1949.
4. A recent exposition of left-wing thought on British defence policy raises, not for the first time, the idea of disengagement from NATO, but argues that 'it is not in any effective sense on the political agenda in Britain'. See Dan Smith, *The Defence of the Realm in the 1980s* (Croom Helm, 1980).
5. When the rise of the Left split the British Labour party and reduced the prospects of its electoral success.
6. This attempt to save money and promote exports by adopting a common design for the warships of the two navies foundered on objections from the British Ministry of Defence that did not reflect any major national interest.
7. Pierre Mauroy, 'La cohérence d'une politique de défense', *Défense Nationale*, October 1981, p. 22.
8. David Greenwood, *Reshaping Britain's Defences, Aside, no. 19, Aberdeen Studies in Defence Economics* (Centre for Defence Studies, Aberdeen 1981) p. 8.

9. *The Times*, 21 May 1981.
10. House of Commons Defence Committee, *Fourth Report Strategic Nuclear Weapons Policy*, 36 (HMSO, May 1981) p. xviii.
11. See Walter Lacqueur, 'Hollanditis: a new stage in European neutralism', *Commentary* (New York) August 1981, pp. 19–26. Professor Lacqueur is also a specialist in Finlandisation.
12. Although Tirpitz succeeded, as early as 1899, in squashing the half-baked German plans for an invasion of the British Isles, this contingency continued to preoccupy all the British authorities concerned up to the eve of the First World War. It featured in the British naval manoeuvres of 1912 and 1913, for instance, and the Army kept troops at home to deal with it throughout the war. See P. M. Kennedy, 'The Development of German Naval Operations Plans against England 1896–1914', in Paul M. Kennedy (ed.), *The War Plans of the Great Powers 1880–1914* (George Allen & Unwin, 1979) and Arthur J. Marder, *From the Dreadnought to Scapa Flow, vol. I* (OUP, 1961).
13. Roskill implies that the Admiralty first addressed themselves to the problem in May 1940, when they were guided primarily by the precedents of the First World War. It is scarcely surprising that many weeks of argument followed between the Admiralty and the Commander-in-Chief Home Fleet concerning the best dispositions to adopt. Captain S. W. Roskill, *The War at Sea 1939–1945 Vol. I: The Defensive* (HMSO, 1954) pp. 247–53. For Raeder's order see Peter Fleming, *Invasion 1940* (White Lion, 1975) p. 36.
14. Quoted in Fleming, op. cit. p. 37.
15. Captain A. T. Mahan, *Naval Strategy* (Sampson Low, Marston, 1911) p. 219.
16. General Sir Peter Whiteley, 'Navies and the Northern Flank', in Captain John Moore (ed.), *Jane's 1981–82 Naval Annual* (Jane's, 1981) p. 112.
17. After the Russian Baltic Fleet, which the Admiral commanded, on its way to annihilation at Tsushima, had mistakenly fired on British fishing boats in the North Sea.
18. Herbert Rosinski in B. Mitchell Simpson III (ed.), *The Development of Naval Thought* (Newport, Rhode Island: Naval War College Press, 1977) pp. 54–5.

Chapter 11: Doing Without a Navy

1. Quoted in Sir Roderick Barclay, *Ernest Bevin and the Foreign Office 1932–1969* (Latimer: Barclay, 1975) p. 67.
2. See James Cable, *Gunboat Diplomacy 1919–79* (Macmillan, 1981) Appendix One, *passim*.
3. Ernest Bramah, *Kai Lung Unrolls His Mat* (Penguin, 1937) pp. 102–3.
4. Ministry of Defence News Release 33/81, 17 August 1981.
5. Dan Smith, *The Defence of the Realm in the 1980s* (Croom Helm, 1980) pp. 234–5.
6. Correlli Barnett, letter to *The Times*, 22 December 1980.
7. Garrett Mattingly, *The Defeat of the Spanish Armada* (Jonathan Cape, 1959) pp. 191–2.

8. See Chapter 7.
9. Mattingly, op. cit.
10. Vice-Admiral Ronald J. Hays, USN, 'Sea Power and World Affairs', in Captain John Moore (ed.), *Jane's Naval Annual 1981–82* (Jane's, 1981).
11. Nelson, quoted in Captain A. T. Mahan, *Naval Strategy* (Sampson Low, Marston, 1911) p. 431.

Chapter 12: Towards an Uncertain Horizon

1. Quoted in Captain A. T. Mahan, *Naval Strategy* (Sampson Low, Marston, 1911) p. 20.
2. Michael Baily, 'Can British shipping keep afloat?' *The Times*, 21 September 1981.
3. A letter to *The Times* of 9 February 1982 from Mr Robert Battersby, Chairman of the Fisheries Working Group in the European Parliament, gave the following figures: 23,000 fishermen and 7,200 vessels (more than in the sixties but less than in the thirties) catching the same million tons of fish as in 1913 or 1937. In terms of fish caught, Britain, in 1976, ranked nineteenth among the nations, just after Iceland.
4. Admiral Lord Beresford did not allow his command of the Channel Fleet to interrupt his sustained, violent and much publicised campaign against Fisher as First Sea Lord.
5. Richard Hough, *Admirals in Collision* (Hamish Hamilton, 1959) pp. 15–21.
6. Paul Kennedy, *The Rise of the Anglo-German Antagonism 1860–1914* (George Allen & Unwin, 1980) p. 385.
7. Lt.-Col. V. M. Bondarenko, quoted in Roman Kolkowicz, 'U.S. and Soviet Approaches to Military Strategy', *Orbis*, Summer 1981.
8. George Thomas Kurian, *The Book of World Rankings* (Macmillan, 1979).
9. IISS, *The Military Balance 1981–2* gives the figures as Britain 28,660 million dollars, France 26,008 and Germany 25,000 (p. 112). The *Statement on the Defence Estimates 1981*, Cmnd 8212–I (HMSO) gives no figures later than 1980, for which year it estimates defence expenditure by the three countries as being almost exactly equal (p. 67).
10. Estimate kindly communicated to the author by David Greenwood of the Centre for Defence Studies, Aberdeen.
11. *Statement on the Defence Estimates 1981, Part 2*, Cmnd 8212–II, pp. 18 and 22.
12. *The Times*, 21 May 1981.
13. The author was furnished with these estimates by David Greenwood, who emphasised that they represented an arbitrary, notional and coarse attribution of total defence expenditure to particular strategic functions. The difficult task of distributing support costs has understandably not been attempted by the Ministry of Defence, hence their much lower figure of 2 per cent for the present cost of the nuclear deterrent. But, where the Gods refrain, mortals must adventure, and David Greenwood's estimates are easily the best available.
14. Ian Bellany, 'Sea Power and the Soviet Submarine Forces', *Survival*, January/February 1982, pp. 3–4.

15. Edward Wegener, *The Soviet Naval Offensive* (German original 1972; Annapolis, Maryland: Naval Institute Press, 1975) p. 83.

16. Quoted by George E. Hudson, 'Soviet Naval Doctrine and Soviet Politics 1953–1975', *World Politics*, vol. xxix, (October 1976) no. 1, p. 104.

17. As Foreign Secretary when addressing the House of Commons in 1848, quoted in Philip Guedalla, *Palmerston* (Ernest Benn, 1926) p. 281.

Select Bibliography

This is not a complete list of works cited in the text, but of those deserving to be read for their independent contribution to the subject. For others see Index.

Barnett, Correlli, *The Collapse of British Power* (Methuen, 1972).

Bartlett, C. J., *The Long Retreat: A Short History of British Defence Policy 1945–70* (Macmillan, 1970).

Bertram, Christoph and Holst, Johan J. (eds), *New Strategic Factors in the North Atlantic* (Guildford: IPC Science and Technology Press, 1977).

Clausewitz, Carl von, *On War* (trans. ed. Anatol Rapoport) (Penguin, 1968).

Cook, Robin and Smith, Dan *What Future in NATO?*, Fabian Research Series 337 (1978).

Corbett, Sir Julian, *Some Principles of Maritime Strategy* (Conway Maritime Press, 1972).

Dismukes, Bradford and McConnell, James (eds), *Soviet Naval Diplomacy: From the June War to Angola* (Pergamon, 1979).

Freedman, Lawrence, *Britain and Nuclear Weapons* (Macmillan, 1980).

Gorshkov, S. G., Admiral of the Fleet, *The Sea Power of the State* (Pergamon, 1979).

Howard, Michael, *The Continental Commitment* (Temple Smith, 1972).

Kaldor, Mary, Smith, Dan and Vines, Steve (eds), *Democratic Socialism and the Cost of Defence* (Croom Helm, 1979).

Kennedy, Paul M., *The Rise and Fall of British Naval Mastery* (Allen Lane, 1976).

Labour Party Defence Study Group, *Sense About Defence* (Quartet, 1977).

MccGwire, Michael, Booth, Ken and McDonnell, John (eds), *Soviet Naval Policy: Objectives and Constraints* (New York: Praeger, 1975).

McConnell, James, *The Interacting Evolution of Soviet and American Military Doctrines* (Virginia: Center for Naval Analyses, 1980).

Mahan, Captain A. T., *The Influence of Sea Power Upon History* (Boston: Little Brown, 1940).

Mahan, Captain A. T., *The Influence of Sea Power Upon the French Revolution and Empire 1793–1812* (Sampson, Low, Marston, Searle & Rivington, 1892).

Martin, L. W., *The Sea in Modern Strategy* (Chatto & Windus, 1967).

Moulton, J. L., *The Norwegian Campaign of 1940* (Eyre & Spottiswoode, 1966).

Murphy, Paul J. (ed.), *Naval Power in Soviet Policy* (Washington DC: US Govt. Printing Office, 1978).

Myers, Kenneth A. (ed), *NATO: The Next Thirty Years* (Croom Helm, 1980).

Myers, Kenneth A., *North Atlantic Security: The Forgotten Flank*, A Sage Policy

Paper (Center for Strategic and International Studies, Georgetown: Sage Publications, 1979).

Nathan, James A. and Oliver, James K. *The Future of United States Naval Power* (Indiana University Press, 1979).

Nitze, Paul H. and Sullivan, Leonard, Jr., *Securing the Seas: The Soviet Naval Challenge and Western Alliance Options* (Boulder, Colorado: Westview Press, 1979).

Pierre, Andrew J., *Nuclear Politics: The British Experience with an Independent Strategic Force 1939–1970* (OUP, 1972).

Quester, George H., *Navies and Arms Control* (New York: Praeger, 1980).

Rosinski, Herbert in B. Mitchell Simpson III (ed.), *The Development of Naval Thought* (Newport, Rhode Island: Naval War College Press, 1977).

Roskill, Captain S. W., *The Strategy of Sea Power* (Collins, 1962).

Rouse, Lt.-Comm. F. C. (ed.), *To Use The Sea* (2nd edition), Readings in Sea Power and Maritime Affairs, (Annapolis: Naval Institute Press, 1977).

Smart, Ian, *The Future of the British Nuclear Deterrent: Technical, Economic and Strategic Issues* (RIIA, 1977).

Smith, Dan, *Defence of the Realm in the 1980s* (Croom Helm, 1980).

Till, Geoffrey, *Maritime Strategy and the Nuclear Age* (Macmillan, 1982).

Zumwalt, Admiral Elmo R., Jr., *On Watch* (New York: Quadrangle, 1976).

Index

Authors cited are normally indexed on their first appearance in the Notes.

Admirals
  anguish of American, 2
  ardent, 28, 176
  doctrinal preconceptions, 44
  don't need advice, ix
  gobbled unripe scenario, 104
  helpful, ix
  irritated, 1, 190, 203
  lacking forces for Narrow Seas, 60
  monopoly of strategic thought, 7
  outnumber ships, 126, 199
  seldom go to sea, 1
  should have written the book, 9
  taciturn, 108, 130–3
  unduly aged, 14
Admiralty
  Beresford rages against, 175
  chooses wrong threat, 119
  fails to read Mahan, 16
  and invasion, 202
  revolutionary steps, 176
  shot by an indignant people, 176
Aircraft
  against ships, 38, 40–1, 63, 185, 197
  against submarines, 98–9
  BACKFIRE bomber, 100, 102, 197
  and ports, 102
  replace ships, 170
  unsuitable instruments of limited force, 121
Aircraft carriers
  British, xi, xiii, 7, 18, 77, 127, 143
  in Second World War, 40
  Soviet, 120
  task forces, 41

US, 59, 87, 112, 118, 121, 127, 137–8, 152
Alford, Jonathan, 82, 195
Alliance
  bluff and paradox, 153–4, 162, 167–8, 178, 184–5, 187
  burden-sharing, 88, 158, 181–2, 186–7
  Central Front incidental, 102–4, 187
  consequences of defeat, 150–4, 178
  deterrent effect of, 106, 111, 163, 186
  division of, 111–16, 138, 150, 155–9
  European support for, 156
  fallibility of, 62, 153, 159
  hostages to, 185
  if it fails, 63, 106, 124, 150–64, 187
  looser at sea, 125, 144
  need for choice in, 105, 152–4, 185, 187
  remarkable survival of, 155, 159
  risks of change, 183–4, 187
  serves national interest, 109, 124, 152, 163
  some conflicts divide, 156, 159
  see also under NATO
Alliance war
  choosing threat in, 105–24
  orthodox case, 86–104
  tasks and resources, 125–39
Allies
  alienation, 159
  asking too much, 147, 158
  asset or liability, 178
  Europe first, 148, 155–8

Allies – *continued*
  gratitude of, 142, 147
  limitations of, 61, 90, 94
  and limited naval force, 148
  refusal of facilities for, 155
  replacing British forces in Germany, 181–5
  superrogatory aid to, 142, 146–7
  unreliable, 62, 97, 148–9, 153
Ambrose, Professor, 190
Amphibious operations
  future, 46, 115, 119–20, 162, 169, 185
  inadequate preparation for, 63, 117–18
  manoeuvres, 113–20
  in Second World War, 40, 119, 161
  Soviet capability, 120, 161–2
Anti-submarine warfare
  British weapons inadequate, 99–100, 130, 197
  escort of US carriers, 138
  likely balance in Atlantic, 98–9, 131–2
  main task, 87–8, 185
  and Royal Navy, 41, 87–8, 98–102, 128–32, 137–8, 185
  tactics, 98–102
Arab–Israeli war
  European attitudes, 62
  lessons of (1967), 1, 58, 62; (1973), xii, 1, 58, 62, 101, 173
  and NATO (1967), 156; (1973), 111, 156
  Super-Power threats in, 119
Atlantic ocean
  bridgehead, 150
  comfortable insulation for US, 110
  Eastern, 5, 59–60, 94, 97, 185
  Fleet, 2
  future war in, 6, 44, 59–60, 96–102, 107, 136–8, 151
  islands in, 87, 114, 137, 185
  Royal Navy in, 12, 94, 97, 102, 107, 136–8, 168, 170, 182, 185
  Standing Naval Force, 126, 132
  Strike Fleet in, 46, 59, 127–9, 138
  transatlantic lifeline, 94–6, 136–7
  US attitudes to, 59, 97, 124, 138

  warning time, 138, 141
  withdrawal from, 168, 172
  see also under South Atlantic; Supreme Allied Commander

Bacon, Francis, 192
Ball, Desmond, 193
Baltic Sea
  beyond control, 37
  exit from, 21
  and NATO, 145
  possible Soviet aims in, 114, 123, 186
  Royal Navy in, 12
  Soviet exercises in, 120
  Soviet fleet, 112
Barclay, Sir Roderick, 202
Barnett, Correlli
  Collapse of British Power, 22, 205
  economic expansion in war, 27, 30
  favours naval reductions, 3, 167, 189
  limitations, 29
Bartlett, C. J., 190
Beatty, Admiral of the Fleet, Lord, 30, 190
Bellany, Professor Ian, 186, 203
Blechman, Barry M., 199
Blockade
  and command of sea, 39–40
  and Cuba, 1
  difficulties of, 16
  failure of, 17, 38
  in First World War, 38
  future, 46, 128, 149
Braisted, William R., 190
Brezhnev, President, 194
British Army
  different strategic assumptions, 179
  financial constraints on, 182
  in Germany, 90, 107, 178–9, 181–5, 198
  limited war, 63
  and Royal Navy, 165, 176, 179–82, 185
  soldiers abroad as hostages, 185
  withdrawal, 181
British Defence Policy
  aberrations, 63

British Defence Policy – *continued*
commitment to NATO, 4, 60, 78, 88, 107, 125–7, 139, 157–9, 187
contraction of effort, 4, 109, 121–2, 134, 170
economic constraints on, 27–35, 80, 133–5, 158, 178, 182, 184
expenditure, 4, 28, 78–82, 133–5, 158, 181–2, 185, 203
failure to predict results, 134
four pillars of, 5, 7, 177–87
impact on NATO, 121–2, 158–9
and Navy, 108, 127, 139
nuclear forces, 66–9, 71–85, 160
out of area activities, 60, 129, 141–4, 146–7, 156
political attitudes to, 4–9, 21–35, 81–2, 133–5, 158
priorities, 64, 80, 107, 130, 134, 139, 141
realignment of, 185–8
rearmament, 33
relevance of conventional war, 58, 139
should be about survival, 82, 177, 187
subordination to Americans, 75–6, 84–5, 146
Suez failure, 63, 111, 166
tokenism, 185
see also under Defence Estimates and Statements; Nott
British Economy
benefits from war, 27, 30
capacity for war, 26, 28–9
comparisons, 19, 28–32, 181
decline of, 29, 31, 134
growth inverse to defence expenditure, 29–35
historical dependence on naval strength, 13–14
impact of Korean War, 33–4
influence of theories on, 24
limitations of, 27–35: absolute, 27–8; relative, 27, 29–35, 134
maritime capacity of, 174–5
political perceptions of, 21, 85, 134–5

recession and rearmament, 30, 33, 80
see also under Treasury
British nuclear forces
controversy concerning, 66–85, 139, 167–70, 178–9
deterrent functions, 49–56, 66, 69–70, 73–6, 78, 83–5, 160, 179
dying bee argument, 51
financial cost of, 77–81, 182
history, 66, 75, 84–5, 157, 195–6
incredible against conventional attack, 94, 160
independence of, 69, 75, 78, 85, 160
monopoly desirable, 74–6, 179
not needed by NATO, 78
official justification, 67–9
political costs of, 78, 84–5
renunciation of, 7, 69–71, 76–7, 81–2, 139, 167, 178–9, 184, 194
survivable, 55, 66, 69–70
threaten conventional strength, 77–82, 139, 179
weapon of last resort, 78, 84–5, 151, 160
see also under Deterrence; POLARIS; TRIDENT
British political attitudes
alienation, 175
change in, 21–7, 107, 134–5, 156–8, 172–3, 175, 177–8, 187
cynicism, 24–7, 175–7
defence priorities of, 64, 80–2, 177
fear less effective, 25
guns or butter, 21–6
happiest in (1940), 177
and mass media, 175–6
Navy must not disregard, 133, 175–9, 185, 187
to NATO, 62, 91, 155–9, 167–8, 170, 176–7, 186–7
nuclear weapons, 76, 80–2, 167–70, 178–9
open government, 68
readiness for risks, 50
response to challenge, 21–35, 177
scepticism of threats, 24–6, 133

British political attitudes – *continued*
why no win?, 26–7, 32, 175
see also under Conservative Party;
Labour Party
Brown, Harold, US Secretary for
Defense, 192
Bryant, Sir Arthur, 190
Bundy, McGeorge, 194

Carr, E. H., 201
Carver, Field Marshal, Lord, 103, 198
Central Front
airborne reinforcement of, 96–7
consequences of collapse, 94–6,
104, 109, 162
defence of, 89–91, 125, 183, 187
demands on British forces, 107–9,
162, 182, 184–5, 187
as deterrent, 91, 183–4
endurance, 91, 101–3, 196–7
and France, 106
and Germany, 184
land lines of communication, 102–3
many members of NATO make no
contribution to, 187
no sea breezes blow, 103–4
obsession with, xiii, 103–4, 109,
129–30, 170, 178, 183–4, 187
offensive against, 60, 89, 92, 103,
111, 113–14, 180
pre-positioned equipment, 96–7
seaborne reinforcement of, 59–60,
87–104, 107–9, 130, 134,
136–7, 168, 173, 185
secondary for Britain, 86, 94,
102–4, 124, 187
symbolic naval contribution to,
103–4
task for other Allies, 181–5, 187
Treaty commitment to, 125
see also under Continental commitment; NATO
Chatfield, Admiral of the Fleet, Lord,
ix, 17, 189
Clausewitz, Carl von
and allies, 97
indifferent to catastrophe, 192
Vom Kriege, 192, 197
war as political instrument, 49

Clerk, John of Eldin, *Essay on Naval
Tactics*, ix–x
Close, General Robert, 196–7
Coastal defence, 45, 124, 169, 172: and
ceremonial squadron, 172
Coercive diplomacy, 110–14, 119–24,
128, 132, 135–6, 142, 159, 162–3,
169–70, 173
see also under Limited naval force
Command of sea
Corbett on, 39
decline of concept, 44–6
equivalent to control, 37
imperfections of, 40–1
Mahan on, 39
and maritime communications, 37
product of success, 40
sufficient objective, 39, 43–6
see also under Sea control; Sea
denial; Naval Strategy
Conservative Party, British
allocation of defence savings, 31,
81, 158
and defence, 23, 79, 81, 107, 133–4,
158
electoral success (1979), 23
and next election, 178
and nuclear weapons, 67, 81
see also under British political
attitudes
Continental commitment
anachronistic gesture, 187
British attitudes to, 108, 158, 165,
168, 170
consequences of, 106, 162, 173
cost of, 78, 158, 181–2
cost-effectiveness of, 182
Howard, Michael, 189
and NATO strength, 182
needs more money if retained, 185
reduction of, 147, 155, 158, 179,
181–7
and Royal Navy, 179, 181–2, 185–7
in Second World War, 38–9, 106
subsumes defence of British Isles,
167, 170
see also under Central Front
Contingencies of conflict
broken-backed war, 51–2

Contingencies of conflict – *continued*
  failure of Alliance, 62–3
  fluidity of, 56
  general, 48–65
  maritime, 139
  national, 61–5
  purely maritime, 56
  see also under Conventional;
    Deterrence; Limited; Nuclear;
    Total
Conventional war
  after collapse of Central Front, 109,
    150–2, 160–4
  balance on Central Front, 183
  can be won, 58–60
  definition, 56
  global and protracted, 151, 161,
    170, 173
  important to Royal Navy, 58–65
  Iraq–Iran, 60
  and Norway, 115–19
  reaction to defeat in, 57, 150–4
  ruling out, 169–70, 180
  short?, 109, 137, 151, 161, 165, 170,
    178–9
  uncertain outcome of, 139
  see also under Central Front;
    Contingencies; Limited
Conventional wisdom, xiii–xiv, xvi,
  32, 105
Convoy system, 16, 37, 46, 98, 149,
  166, 171
Cook, Robin, MP, 198
Corbett, Sir Julian
  command of sea, 37, 39–40, 46
  lectured at Greenwich, 7
  mistaken judgment, 40
  Principles of Maritime Strategy, 7,
    189
  sense of purpose, 43
Cyprus, 1, 62–3, 123, 145, 148, 156,
  198

Defence Estimates and Statements
  Future UK Strategic Nuclear
    Deterrent (1980), 69, 194
  Outline of Future Policy (1957), 1,
    189
  Statement (1956), 63, 193
  Statement (1966), 67, 193
  Statement (1970), 67, 193
  Statement (1971), 67, 193
  Statement (1975), 67, 107, 194
  Statement (1979), 67, 191, 194
  Statement (1980), 68, 72, 79, 88,
    107, 193–5
  Statement (1981), 68, 71–2, 88–90,
    131, 194–5
  Statement (1982), xi, xiv, 189
  The Way Forward (1981), 79, 108,
    129–31, 143
Democracy and Defence
  general, xv, 24–5
  popular governments, 23
  popular right to influence vital
    choices, 121
  and strategy, 174, 187
  and television, 113, 120–1
Denmark
  and Danish Straits, 87, 129, 137–8
  need for reassurance, 123
  and Norway, 121
  political attitudes, 155
  see also under Baltic Sea; Norway
Deterrence
  British nuclear, 49, 56, 66, 69–70,
    73–6, 78, 83–5, 160, 169, 179,
    184
  constituents of, 86
  discussion of, 6
  doubts concerning, 53–5, 68, 157,
    160, 180–1
  and Europe, 84, 88–9, 157
  failure (1914), 38, 74, 164; (1939), 38
  gambling on, 39, 170, 178
  limits to, 58, 120, 123
  must reward abstinence, 74, 76
  naval, 163–6, 168, 170–3
  in Soviet Union, 57, 84, 160
  in territorially limited nuclear war,
    54–6, 66, 69–70, 73–6, 78,
    83–5, 160, 179, 181
  uncertainty not advantageous, 74,
    160
  US nuclear, 49–58, 105, 160, 183
  see also under British nuclear;
    Limited war; Total war

Dismukes, Bradford, 200

Eberle, Admiral Sir James, 43, 192
Empire, British
  association with Royal Navy, 3,
    11–17
  death duties of, xiv, 61–2, 148–9,
    159
  emotional legacies of, 30
Equal Misery
  doctrine of, 5, 81, 182, 184
  and salami-slicing, 5, 79, 170, 172,
    177, 184–5, 187
  threat to, 107
Erickson, John, 52, 193
European Economic Community, 3,
  8, 107, 156, 175, 177

Falkland Islands
  Allied attitudes, 147, 159
  and Argentina, x
  attitude of British government, xi
  battle of (1914), x
  commitments to, 61, 148
  conclusions still premature, xii–xiii
  fait accompli, 61
  General Galtieri, xi–xiii
  naval lessons of, xii
  seized after book completed, x
  threat to, 170
  unique nature of conflict, xi–xvi
  war (1982), x–xvi
Finland, 110, 112, 154: 'Finland-
    isation', 159
First World War
  American dependence on foreign
    matériel, 18
  economic development in, 30
  German submarines in, 37, 63, 98–9
  invasion threat, 161, 202
  prior British attitudes to, 26, 63, 161
  and sea power, 16, 37–8
  strategic errors, 38, 63
Fischer, Robert Lucas, 196
Fisher, Admiral of the Fleet, Lord
  battle ground and drill ground, 144,
    200
  predicts Bank Holiday war, 93
  reorganises navy, 15–17, 201

right about war on trade, 40
Fleming, Peter, 202
France
  and Algeria, 30, 61, 156
  alliance with, 17, 155
  British attitudes to, 15
  defence expenditure, 23, 29–31, 77,
    181, 203
  economy, 31
  example of, 154, 178
  limited deterrent of, 55, 84
  no assistance from Allies, 61–2
  nuclear capability of, 50–1, 55, 74,
    157
  perceived resolution of, 50
  policy of, 55, 68, 70, 85, 106–7,
    145–6, 155, 157, 178, 201
  rivalry with, 13–14
  and Suez, 111
  target for Soviet nuclear attack, 51
  western ports of, 152
  see also under French Navy
Freedman, Lawrence, 82, 192
French Navy, 142, 144–6, 200
Fullick, Roy and Powell, Geoffrey,
  193

Gaullism, 68, 78, 85
Germany
  attacks Belgium (1914), 50, 55
  British forces in, 90, 107, 178–9,
    181–5, 198
  defence expenditure, 23, 29–31,
    181, 203
  effects of rearmament in, 30, 33
  invades Soviet Union (1941), 38
  naval challenge of, 15–17, 32
  naval strategy of, 38, 163
  policy, 184
  submarine offensive, 16, 37–8, 40,
    63, 98–9, 171
  see also under Central Front;
    Continental commitment
Gorshkov, Admiral of the Fleet,
    Soviet C. in C.
  and British survival, 94
  and command of the sea, 43
  creator of modern navy, 2
  doctrines of not universal, 46, 192

Gorshkov – *continued*
  and maritime communications, 197
  most effective units, 113
  Sea Power of the State, 192
  and strikes from the sea, 45
  territorial changes, 45, 113, 199
  visible warships, 113
  well-balanced fleet, 186
  see also under Naval Strategy;
    Soviet Navy
Gowing, Margaret, 193
Greenland–Iceland–UK Gap, 88, 98,
  100, 115, 128–32, 136–7, 152
Greenwood, David, 78–9, 82, 130–1,
  133–4, 146, 195, 199, 203
Guedalla, Philip, 204

Hanks, Rear-Admiral Robert J., USN,
  200
Harrod, R. F., 191
Hays, Vice-Admiral Ronald J., USN,
  87, 196
Hibbits, John G., 197
Hicks, Ursula K., 191
Hill-Norton, Admiral of the Fleet
  Lord, 200
Holloway, Admiral, USN, 37, 43, 192
Holst, Johan Jørgen, 192
Hough, Richard, 190
House of Commons
  Defence Committee, 197, 202
  Expenditure Committee, 197, 199,
    200
  no debate in, 67
Howard, Michael, 189
Hudson, George E., 204
Hugo, Grant, 48, 92, 200

Iceland, 1, 42, 62, 87, 114, 121, 148,
  155–6, 166
Indian Ocean, xi, 18, 59, 112, 124,
  143–4
Indonesia, confrontation with, 111,
  166, 200
Invasion
  of British Isles, 38–40, 94–5, 138,
    159, 161–2, 202
  Dartmouth's failure to prevent, 12,
    138, 190

deterrence of, 17, 162, 170
indifference to, 4, 13, 20, 161–2
of Norway (1940), 37
possibilities, 28, 114–19, 159,
  161–2
scares, 15

Jane's Fighting Ships, 191
Japan, 15, 17, 29, 38, 40, 43
Jellicoe, Admiral of the Fleet, Lord, 1,
  16, 190

Kaplan, Stephen S., 198–9
Kennedy, Paul
  on German Plans, 202
  *Rise and Fall of British Naval
    Mastery*, 10–16, 36, 189, 200
  on sea power, 36
Keyes, Admiral of the Fleet Sir Roger,
  136, 200
Keynes, John Maynard, 33, 189, 191
Khruschev, N. S., 2
Kissinger, Dr Henry
  on European dream, 54
  launch on warning, 193
  on limited war, 53
  on value of US nuclear guarantee,
    54
Kolkowicz, Roman, 203
Korean War, 33–4, 57, 111, 156

Labour Party, British
  allocation of defence savings, 31,
    81–2
  Callaghan and continental commit-
    ment, 183
  defence expenditure under, 79, 82
  and Europe, 107, 156, 158, 184, 198
  internal developments in, 156, 201
  and NATO, 154–6, 158, 198
  opposition to nuclear weapons, 7,
    67, 70, 81–2, 107, 155
  Sense About Defence, 6, 82, 189
  see also under British political
    attitudes
Lacqueur, Walter, 202
Lawson, Nigel, Financial Statement,
  196
Litchfield, Captain John, RN, 189

Limited Naval Force
  against Britain, 94, 147–9, 170
  on Alliance basis, 144–7
  characteristics, 145, 148–9
  fait accompli, 61
  future use of, 46, 112, 119–24,
    147–9, 171, 173, 185–6
  limitations of, 144–5
  naval requirements for, 41, 120–1,
    132, 135, 170
  need for, 61, 64, 121–4, 144–9
  past use of, 1, 142, 144, 147–8
  tactics of confrontation in, 121, 132,
    135, 171
  see also under Coercive diplomacy;
    Naval deployment
Limited war
  Alliance shield against, 163
  inadequate preparations for, 63
  in Korea, 57
  lightning campaign in, 115, 153
  not excluded by theatre nuclear
    weapons, 54
  nuclear, 52–7, 84, 150, 155, 160, 193
  possibility of, xiv, 61, 83, 160, 170
  territorially limited, 53–6, 66,
    69–70, 73–6, 78, 83–5, 89, 151,
    155, 160, 173, 179
  in Vietnam, 57
  see also under Conventional war
Longford, Elizabeth, 190

McConnell, James, 84, 196
MccGwire, Michael, 43, 192
Mackinder, Halford, 10, 15, 189
McLaughlin, Redmond, 198
McNamara, Robert, 194
Mahan, Captain A. T., USN
  causes of British naval superiority,
    17, 46, 175
  England *the* sea power, 12
  far-distant ships, 13
  and imperialism, 3
  *Influence of Sea Power Upon
    History*, 15, 190
  Kaiser reads, 15–16
  overbearing power at sea, 39, 46
  popular governments, 22–3
  quotes Nelson, 162

  sense of purpose, 43
Marder, Arthur, J., 24, 190
Maritime communications, 37–8, 44,
    59, 92, 94–6, 101, 104, 128–9,
    136–7, 151, 179, 185
  see also under Central Front; Naval
    Strategy
Matériel
  actual deficiencies of, 100, 130, 137,
    166, 182, 197
  British preoccupation with, xiv,
    6–7, 38, 42, 130
  cheap, simple ships, 169, 171
  historical deficiencies of, 17, 130
  sophistication price of versatility,
    171
Mattingley, Garrett, 83, 189
Mauroy Pierre, 201
Mediterranean Sea
  coastal states of, 123
  future war in, 44, 59, 87
  inappropriate theatre for British
    efforts, 124, 152
  Italy, 17, 32, 155
  Libya, 125, 145
  reinforcement of, 127
  Royal Navy in, 12, 17
  in Second World War, 17, 40
  in Treaty area, 86, 125, 156
  Turkey, 1, 62, 123, 152, 155
  US Navy in, 123–6
  Yugoslavia, 60
Mines, 38, 41, 102, 137
Ministry of Defence, British
  concern for American suscepti-
    bilities, 67–8, 75–6
  curious conception of their country,
    107, 198
  and Falklands, xiii
  feelings about NATO, 8
  financial cosmetics of, 77–82
  lacks credibility, 179
  narrow views of, 130, 133
  and Norway, 129
  respect for realities, 141
  shuns strategic discussion, xv, 8,
    66–8, 133, 179
  on submarine threat, 99
  and Treasury, 32–3

Ministry of Defence – *continued*
  unique responsibility for expo-
    sition, 135
  see also under British Defence
    Policy; Defence Estimates
Missiles, 41, 48–52, 57, 70–5, 161, 194
  see also under Nuclear weapons;
    Submarine launched
Mitchell, Joan, 34, 191
Montgomery, Field Marshal Lord,
  198
Moore, Captain John, RN, 200
Myers, Kenneth A., 196

Nailor, Peter, ix, 82, 195
Narrow Seas
  and Central Front, 94
  concentration in, 16
  control in, 43
  expansion from, 17
  from Finisterre to Norway, 12
  loss of supremacy in, 20, 60
  Masters of, 11–12, 28
  options wider in, 187
  priority for, 149
  readiness in, xiii, 5
  Standing Naval Force Channel, 126
  survival in, xiv, 162
  see also under North Sea
Nathan, James A. and Oliver, James
  K., 192
National insurance (naval), 76–7,
  139, 159–64, 166, 187
NATO
  and Algeria, 193
  British dependence on, 78, 121,
    152–3, 158, 161, 167–8, 170,
    187
  British naval contribution to, 59,
    102–4, 124, 134, 182
  British nuclear contribution to, 67,
    168
  demands on Royal Navy, 60, 88,
    107, 124–39, 182
  divided, 62, 111–14, 122, 145, 150,
    153, 155–9
  and Falklands, xii
  flexible response, 122–3, 157, 170

general strategy, 4, 7, 84, 88, 90, 96,
    105, 139, 155–9
  mutual loyalty strained, 62, 147,
    153, 155–9
  naval strategy, 4, 45–6, 87, 100,
    126–32, 135–9
  necessary cement of, 154
  and Norway, 115–18, 121–4,
    127–9
  and nuclear choice, 105
  possible impact of change, 7–8, 124,
    150–9, 183–5, 187
  realigning British contributions,
    185–7
  reluctance to consider Yugoslavia,
    60, 123
  resistance to Soviet blandishment,
    154–5
  risk for Britain, 167, 170, 178, 187
  Southern Flank, 123–4, 145
  Strike Fleet, 46, 59, 127–9
  Treaty area, 86, 122, 145, 156, 196
  treaty commitments, 60, 62, 125,
    152–3, 193
  unravelling, 63, 121–2, 150, 155–9,
    183–7
  withdrawals from, 63, 122, 155, 159,
    170, 183–7, 201
  see also under Alliance; Central
    Front; Continental
Naval deployment
  diplomatic need for, 163
  opportune presence, 149, 201
  side effects of, 144
  subject to change, 2, 14, 17, 20, 87
Naval exercises
  benefits of, 176
  escalation no answer to, 123
  insufficient publicity for, 118, 176
  location, 143, 200
  NATO, 117–18, 152, 166
  neglect invasion, 161, 202
  reassuring, 122
  should not constitute commit-
    ments, 152
  Soviet, 113, 119–20, 148
  use in coercive diplomacy, 119–20,
    123, 148
Naval Staff, responsibility of, xvi, 173

Naval Strategy
  appropriate force, 42
  balanced fleet, 128, 186
  Central Front secondary for,
    103–4, 109
  doctrinal influence on tactics, 44
  in First World War, 37–8, 40
  fleet in being, 109, 128, 135–6,
    162–4
  flexible response, 122–4, 172–3,
    187
  and foreign policy, 174–5, 186–8,
    201
  lacks clarity, 43, 87, 126–34, 165
  most glorious victory, 121
  neglect of, 6–7, 16, 43, 129
  pace of change in, 42–3
  and resources, 174
  Risikflotte, 163–4
  in Second World War, 38–40
  sequential operations, 44, 124, 132
  survival of Navy depends on
    plausible strategy, 187
  theories of, 36–47, 163–4
  see also under NATO; Strategy
Naval superiority
  balance of, 44, 95, 101, 109, 121
  control rewards, 37, 39
  invulnerability of fleet, 40–1, 46
  political response to, 3, 32, 177
  Risikflotte riposte, 163–4
Naval war, 1, 59, 96–102, 140–1, 149,
  151, 169
Navalism, 3, 22, 24, 27, 99, 140, 176
Navies
  built on speculation, 1–2, 100–1
  Central Front secondary for, 103–4
  flexibility of, 172–3
  instruments of national policy, 87,
    124–7, 186–8
  mobility of, 87, 126–7
  permit avoidance of precipitate
    choices, 121
  pose threats in any sea, 123
  see also under French; Royal;
    Soviet; United States
Nelson
  battle ground and drill ground, xi,
    144

  beaten me soundly, 162
  influenced by civilian writer, x
  something must be left to chance,
    173
Neutrality, 89, 112–13, 148, 150, 153,
  156, 162
Nitze, Paul and Sullivan, Leonard
  Securing the Seas, 96–102, 196
  on swing strategy, 199
  on TRIDENT, 196
North Sea
  concentration in, 15
  importance to Britain, 162
  need for deployment in, 87–8, 146
  oil, 35, 80, 88, 123, 128
  operations in, 107
  Russian Fleet in, 202
  see also under Narrow Seas;
    Norway
Norway
  airfields, 87, 115–18, 129–30, 137,
    151
  importance to Britain, 121, 124,
    129, 151–2, 163, 185
  invaded (1940), 37, 119–20
  manoeuvres against, 113, 119, 132
  and NATO, 115–18, 121–4, 127–9
  need for peace-time reassurance,
    121–2, 130, 132, 171
  policy, 114, 117
  possible Soviet demands on, 114,
    120, 122
  possible Soviet invasion of, 114–19,
    122
  radar chain in, 115–16
  reinforcement of, 115–18, 121–2,
    128–30, 152, 168, 185
  vulnerability of, 60, 117–19
  warning time, 115–18
  see also under British Defence
    Policy
Norwegian Sea, 21, 86, 100–2,
  114–15, 118, 124, 186, 199
Nott, John, Secretary of State for
  Defence
  considers reinforcement irrelevant,
    91
  maritime strategy of, 129
  merchant banker's eye, 134

Nott, John – *continued*
  naval economies of, xiii, 101,
    130–1, 133–5
  policy of, xiv, 7–8, 80–1, 130,
    133–5
  and short war, 94–5
  see also under British Defence
    Policy; Ministry of Defence
Nuclear escalation, 45, 48–56, 58,
  90–1, 103–4, 114–16, 120, 123,
  138–9
  see also under Deterrence
Nuclear war, 48–58, 86, 98, 150, 179,
  193
  see also under Limited; Total
Nuclear weapons
  actual and prospective possessors,
    70
  as bargaining counters, 52
  confined to sea, 56
  dangers of American monopoly,
    71–6, 160, 179
  essential characteristics, 58
  fire-break concept, 52, 56, 58
  French, 50–1, 55
  naval (tactical), 98, 121
  opposition to, 155–7
  proliferation, 69–70
  renunciation of, 7, 69–71, 158
  and sea power, 41, 49–56
  tactical and strategic, 57–8, 90
  theatre, 54, 70–5, 90
  unequal advantage in using, 57
  US, 49–58, 155
  see also under British nuclear forces

Ocean-going navy, xiii, 3, 64, 149,
  167–8, 170
  see also under Out of Area; Royal
    Navy
Office of Technology Assessment, 193
Out of Area Activities
  avoidance of commitment, 149
  British partiality for, 129, 143–4
  drain on resources, 146
  general, 140–9
  importance to US, 126
  limited war, 141

and NATO, 86–7, 111–14, 122,
  141–7
Persian Gulf, 14, 60–1
policy, 61
political purpose critical, 149
prolong warning time, 143
and Soviet Navy, 186
  see also under British Defence
    Policy; Royal Navy

Pacific Ocean
  American preference for, 97, 124,
    138, 199
  comfortable insulation for US, 110
  Fleet, 2, 18
  future war in, 44, 59
  Second World War in, 18, 37
Palmerston, Lord, 19, 188, 204
Pierre, Andrew J., 196
Poland, 90, 93, 110, 113, 123
POLARIS, 67, 72–3, 75, 77–8, 82–3,
  139, 167, 178–9, 181, 196
  see also under British nuclear forces
Powell, Enoch, 86, 196
Powley, Edward B., 190
Pym, Francis, 194

Rodgers, William, 82, 195
Rosinski, Herbert, 36, 46, 191
Roskill, Captain Stephen, RN, 36–7,
  46, 98–9, 190, 191, 197, 202
Rowse, A. L., 190
Royal Air Force
  and British Isles, 107–8, 128, 162,
    170, 179, 182
  and Central Front, 107, 137, 162
  financial constraints on, 182
  and maritime communications,
    102, 128
  and Norway, 124, 128
  prevents invasion (1940), 95, 161
  and Royal Navy, 165, 179
  strength of, 130–1, 179, 182
  see also under British Defence
    Policy
Royal Navy
  and anti-submarine warfare, 41,
    87–8, 98–102, 128–32, 137–8,
    185

Royal Navy – *continued*
arguments for reduction of, 3, 130, 162, 167–73, 185
in broken-backed war, 51–2
and conventional war, 58–65, 86–139, 141, 151–4, 159–64
deficiencies of, 100, 130, 137, 141, 166–7
deterrence, 49–56, 66, 69–70, 73–6, 78, 83–5, 139, 141, 144, 154, 160, 163–6
does not depend on Central Front, 102–4, 151, 153, 185, 187
and Empire, 3, 11–17, 148
and Falklands War, xii–xiii
history, xii, 10–20, 37, 98, 161
in isolated combat, 62, 138, 159–64
and NATO, 60, 86–139, 178, 181–2, 185–7
neglect of strategic thought, 6–7
nuclear trigger, 49, 72, 76
options, 64, 136, 139, 153, 168–9
orthodox arguments for, 4, 86–104
purely national functions, 127, 145, 147–9, 160–4, 166, 171–3, 178, 186–8
roots of, 20, 174, 203
sentimental influence on, 3, 5, 187
Spanish irony might be needed by, 171
strength of, 2, 14, 18–20, 125–39, 149, 175, 182, 185
tasks, 128–9, 135–9, 145, 148–9, 151–4, 156, 160–4
transformation of, 1–3, 25, 162, 168–9, 172
in total war, 1, 49–52
versatility, 171, 173
and violent peace, 64–5, 122, 141–9, 201
what could it do?, 9, 31, 35, 52, 59, 64–5, 84–5, 102–4, 119, 122–4, 127, 139, 149, 160–4, 165, 175, 177, 187–8
yields precedence, 18–20
see also under British Defence Policy; Naval Strategy

Sea control, 37, 39–46

Sea denial, 37–41, 43–6
Sea power
British, 10–20, 37–40
concept of, 10, 12–20, 36–48, 95, 175
and nuclear war, 41–58
see also under Naval Strategy
Second World War
lessons of, 94–5, 123, 171
naval history, 17–18, 37–40
strategic errors in, 38–9, 63
Secrecy, cult of, 8, 67–8, 131–5, 175–7, 187, 194
Single scenario, xiv, 87, 93, 165, 173
Smart, Ian, 77, 82, 195
Smith, Dan, 167, 194, 201
Smith, Peter C., 190
South Atlantic, cruises in, xi, 143
Soviet Navy
battle of first salvo, 99, 121
better equipped for nuclear war, 98–9, 121
building programme, 7, 113, 185
interdiction of maritime communications, 92–104, 197
KIROV, 2, 42, 93, 120
Kola base, 115–16, 129, 138
limited naval force, 119–24, 144, 148, 186
and mining, 137
Northern Fleet, 59, 88, 95, 102, 112, 120, 132
and Norway, 113–20, 122
objectives, 59, 100–2, 186
peace-time activities of, 1, 60, 112–14, 119–20, 135, 148, 186
strength of, 2, 19, 100, 186
submarines, 93, 98–102, 115, 137, 185–6
Soviet Union
accretion of strength, 25
and Afghanistan, 110
attitudes to nuclear war, 49–58, 70–1, 73, 84, 107, 121, 180, 194
and Berlin, 33, 110
cautious policy of, 26, 93, 109–11, 135, 154, 180
and China, 51
commitments of, 28

Soviet Union – *continued*
and Czechoslovakia, 33, 90, 93, 110
economic advantages of, 28, 181
and Europe, 88–93, 103–4, 110–14,
154
and limited war, 52–6, 84, 92–4,
107, 114–19, 135, 180
military doctrines, 53, 56–7, 84, 92,
107, 111, 180
naval concepts, 2, 45, 56, 92, 113,
186
only enemy, xiii, 155, 159, 170
perimeter of, 110–14
political offensive by, 154–5
threat presented by, 6, 33, 48–61,
87–104, 109–24, 147–8,
159–64, 180–3, 185–6, 198,
201
see also under Super-Powers
Strategy
alternatives, 8–9, 107, 152–4,
157–64, 167–71, 177, 185–8
armchair, xv
British neglect of, xiv–xv, 5–9, 130
collective or national, 178, 181–8
errors in, 38–9, 179
flexibility and Navy, 172–3, 187
and foreign policy, 178, 185–8
maximum force no longer axiomatic, 180
mobilisation, 90, 96, 103, 117, 120
need for public discussion, xv–xvi,
8–9, 33, 68–9, 131–5, 175, 177,
187
not only nuclear, 43
obsolescence in, 135
political objectives of, 39, 152–4,
157, 171–4, 177, 185–8
preservation of options, 169–73,
187
reappraisal in crisis, 152–4, 187
tokenism, 185
value of a military force, 184
see also under Deterrence; Naval
Strategy
Submarines, 16–17, 38, 40–2, 63, 88,
98–102, 120–1, 136–8, 170–1,
197
Submarine launched ballistic missiles,

49–56, 66, 69–70, 73–4, 84, 115,
127, 160
Suez crisis (1956), 62–3, 111, 147, 156,
166, 200–1
Super-Powers
aspire to global influence, 110, 156
attitudes to allies, 49–58
and Cuba, 1, 110, 156
doctrines of, 56
and Europe, 57, 156–8
first use of nuclear weapons, 57,
70–1, 194
and limited war, 53–8, 73, 83–4,
150
monopoly of nuclear victory, 58
and naval deployments, 58, 119
and nuclear war, 49–58, 105, 150,
180
reciprocal threats, 119
reluctance to accept defeat, 150
sanctuary of metropolitan territory
of, 53–8, 73, 83–4
transcending British power, 66
see also under Soviet Union; United
States
Supreme Allied Commander Atlantic,
64, 118, 124, 127
Surface warships, 2, 18, 32, 42, 93,
113, 120–1, 128–9, 130, 136, 169,
171, 185
Surprise attack, 92–3, 116, 138, 144,
192
Swarztrauber, Rear Admiral Sayre A.,
USN, 197

Technology, 7–8, 14, 25, 31, 35, 41
see also under Matériel
Terraine, John, 190
Thompson, E. P. and Smith, Dan,
194
Threats
choosing, 63, 105–9, 122, 132,
138–9, 141, 145, 170, 173, 185
failure to meet, 121–2, 124, 169–70
gravest, 64, 105–8
ideological, 21
ignored by NATO, 62, 159
maritime, 109, 122–4, 138–9, 185
to Moscow, 49–55, 160

Threats – *continued*
  need to demonstrate, 33
  nuclear, 49–56, 160
  predicted terminal situation, 106,
    132, 134, 138–9, 149, 185
  remote, 106
  scepticism concerning, 26
Tirpitz, Grand Admiral, 42–3, 45,
    163, 202
Total war
  and Britain, 49–52, 58, 70, 78,
    83–4, 150
  characteristics, 48–52
  deliberate, 50, 192
  improbability of, 49, 180
  naval forces in, 1, 49–52
  risk of encourages use of limited
    force, 180
  US responsibility, 105
  see also under Nuclear war
Trade, 11–14, 20, 28, 37–40, 45, 63,
    93–4, 149, 161, 170–1
Train, Admiral Harry D. II, USN, 199
Treasury, British, 5, 29–32, 51, 85, 175
TRIDENT, 7, 72, 78–85, 133–5, 139,
    158, 167–8, 178–9, 181, 196
Turner, Admiral Stansfield, USN, 43

United States
  attitudes to Britain, 19, 59, 70,
    141–3, 145, 147–8, 155–6,
    160, 200–1
  British attitudes to, 15, 67–8, 75–6,
    84–5, 146, 156, 176
  coercive diplomacy of, 111, 198–9
  defeat in Vietnam, 58
  economic advantages of, 19, 28, 30,
    181
  global contest, 148, 155–6
  lesser ally (1917), 18
  and NATO, 62, 88, 91, 111, 135–6,
    151, 156–8, 183

naval concepts, 2, 37, 41, 44, 58–9,
    124
  nuclear forces of, 49–58, 157
  perpetual ally, 19, 28, 160, 168, 188,
    201
  and territorially limited nuclear
    war, 54–6, 66, 69–70, 73–6,
    78, 83–5, 157
  troops in Europe, 88, 91, 95, 114,
    155, 183
  see also under Super-Powers
United States Navy
  achieves supremacy, 17–20
  attitudes to Britain, 19, 59, 135–6
  diversion of, 60, 112, 118, 135–7
  limitations of, 41, 97
  loss of assured supremacy, 44
  in Mediterranean, 123–6
  peace-time activity, 142, 144
  priorities, 97, 124, 133, 137–8
  projection of power ashore, 45–6
  reluctance to accept British help, 18,
    59
  in Second World War, 18, 37, 40
  strength of, 2
  swing strategy of, 44, 124, 132, 138,
    199
  see also under Naval strategy

Vietnam, 1, 30, 52, 57, 58, 111, 183
Violent peace, 41, 60, 64, 141–9, 156,
    165, 168–70
  see also under Coercive diplomacy;
    Limited Naval Force

Wegener, Admiral, 186, 203
Wettern, Desmond, 199
Whiteley, General Sir Peter, 202
Winton, John, 190

Zumwalt, Admiral Elmo R. Jr., USN,
    125, 132–3, 199